D1262373

BUTTERFLY GARDENING

THE NORTH AMERICAN BUTTERFLY ASSOCIATION GUIDE

BUTTERFLY GARDENING

THE NORTH AMERICAN BUTTERFLY ASSOCIATION GUIDE

JANE HURWITZ

Princeton University Press

Princeton and Oxford

Published by Princeton University Press,
41 William Street, Princeton, New Jersey 08540

In the United Kingdom: Princeton University Press,
6 Oxford Street, Woodstock, Oxfordshire OX20 1TR

press.princeton.edu

ISBN (pbk.) 978-0-691-17034-3

Library of Congress Control Number: 2017958516

British Library Cataloging-in-Publication Data is available

This book has been composed in Avenir (headings), Melior (text and captions), and Gill Sans Std (boxes)

Printed on acid-free paper. ∞

Photograph previous page: Orange Sulphur nectaring.

Designed by D & N Publishing, Baydon, Wiltshire, UK

Printed in China

10 9 8 7 6 5 4 3 2 1

CONTENTS

CONTENTS

PREFACE

If you have picked up this book, you are probably drawn to the delicate beauty of butterflies. You probably also enjoy gardening to some degree, or at least have gardening ambitions. How butterflies and gardens intersect and how we can maximize this intersection in ways that benefit both people and butterflies is the basis of this book. Whether you are already a butterfly gardener, know someone who is, or are just curious about the topic, this book will inform you about the many ways we can each help butterflies survive and thrive, and derive endless hours of fascination and enjoyment in doing so. The book emerges from my own love of gardening and butterflies, but it is also a community product of sorts. Much of it emerges from the varied experiences of many other members of the North American Butterfly Association who have put their interest in butterflies into action by transforming gardens into butterfly habitat. Every butterfly gardener has experiences worth sharing, and even after fifteen years of associating closely with fellow NABA members in a variety of settings, I still continually learn new things from them.

I can trace my own first encounters with butterflies to my father's daily homecoming from his work commute on a Kansas highway. In warm weather, my sisters and I would run out to greet his car upon its nightly return. Although happy to see my father, I was more interested in what he brought home each evening. Conveniently at eye level for a child of five or six was the large metallic front grille of my father's Chrysler, and splayed and splattered across it were dozens (even hundreds?) of grasshoppers and butterflies. The grasshoppers were enormous and varied in size and color, but what most attracted my eye were the yellow, white, and occasional orange butterfly wings that made a mosaic pattern across the front of the car. No sibling or schoolyard friend had yet told me that bugs were "gross," and no squeamish parent stopped me from touching the wing-encrusted car grille. I was allowed to observe and explore what caught my attention and it made an impact on how I viewed the insect kingdom, and the natural world in general, that proved formative for me. I cultivated my first garden at age eleven in the scorching Kansas sun, and my interest in insects and especially butterflies continued unabated. But it was only decades later that I discovered the blindingly obvious: that gardens and butterflies go together, and that gardening for butterflies adds a rich new layer of enjoyment and satisfaction to the gardening experience. If this book succeeds in communicating even a fraction of that enthusiasm and enjoyment to interested readers, it will have been more than worth the effort.

How and why do people connect with the natural world around them, how do they come to embrace its beauty, and what do they do to promote and protect it? A bug-encrusted car grille may not spark lifelong curiosity about nature and fascination with butterflies in everyone, but that was my experience. A spectacle of smashed butterflies somehow transmuted into a desire to save butterflies. "If we can save butterflies, we can save ourselves" is NABA's motto, and this book serves as an initial guide by providing the background information that will allow you to take that sentiment and create what is appropriate for your particular lifestyle to enable butterflies to flourish.

BUTTERFLY AND PLANT NAMES USED IN THIS BOOK

Common butterfly names used throughout this book are from the *NABA Checklist & English Names of North American Butterflies*. Common butterfly names mentioned in this book along with their respective scientific names are listed at the end of the book.

Plants discussed in the book use common names listed by the USDA on its website, www.plants.usda.gov. When a different common name is used in the text, the USDA name is given first with the secondary name noted afterward (for example: palmleaf thoroughwort, commonly known as Gregg's mistflower). A plant inventory list at the end of the book links common names to scientific names.

ACKNOWLEDGMENTS

The material in this book is a synthesis of ideas gathered over a decade-plus tenure with North American Butterfly Association, during which I had the opportunity to spend my days thinking of, talking about, and promoting butterfly gardening. For this I am grateful to NABA President Jeffrey Glassberg as well as to the other officers and directors of NABA for their indefatigable efforts to promote butterfly conservation on all levels.

This book would not exist without NABA members—many have shared their stories and photographs with me for this project and many others provided information and suggestions along the way. This book is about and dedicated to this community of individuals who share ideas and information about butterfly gardening in particular and a love of nature in general. I encourage you to join NABA and experience the world of butterflies.

ACKNOWLEDGMENTS

A dedicated group of supporters read drafts, listened to complaints, and cheered me on when the work got tough. Without them, I would not have completed this task. Incalculable amounts of thanks to Anne Christie, Jane V. Scott, Ann Shrevens, Jim Springer, and in particular the greatest supporter/cheerleader of all, Sharon Wander.

Finally, I would like to thank my visionary editor, Robert Kirk, for commissioning this book and shepherding it through to completion.

THE BASICS OF BUTTERFLY GARDENING

PART I

CHAPTER ONE

GETTING STARTED

PREVIOUS PAGE: Be sure to include seating areas in your butterfly garden. If you feel there is never time to sit still during the garden season, watching butterflies will give you the needed excuse to sit and watch what unfolds. This southern California garden is awash with flowering nectar-producing plants that draw butterflies close to view.

Butterfly gardening melds two distinctly different activities, butterfly watching and gardening. Gardening involves planning, digging, weeding—more weeding!—watering, and some cleaning up at the end of the season. Gardening is a satisfying and joyful endeavor, despite—or because of—the physical exertion it requires. It creates a version of nature that pleases the gardener. Butterfly watching, even more than gardening, can be tailored to one's love of, or aversion to, physical exercise: it can entail a simple visit to a public garden to see what butterflies it attracts, or it can involve a daylong hike in a wild area in search of specific butterflies. Whatever the amount of energy one chooses to invest, the goal is to view butterflies, whether for the pleasure of observing their beauty or for the challenge of identifying their species. Gardening always includes some output of physical energy, while butterfly watching might require only the heft of binoculars on the wrist—and some close-range butterfly viewing binoculars are pretty lightweight.

While the number of people who garden far exceeds the number who watch butterflies for recreation, once focused awareness of butterflies enters your gardening world, the interest and excitement that butterflies add to the garden will soon have you hooked. One more activity will be added to your yearly garden routine—but at least watching different species of butterflies flutter around your garden, visiting the flowers you have grown for them, is a task that you can accomplish while relaxing in a lawn chair.

Butterfly gardening is perhaps best defined on the sign that has long been in use by North American Butterfly Association's Butterfly Garden and Habitat Program, which states: "This garden provides resources that increase the world's population of butterflies." The resources in question need not be extensive or elaborate; you can start butterfly gardening by including a few nectar plants and a few caterpillar food plants in an existing garden, in a school garden, or even in patio planters. This simple goal is achievable by almost anyone; even a small garden can play a part in creating habitat for butterflies—you do not need vast amounts of land in order to create a home for these beautiful creatures.

CONSERVATION

The North American Butterfly Association (NABA) has been promoting the conservation of butterfly habitats since the 1990s. This concept may not be foremost on anyone's mind when they browse colorful plant catalogs because, for many people, nature conservation can evoke images of long hikes with groups of sweaty, flannel-clad enthusiasts striking out through bogs with the goal to plant twig-sized saplings for future generations. Yet conservation can also be a simple, uncomplicated act, such as making careful choices of what we plant in our gardens and yards. It is an opportunity; it is something in which just about everyone can participate if interested. You don't need to feel that conservation is a burden you are shouldering as a remedy for all the world's

Tiger Swallowtails, like this Western Tiger Swallowtail, are found in virtually all parts of the United States. Swallowtails are easily recognized common garden butterflies and are thus part of NABA's logo.

IMPROVEMENTS MADE TO LOCAL HABITATS will benefit common butterflies, but not all butterflies can be considered common. About 722 butterfly species have occurred naturally in North America, north of Mexico. Many of these butterflies have such specific habitat requirements that a butterfly garden is unlikely to attract them.

Regal Fritillary is a prime example of a butterfly species whose reliance on a unique habitat has directly influenced its population size and density. Once ranging from Maine west to Montana and south to North Carolina and Oklahoma, Regal Fritillary was considered a widespread and common butterfly. However, its livelihood is tied to grassland ecosystems, and this reliance on a disappearing habitat type has precipitated the Regal's downfall, to the point where substantial populations remain only in Midwestern remnants of tallgrass prairie. In addition, to support Regal Fritillary populations, not just any tallgrass prairie will do; it must be

Regal Fritillary visiting milkweed, an essential plant of the tallgrass prairie habitat and among the preferred nectar plants of Regal Fritillaries.

"high-quality" tallgrass prairie, meaning that these butterflies are discerning about their prairie homes. A high-quality tallgrass prairie will encompass a diversity of both native grasses and forbs, which include familiar flowering plants such as iconic sunflowers and Monarch-friendly milkweeds, and of course violets, the Regal's caterpillar food plant. Fire is another critical feature of a healthy tallgrass prairie; periodic burning of the grasslands unlocks nutrients and rejuvenates the soil surface by clearing away large amounts of dead and decaying plant material, allowing new plants to see the sun, and stimulating seeds to germinate.

When flying about looking for the right habitat, Regal Fritillaries do not carry a checklist of home-buying must-haves tucked under their wings; they decide where to lay eggs based on instinct. All butterflies are hardwired to know what "looks" and smells like a home, and that will be different for each butterfly species. Regal Fritillaries will stop and mate when there is a vast expanse of tallgrass prairie that contains ample amounts of their preferred caterpillar food plants—birdfoot violet and prairie violet. In addition, enough nectar plants of the right type must be available; not enough food or not enough space and Regal Fritillaries will look for their home elsewhere, even if it no longer exists.

Although native prairies are now extremely fragmented and the Regal Fritillary population has dramatically decreased, conservation efforts are underway to protect remnant patches of prairie, and to develop land-management methods that encourage Regal Fritillaries. One of the last Regal Fritillary populations in the East is protected and monitored by the United States Army on the Fort Indiantown Gap National Guard Training Center near Annville, Pennsylvania. This isolated population is stable, and researchers are studying ways to increase eastern Regal Fritillary populations.

Less common butterflies that require specialized habitats do sometimes arrive in gardens but it is not the norm. If your garden is near an already existing population, an uncommon species may stop by, but even then, it takes a perfect alignment of location, weather, plant materials, timing, and luck to entice some species into a garden. Usually if an uncommon butterfly visits a butterfly garden, it is just that—a fleeting visit—rather than the beginning of a breeding colony.

In the spring, dried plant material left over from the winter will be burned off this Kansas prairie remnant that Regal Fritillaries call home.

environmental abuses; rather, view it as a series of small steps that can go in many directions based on your interests, resources, and needs. Whatever level you take it to, conservation is something that can have a real impact both now and for future generations.

Is conserving butterfly habitat the same as conserving butterflies? In many cases it is the same, since butterflies are so deeply dependent on their habitat. As more suburbs, office buildings, and their attendant roads and small businesses are built, fewer fields, wetlands, and woodlands are left. Suburban development replaces wild spaces with a new, monotonous landscape of concrete, grass lawns, and a small selection of ornamental trees and shrubs, almost none of which supply either nectar for adult butterflies or the specific food plants that butterfly caterpillars need to survive. This loss of habitat reduces the populations of almost all butterflies. Some species, though, which can be called common garden butterflies, normally travel surprisingly long distances to find appropriate food and shelter. Their caterpillars are able to eat either a wide variety of plants or plants that are common even in developed locations. Because of their widespread populations and accommodating lifestyles, common butterflies should be the target group of butterflies to attract for a beginning butterfly gardener.

While many butterfly species are threatened by habitat loss, Monarchs probably receive the most widespread attention of any of the butterflies in this predicament, and in fact, they have become the focus of a conservation effort that spans the entire continent. This effort mainly involves restoring milkweeds, which Monarch caterpillars require as their food plant, but has also brought attention to other Monarch population problems: parasite infestations that increase mortality, lack of nectar availability along migration routes, and even the possible impacts of climate change on Monarch overwintering sites. What makes the Monarch conservation effort so compelling is the Monarch migration—Monarchs fly through much of the United States twice a year on their journey to and from their wintering grounds in Mexico and California. While the overall Monarch population is not in danger of extinction, the spectacular migration could be in danger of disappearing if habitat along the migration route is not protected and improved.

Encouraging and educating gardeners to plant regionally native milkweeds throughout the Monarch migration route is one conservation practice that is simple and can be accomplished in a variety of settings. Since Monarchs inhabit much of the land in the United States, gardeners everywhere can participate in conservation efforts by planting milkweed—home gardeners, schools, highway roadside managers, and nursing homes are some of the places where land has been planted for Monarchs. In addition to providing essential caterpillar food for Monarchs, milkweeds attract many butterflies and pollinators to their flowers, so even if you are not in the thick of the Monarch migration route, milkweeds are an important plant for butterflies.

The interaction between milkweeds and Monarchs starts as soon as milkweed shoots push through the earth in spring—Monarchs may be seen laying their eggs on milkweed plants that are just inches tall. There are many different types of milkweed that are native to different regions of the United States, so it is easy to find one that suits each specific gardening need.

As Monarchs begin their migration northward, milkweed plants are just breaking ground. Typically among the later perennials to appear in the spring, milkweeds can be a source of consternation to new butterfly gardeners, who might wonder whether their plants survived the winter. You can cope with this spring shyness by marking your milkweed patch in the fall before the vegetation dies down so the area can be left undisturbed in the spring until the new shoots emerge.

Although formerly considered a common garden butterfly, Monarchs have become much less so as their migration numbers have decreased—so perhaps it should be the first butterfly to consider when planting a garden. Luckily for gardeners, the hardest part of planting for Monarchs might be finding milkweeds to plant, since the conservation effort to save the Monarchs' migration has created more demand than supply of these very popular garden plants. Milkweed seeds are plentiful, so consider propagating plants from purchased seeds.

Monarchs on their spring migration northward have deposited eggs on young shoots of common milkweed in central Kansas.

CONSERVATION STARTS AT HOME

If you are interested in promoting butterflies and their habitat, how do you create "butterfly habitat"? To start, look around at what is near you already. Some weeds, tree foliage, and wildflowers are eaten by caterpillars of common garden butterflies, as well as of many less-common species. Learning to recognize and protect the different species of trees and flowering plants that are already on your property and used by butterflies is a relatively quick way to start helping butterflies. The protection of existing butterfly-friendly trees, weeds, and wildflowers should be the first step in creating your butterfly habitat without having to buy anything or dig a hole.

Already existing butterfly gardens can be certified by NABA. Certification signs help begin conversations that can inform others about habitat conservation for Monarchs as well as all butterflies.

START WITH SIMPLE GARDENS

For nearly a decade, the North American Butterfly Association has promoted a program that certifies butterfly gardens. The requirements are easily manageable—the garden needs only three different butterfly nectar plants and three different caterpillar food plants to become certified. Information on choosing regionally useful plants for butterflies is provided on NABA's website, and NABA chapters serve as resources for beginning butterfly gardeners.

Three different butterfly nectar plants and three different caterpillar food plants in one small garden, or even a patio planting, is not going to decisively tilt the balance of habitat loss. However, it is a starting point for shifting perceptions and habits. Learning to incorporate three different nectar plants in the landscape initiates a change in the way we choose plants. Nectar plants can be beautiful as well as useful—pleasing the gardener while also sustaining wildlife. Caterpillar food plants are often less visually dramatic than nectar plants but can still complement a garden scheme. Using certain shrubs, trees, and vines in addition to flowering perennials and annuals makes it easy to accommodate caterpillars in a garden layout.

RIGHT: Common buttonbush needs a moist site to thrive—a rain garden would be ideal. The summer-blooming flowers are fragrant to humans and butterflies and provide nectar over a long period. Two Eastern Tiger Swallowtails are nectaring on this plant—the yellow individual on the left shows the common coloration, while the "dark morph" on the right exhibits a coloration seen only in female Eastern Tiger Swallowtails where the yellow wing color is replaced with black.

TRANSFORMING A GARDEN INTO A HABITAT

The Environmental Protection Agency defines pesticides in part as "any substance or mixture of substances intended for preventing, destroying, repelling or mitigating any pest"—a pretty broad definition that encompasses many substances important to public health and safety. The EPA considers antibacterial soap to be a pesticide but it would not be prudent to suggest that hospitals stop using these soaps just because they are called pesticides. Clearly, great care is warranted when considering the use of any pesticide, particularly in gardens, because one person's pest (and the caterpillars of some butterflies can be considered pests) might be the creature that you are trying to encourage.

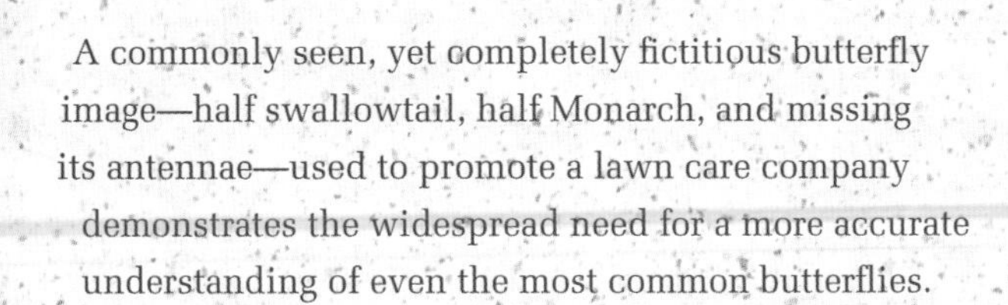

A commonly seen, yet completely fictitious butterfly image—half swallowtail, half Monarch, and missing its antennae—used to promote a lawn care company demonstrates the widespread need for a more accurate understanding of even the most common butterflies.

The home gardener can choose from a multitude of products to control both insects and weeds. But when gardens are treated as habitat and the goal is to increase local butterfly populations, many fewer of these products fit into the scheme of butterfly gardening and many of them should be strictly avoided. To put it mildly, the butterflies that visit our gardens do not benefit from applications of lawn and garden chemicals. What butterflies do need is an abundance of caution when it comes to what is sprayed, dusted, or otherwise applied to their environments. Be aware that in your gardening endeavors you are creating a season-long buffet line for the insect's entire life cycle, from the smallest caterpillar to the largest butterfly. Home and garden pesticides have no place in that banquet.

ISLANDS OF HABITAT

Butterflies, in varying concentrations, can be found throughout the United States. Even in cities, surrounded by concrete, a few species can survive. It might be harder to attract them, and you will have to search harder to see them flitting around your neighborhood, but they are there. In general, butterflies will not be as plentiful in urban areas as in the surrounding leafy suburbs. Move even farther out to the exurbs, which are greener, wilder areas beyond the suburbs, and butterflies will be still more plentiful. The route from urban area to suburb to exurb may cover only 50 miles and may experience the exact same climate throughout. Yet the more buildings, roads, and lawns occupy the landscape, the more butterfly habitat becomes patchier to nonexistent. Small plantings of butterfly habitat, such as those encouraged by NABA, are one way to combat the uneven distribution of homes for butterflies. Each small butterfly garden is complemented by gardens and wild spaces in the same general area to create a mosaic of welcoming spaces for butterflies to reproduce.

Helping butterflies to move between patches of environmentally suitable lands can be accomplished in many ways. Habitat corridors are passageways that allow wildlife to move between suitable environments embedded within unsuitable areas. Such corridors need not be pristine, wild spaces. Drainage

NEONICOTINOIDS, also commonly referred to as neonics, are a group of insecticides widely used in farm, home, and garden applications for the control of leaf-chewing and sap-sucking insects. Once a plant or seed is treated with neonics, the insecticide is found throughout the entire plant, not just in the leaves or sap, and remains active throughout the growing season. For caterpillars, which are leaf-chewing insects, a plant treated with neonics is a death sentence. And without caterpillars, there are no butterflies!

For butterflies and other pollinators such as bees that drink nectar, the threats associated with neonic-treated plants are harder to quantify—since neonics are present in all parts of a plant, the insecticide can also exist in flower nectar. The levels of neonics found in nectar are considered sublethal; but even at a low level, the effects of neonics on insect health, behavior, and reproduction are not known.

In order to protect butterflies and their caterpillars:

~ Avoid applying neonics in your yard and garden.

~ When purchasing new plant material, be certain to check that it is labeled as neonicotinoid-free. With each passing growing season, ornamental plant producers and plant nurseries are improving their labeling to show which of their plants are safe for pollinators. Labels are not standardized and must be read carefully to determine if they are declaring the product to be "neonicotinoid-free" or not.

~ If a pest-control professional treats your home or lawn, ask that they use alternatives to neonicotinoid insecticides; neonicotinoids include the chemicals imidacloprid, clothianidin, thiamethoxam, acetamiprid, and dinotefuran.

culverts in southern California serve as passageways for deer, coyotes, and many other animals to navigate between the concrete barriers of roads and buildings for access to whatever limited green spaces are available. For butterflies, though, habitat corridors work best when they approximate recognizable butterfly habitat. As you can imagine, butterflies are more likely to fly through a flower-filled backyard than through a concrete rainwater channel. Butterfly gardening emphasizes both creating pockets of habitat and linking habitats together.

Consider how the garden you create relates to other possible butterfly habitat in your neighborhood. Is there a line of trees and shrubs running down one of your property lines? Adding nectar-producing shrubs to that mix is just one more step to enlarging habitat and promoting connection between habitats. Even nongardeners can ask their town councils to replace some of the sterile lawnscape of parks with plants specifically needed by local butterflies.

LEFT: Spicebush Swallowtail flies in the eastern half of the United States. It is easily distinguished from other black-colored swallowtails by the "missing" orange spot on the hind wing below in the row of orange spots closest to the body. Loved by swallowtails and by hummingbirds, cardinalflower is a good choice for fire-engine-red blooms in midsummer gardens. The caterpillar food plant for Spicebush Swallowtail, northern spicebush, is a much more understated plant, although its haze of tiny yellow flowers in early spring is always a welcome sight and provides nectar for Spring Azures.

The next time a foundation shrub—one of those nondescript bushes that was planted along the front of your house when it was built—finally dies, replace it with a butterfly-friendly plant. In the East, planting northern spicebush to provide food for Spicebush Swallowtail, or redosier dogwood for Summer Azure are possibilities. In southern Florida, you could plant coontie, the sole caterpillar host for the Atala hairstreak.

When considering how to promote islands of habitat, it is apparent that moving beyond the boundaries of our homes and linking up pockets of habitat is essential. The more fully the mosaic of habitat is filled, with either new habitat or improved existing habitat, the easier it is for butterflies to find homes where they can reproduce. The key to helping butterflies in all locations is to provide food. Butterfly gardening requires providing food for two of the four life stages of a butterfly: nectar for adult butterflies and specific plants for caterpillars to eat. Most people start by focusing on nectar-producing flowers, then based on what butterflies they see, go on to provide the food needed by the caterpillars of those species. Once both food sources are in place, an island of habitat has been created.

WHERE ARE THE BUTTERFLIES?

Butterflies are wild animals and the factors that influence their population numbers from year to year, or even season to season, are myriad. Even on a warm summer day, the most desirable habitat may seem to lack abundant flying butterflies. Weather is assumed to be an important determinant of the size of butterfly populations, although it is difficult to show direct cause and effect. Adverse weather that impacts butterfly populations can include a brutally frigid winter, which may decrease the number of overwintering eggs, caterpillars, and chrysalides. A long stretch of cool weather in the spring or summer that coincides with a mating cycle can suppress a butterfly population to the point where butterfly watchers will notice a downtick in numbers; cold butterflies become semidormant and lack the energy to fly vigorously looking for a mate.

THE SPECTACULAR ATALA HAIRSTREAK, once a common butterfly in South Florida, declined to near-extinction as its caterpillar food plant, coontie, was severely depleted. Initially, wild coontie plants were overharvested (for processing into a cornstarch-like flour) at a rate faster than they could regrow. Later, as housing development in South Florida escalated, the native, wild coontie population lost further ground, both literally and figuratively.

Luckily, coontie (a cycad) is now recognized as a valuable landscape plant that can be used as a ground cover or small foundation plant. The popularity of coontie among landscapers and homeowners has helped play a part in the rebound of Atala populations, but a problem remains. Atala females lay numerous eggs (up to 60!) and the growing caterpillars feed for a little over two weeks, during which time the coontie fronds can become quite ragged and tattered, if not completely stripped. Atalas actively breed year-round in South Florida, so caterpillars feast at all times of the year. When confronted with shredded shrubbery, some homeowners start to look for a can of something that will kill the problematic chewing insect. Housing and retail developments have no tolerance for landscape plants that are routinely and actively eaten by caterpillars, so this can be a bigger issue with developments than with individual homeowners. NABA volunteers have rescued both coontie and Atalas from colony sites such as abandoned city lots slated for development, as well as from private homeowners who have not yet learned to appreciate the Atala.

For more than a decade, Sandy Koi and Alana Edwards have spearheaded a group of volunteers from NABA chapters and members of the Native Plant Society in Florida's Miami-Dade, Broward, and Palm Beach counties. Additionally, local Miami-

This newly emerged Atala is nectaring on Chapman's senna. While Atalas are not widespread in South Florida butterfly gardens, Chapman's senna is a good choice for butterfly gardens in South Florida —it is a caterpillar food plant for Cloudless Sulphurs, Sleepy Oranges, and Orange-barred Sulphurs. In addition, as shown here, it provides nectar that attracts a wide variety of butterflies.

These Atalas are just emerging from their chrysalides and will soon fly off in search of nectar. Some dull, speckled orange chrysalides still hang on the coontie frond, a sign that more butterflies will be emerging soon.

Dade County staff have acknowledged and supported the project. The same mission inspires all these volunteers: to reintroduce Atalas into productive South Florida habitat. They focus on creating sustainable Atala colonies at previously occupied colony sites. Locations with suitable habitat adjacent to existing colonies are also used as relocation sites, thus enlarging the corridor of habitat where Atalas can roam.

To accomplish this goal, volunteers identify potential locations by canvassing homes and public locations for appropriate Atala habitat. The suitability of each site is carefully checked: it must have ample stands of coontie, plenty of established and appropriate nectar plants, and shade trees where the Atalas can roost and rest. Once contacted and willing to participate, the keepers of Atala foster gardens also pledge to forgo pesticides and to remain on alert for county mosquito spraying. Gardeners can ask that the county not spray their properties, and they must be careful to cover their coontie plants during any nearby mosquito spraying.

One final request by the NABA chapters is that the garden owners monitor their Atala colonies for at least a year so that more can be learned about which landscape practices promote healthy Atala populations. The accumulating population data, completed garden surveys, and input from the colony site owners help to build a comprehensive picture of what a site needs in order to host a persistent Atala colony.

ANOTHER COMMON BUTTERFLY BEHAVIOR to watch for is basking, which is the act of doing nothing, or at least nothing obvious to the casual observer. Since they are cold-blooded and so cannot generate their own warmth, when encountering sunny but cool conditions butterflies sit still, often with wings spread open, in order to gain warmth from the sun. When basking they position their bodies at an angle toward the sun to soak up the rays, usually in a spot out of the wind. Placing rocks in a sheltered location where the morning sun will shine creates a possible basking spot where you can watch for sunbathing butterflies.

This Silver-spotted Skipper has been caught in the act of nectaring; its tongue is unfurled and is probing each individual purpletop vervain flower. Nectaring (sucking the sweet liquid held within a blossom through a tubular tongue) is how butterflies drink from flowers and can often be seen in flower-filled gardens.

Another factor that may play a role in fluctuating butterfly populations is spraying for mosquitoes and other insects, such as Gypsy Moth, by government agencies. (The spray that kills Gypsy Moth caterpillars kills ALL butterfly and moth caterpillars.) Since the timing and amount of these sprayings may be different each year, their impacts can vary widely.

The best way to get a handle on the location of butterflies is to get outside at various times of the day and observe. Go in the morning when there is still dew on the plants. You might catch a Common Buckeye basking in the morning sun. Walk through your garden right before noon when the air has warmed sufficiently and flower nectar is flowing—Giant Swallowtails may be nectaring on eastern purple coneflowers. Late in the day, be sure to check plants that are catching the last rays of the sun, since some butterflies will still be flying if the air temperature is high enough.

Plan to learn the common garden butterflies and their habits as a first step in butterfly gardening; most of the butterflies mentioned in this book can be found in gardens and are considered common. A list of the most common and widespread butterflies is provided in the next chapter. While their population numbers do vary each year, common garden butterflies are common because they have developed lifestyle strategies that allow them to utilize a variety of habitat features. They are not particularly picky eaters as caterpillars, some overwinter as adults, and many are highly mobile, either through migration or simply as large butterflies that are able to range over wide areas.

While you are learning to attract and feed these common butterflies in your garden, you are certain to notice other butterflies there as well. Looking carefully, you might even find a caterpillar or two munching away at a flowering perennial or shrub. The more time you spend looking for butterflies either in

Giant Swallowtails are strong fliers that may briefly visit gardens before quickly flying away. Regular observations at different times of the day may allow you to see a Giant Swallowtail making a quick stop for nectar, like this one nectaring on milkweed.

The National Butterfly Center's palapa is surrounded by beds filled with native plants that provide nectar and caterpillar food for butterflies. Used for picnics as well as events, the palapa affords a stunning view of Monarchs, Queens, and Soldiers attracted to palmleaf thoroughwort, also known as Gregg's mistflower, in the foreground of the photo.

ONE PLACE TO SEE large numbers of butterflies is the flagship project of the North American Butterfly Association—the National Butterfly Center, located in Mission, Texas. Open 365 days a year, the National Butterfly Center was created and developed by NABA as a 100-acre native-plant and wildlife preserve. This wild butterfly nature sanctuary is devoted to education about, and conservation of, native butterflies.

Strategically located in the Rio Grande Valley, the National Butterfly Center is considered the butterfly capital of the United States. The subtropical climate of South Texas allows the center to remain open year-round, and the variety of butterflies this region attracts is unique for the United States. The valley is the only place in the country where the northernmost range of many Mexican butterflies overlaps with the southernmost range of a number of U.S. butterflies. As a result, more than 300 species of butterflies have been recorded in the valley, among them many rarely seen species as well as first U.S. records.

your garden or out and about, the more you will understand what butterflies live in your area and what plants they use. Start a record of what you see. It can be a simple quick photo with a cell phone, which will give you all the information you need: the butterfly, the location, and the date. Start with the group of common butterflies and you will soon see how much fun it is to expand your butterfly horizons.

FINDING AND NAMING BUTTERFLIES WITH FIELD GUIDES AND TECHNOLOGY

Butterfly field guides are books designed to help the user identify butterflies. Observe a butterfly in nature, and then use the information in the guide to determine the name of the butterfly. All field guides have some similarities; butterflies are grouped and listed by family, all guides feature images of butterflies, and all provide information that will allow the user to narrow down the butterfly they see in the garden to one in the book. However, there are differences between guides; one field guide may show multiple angles of one butterfly species, another may present only one. Some guides use photographs, while others rely on illustrations. The many different guide layouts are a boon for users, making it easy to find a field guide that appeals to each person's needs. Consider the purchase of at least one butterfly field guide as one of the essential items needed for butterfly gardening. As you observe butterflies, either at home or on field trips, use a field guide to work out the name of the butterfly. As your list of identified butterflies grows, you can plant the caterpillar foods required by those butterflies, thereby increasing your chances of attracting more butterflies.

Traditionally designed to be compact enough to take into the field, field guides are usually paperback and small enough to be easily carried when outside. Although the original purpose of guiding a person in the field is still very valid, many people use their field guides as reference books in the comfort of their homes. Given the wide range of inexpensive cameras, from cell phones to point-and-shoot cameras, it can be easier (and fun) to take photos in the field or around the yard and then compare them later to the field guide. If you choose this route, be sure to take a number of photos so that different angles of the butterfly are observable.

Start using your field guide the moment you get it! Look through it carefully so that you become comfortable with how the butterflies are presented. Each guide will have its own style of abbreviations, maps, and species accounts that are displayed in the most compact way possible. It can be a bit like reading a secret code until you become familiar with the style of the particular guide. Keep in mind that many field guides are written for large expanses, like the entire United States, while others have narrowed their focus down to regions or states. Personal preference will play a large role in which guide works best for you. Consider the following when making your decision:

- Are you interested in caterpillar and butterfly egg identification? Perhaps a separate caterpillar field guide will also be necessary.
- Do not discount a state-specific field guide that targets a state other than the one where you live. While a field guide from a different state will not be completely accurate for identifying butterflies in your area, some state field guides go into a lot of detail about butterfly habitat and how to tell the difference between similar butterflies, both of which are topics that will enhance gardening for butterflies.
- A field guide is important to have but there are other books on butterflies, often found under the classification of "butterfly biology" or "butterfly gardening," that can help you learn to identify butterflies. While larger books are not designed to be taken into the field, their size allows more information on butterfly habitats and habits to be presented. In the case of butterfly field guides and their associated reference books, size does not matter; content and how it appeals to an individual are the important factors.
- Field guides assume that you are able to clearly see butterflies but it is often not possible to get close to the butterfly you wish to identify. Close-range focus binoculars magnify butterflies (and other small creatures) and allow butterfly watchers to clearly see field marks referenced by butterfly field guides. These specialized binoculars are available in a variety of prices and many are very lightweight.

Whether your garden attracts scores of active butterflies or leaves you standing alone wondering where the party went is a facet of working with nature. The reality that very little is static in a garden is accentuated when butterflies, or any insects for that matter, become part of the garden's focus. The creation of habitat for butterflies is an ongoing process, not a fixed point that will ever be perfectly attained.

Habitat can mean many different things to butterfly gardeners, and there is even dissent among the ranks of butterfly enthusiasts as to whether butterfly gardening is actually beneficial. For some, butterfly habitat is simply any location that provides nectar for adult butterflies and food for the caterpillar stage of a butterfly's life. This interpretation would certainly be valid for butterflies that are already living and breeding in your immediate location. Others are concerned that a garden designed for butterflies is no more than a trap that attracts them in unnaturally dense numbers, making them easy targets for diseases and for predators such as birds and wasps. The gardener must ultimately decide for him or herself what the butterfly garden will mean and what a butterfly garden is for. The remainder of this book will arm readers with information to develop their own response to the question "What is butterfly habitat?" Spoiler alert: There is no single answer to this question!

CHECKLIST OF ACTIONS FOR GETTING STARTED

- Join NABA! If one is near you, take advantage of the wealth of knowledge and activities offered by NABA chapters or other nature-oriented clubs.
- Identify local trees, weeds, and wildflowers that currently provide butterfly habitat. Nature centers often offer classes on how to identify local plants. Also, check with your state's native plant society for plant identification resources as well as educational walks where plant identification is taught. Use online sources as well as printed plant field guides to become familiar with plants that you see. Decide how these existing plants near your home can be protected or their numbers increased.
- If you have not already done so, consider planting milkweed to support Monarchs.
- Find and visit local or regional gardens that promote butterflies or native plants. When visiting a public garden, take note of the plants being visited by butterflies and consider whether they would work in your garden.
- Eliminate your use of home and garden pesticides. If total elimination is not possible, consider limiting the number of pesticides and always use the smallest amount possible to achieve your goal. Moreover, broaden your tolerance of insects—most of them are beneficial or neutral, so be sure you are targeting a true pest when you deploy your death spray.
- Visit a native plant nursery. Ask what plants are locally important for butterflies in your area. Learn to identify three nectar plants and three caterpillar food plants used by common butterflies in your area.
- As you start to notice butterflies, record your observations either on paper or with photographs.

CHAPTER TWO

BUTTERFLY BASICS

A handful of butterflies can be considered common garden butterflies across the United States. None of their populations are listed as threatened by habitat loss and none need special protective measures or monitoring. Common, however, does not mean unexceptional; it merely indicates that the butterflies in question occur widely across the United States and are securely established within their ranges. In this chapter, we will consider how to make a welcoming place for these common species. If you succeed in attracting and fostering common butterflies, you may have also created hospitable spaces for many more butterflies, whether common or not.

Butterflies broadly distributed across the country generally have lifestyles that allow them to thrive in widely different types of gardens and locations. Some of the common garden butterflies will occur more predictably near wooded areas, while others may greatly prefer wide open spaces, but as a group

Eastern Tiger Swallowtail drinking nectar from fall phlox. White, pink, or lavender are all common colors for fall phlox, which despite its name blooms in the middle of summer.

overall, they are found throughout much of the United States and may be seen over long periods of time during the warmer months of the year.

What this group of butterflies have in common is an acceptance of habitats that are altered by people—lands that probably have little chance of reverting to their original condition. It is in these altered landscapes that butterfly gardens can successfully attract a number of butterfly visitors if they cater to common garden species. Butterflies do not thrive in sterile environments featuring just a few nonnative, traditionally planted shrubs or trees; they need fresh caterpillar food from herbaceous plants, shrubs, and trees. Many caterpillars will only eat and successfully grow on plants that are native to their region. The adult butterflies also need a constantly replenished nectar supply, which means a riot of blooming flowers—and again, nectar plants should be selected from a group of flowering garden plants preferred by butterflies. In short, gardening for butterflies is a way to bring visual excitement to a landscape while improving an environment that previously supported very few butterflies or other wildlife.

Other areas preferred by the common garden butterflies are more transitional in nature, retain some elements of their wild plant life, and have not been irrevocably altered. Edges of agricultural fields, unmowed rural roadsides, and even the land under power lines can help support these butterflies. By working to preserve these semiwild areas in or near our communities, we will benefit butterflies as well as enable other wildlife, such as birds, to make their homes closer to humans. These slightly wilder places might shelter butterflies that will visit smaller gardens for nectar or perhaps to lay eggs on caterpillar food plants. Even if the urban and rural butterfly populations do not mingle, transitional areas can provide us with places to learn about butterfly survival in a natural setting as well as provide recreation for butterfly watchers.

COMMON GARDEN BUTTERFLIES

When starting to watch common garden butterflies, it is handy to remember that the butterflies you will see in the United States are organized into six families: Swallowtails, Whites and Yellows, Gossamer-wings, Metalmarks, Brushfoots, and Skippers. Each time you use your field guide to learn the identity of

Swallowtails, like this Eastern Tiger Swallowtail, are strong fliers and lively garden visitors. This long row of eastern purple coneflower attracts many butterflies.

a new butterfly species, check the guide to see which larger family that butterfly belongs to. By noting the differences and similarities between the butterflies in each family, identifications will become easier and your familiarity with the butterfly world will grow more quickly.

The Swallowtail Family

NABA's *Checklist & English Names of North American Butterflies* lists 34 species of swallowtails occurring north of Mexico. Swallowtail caterpillars feed on a variety of plants. Some, like those of Black Swallowtail, will eat a number of different plants from two different plant families (the Carrot Family and the Citrus Family); however, many swallowtail species specialize on a single plant for caterpillar food. Many of these obligate feeders are tied to plant families considered primitive by botanists: the flowers produced are not brightly colored and many do not produce nectar. Despite the lack of wow-power from bright flowers, these plants are beautiful in the garden for their large leaves, which lend a tropical vibe particularly when the plants are set in groups. Dutchman's pipes (for Pipevine and Polydamas swallowtails); pawpaw (for Zebra Swallowtail); redbay (for Palamedes Swallowtail); and sweetbay magnolia, sassafras, and tuliptree (all three trees feed Eastern Tiger Swallowtails) are all plants to consider if you hope to see as many swallowtails as possible for your location. Northern spicebush, which does not have particularly large leaves, is also in this primitive plant group (the taxonomic subclass Magnoliidae), and should be planted if you live in the range of Spicebush Swallowtail.

Range maps (a feature in all butterfly field guides) show the area where each species of butterfly is known to occur. You can use these maps to help you gauge the likelihood of observing a particular species, although actually finding a butterfly depends on more than using a range map as a predictor. To further narrow the possibility of a seeing a particular butterfly, consider the type of habitat it frequents, the species' abundance, and its flight period. The range map is just the jumping-off point to learning about that specific butterfly. These two range maps show where Western Tiger Swallowtail and Eastern Tiger Swallowtail are likely to be seen. The large irregular-shaped colored areas on the maps indicate where the butterfly's range occurs and how many generations per year a species will produce (in this case purple areas indicate two generations and turquoise areas indicate one generation) while the pink circles mark where a butterfly has been sighted beyond its traditional range.

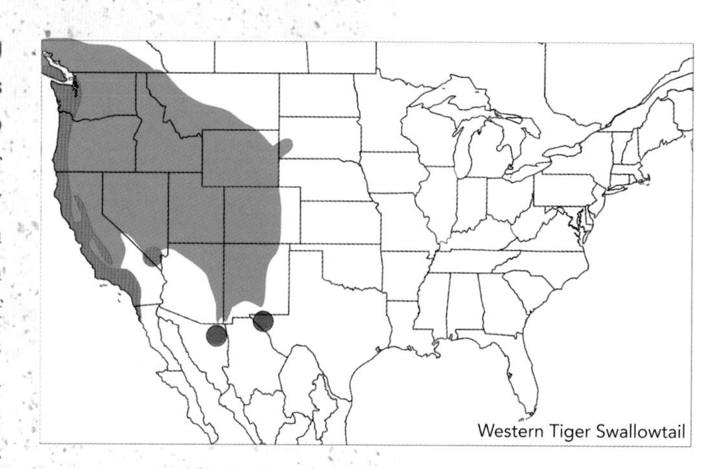
Western Tiger Swallowtail

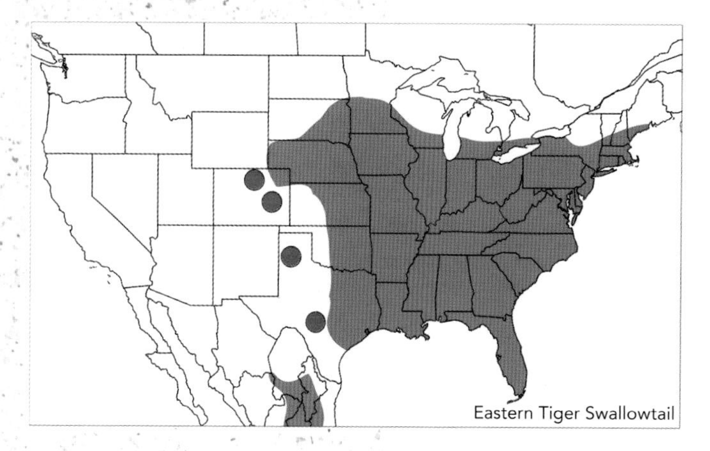
Eastern Tiger Swallowtail

Tiger Swallowtail—Eastern Tiger Swallowtail and Western Tiger Swallowtail

Easily observed because of their size (with a wingspan of 3–5 inches) and bright yellow color with an overlay of black stripes, tiger swallowtails are perhaps the simplest butterflies to identify in gardens. Swallowtails will take nectar from a variety of flowers but are most often seen on large flowers that offer a stable perch to land on. Another life strategy that makes tiger swallowtails so widespread is the ability of their caterpillars to feed on a number of common and widespread trees.

Swallowtails overwinter as chrysalides and emerge in mid- to late spring or early summer. This first generation of the year mates and lays eggs that will develop into a second generation, or brood, of adult butterflies. The two broods may seem to overlap and result in what seems like a continuous population of swallowtails during the garden season. Depending on the species, with careful observation it will be noted that there is usually some time between the broods when no swallowtails of a particular species are flying.

This Eastern Tiger Swallowtail chrysalis spent the winter protected in a glass aquarium inside a garage. When spring finally arrives, the adult butterfly will emerge and begin the first brood of the year.

A BUTTERFLY BROOD is defined as a butterfly generation—a complete life cycle that progresses from egg, caterpillar, and chrysalis to adult butterfly. Some butterfly species take an entire year to complete their life cycle, but many species have multiple broods, meaning that the butterfly population produces more than one generation per year. More specifically, the term *butterfly brood* often refers to the distinct part of the life cycle when adult butterflies are flying. For example, the Eastern Tiger Swallowtails that emerge in late spring to early summer would be referred to as the spring brood. These butterflies mate and lay eggs, which eventually produce adults that fly in midsummer and are referred to as the summer brood.

The Whites and Yellows Family

As the name suggests, the wings of butterflies in this family are primarily white or yellow. Many are trimmed in black, and some have orange bands or spots, but all show a base color of white or yellow. Most butterflies in this group are wide ranging and accept a number of different nectar plants and caterpillar food plants, making them easy garden guests to attract and feed.

Cabbage White

The medium-sized Cabbage White will nectar on small to medium-sized flowers and often visits gardens in large numbers. Because this species is multibrooded, Cabbage White caterpillars can be a persistent pest on homegrown cabbage, broccoli, and kale, but gardeners plagued by the dreaded "cabbage worm" can protect their vegetables by using floating row covers to shield them from hungry caterpillars. Cabbage White may be the first butterfly you notice

When carefully observed, even common butterflies—like this Cabbage White nectaring on whorled mountainmint—show off their beauty. Who knew that Cabbage Whites had such fetching green eyes?

LEARNING THE NAMES OF BUTTERFLIES is an important first step toward communicating about these colorful, day-flying winged insects. But which name to use? Cabbage White is only one of the common names for *Pieris rapae*. Others used for the same insect include European Small White, Garden White Butterfly, and Imported Cabbageworm.

NABA has created a standardized list of butterfly common names—*The NABA Checklist & English Names of North American Butterflies*. The NABA Names Committee, a group of people knowledgeable about and professionally involved with butterflies oversees this publication. The committee continually evaluates both the scientific and common names of the 722 species of butterflies that naturally occur in North America north of Mexico and in Hawaii.

A list of accepted butterfly names is a great help, but it must be used in conjunction with a field guide if one is to be able to match the butterfly with the name. All field guides state the source of common and scientific names used in each particular guide, and not all field guides use names from the same source. One guide that uses NABA names as listed in the *NABA Checklist & English Names of North American Butterflies* is *A Swift Guide to Butterflies of North America*.

flying in the spring and one of the latest to be spotted in the fall. Because they are abundant, Cabbage Whites may not attract much attention, but close observation will prove that even an everyday butterfly can be beautiful.

Orange Sulphur

Although one of the most widespread and common butterflies, Orange Sulphur can also be one of the more confusing to identify accurately with any degree of certainty, at least when one is first starting to identify yellow butterflies. Sulphurs most often land with their wings closed, thereby limiting the chance to discern this species' orange patch of color, which is most clearly seen when the wings are open. Some amount of orange color is visible on the closed forewings, but it can be variable and hard to see, and much depends on the light level, your angle of view, and how old and worn the butterfly is.

A similar-sized yellow butterfly likely to visit gardens is the Clouded Sulphur, which can mate with Orange Sulphurs, creating a hybrid whose appearance can be variable. While the amount of orange on an Orange Sulphur can vary from a lot to a little, Clouded Sulphurs always lack any orange coloration. Females of both species even have a white form that somewhat resembles a Cabbage White. This variation occurs because yellow pigments that color the wings contain nitrogen. A female that displays white wings has used the nitrogen from these pigments to increase her growth rate, which may ultimately lead to that individual butterfly producing larger eggs.

In addition to female white, or "alba," forms, Orange Sulphurs and other related sulphurs display color and size differences by season, with darker butterflies seen in the spring and fall. Rather than be intimidated by the color, size, and hybrid variations of Orange Sulphurs and their relatives, start to look into the possible variations that occur in your location. Armed with a local field guide, observing carefully, and recording what you see, you will find that the sulphurs can provide a window into the changing seasons and conditions in your garden.

The Gossamer-wing Family

To really become familiar with these colorful little butterflies, a pair of close-focusing binoculars will come in handy. All members of this butterfly family are small (about thumbnail-size!) and not always nectaring on a plant within arm's reach or gaze, but the colors and intricate markings of these creatures should not be missed. Many of the butterflies in this large family are "specialists," often requiring a very specific food plant that grows in a very particular habitat. Although these specialist butterflies are unlikely to visit our plantings, a number of gossamer-wings do occur in gardens across the country.

There are no vampire or zombie butterflies, but if you were looking for macabre behavior in the butterfly world, some of the gossamer-wings will provide a bit of gruesome natural history. The Harvester, which is in its own subfamily, is a bright little woodland butterfly with a range over the eastern United States as far west as Minnesota, and south to central Texas and central Florida. Like many gossamer-wings, it is closely tied to specific plants in order to complete its life cycle, although in this case they are not caterpillar food plants—well, at least not directly!

The Harvester is a carnivore; its caterpillar feeds on woolly aphids. While woolly aphids are widespread and comprise many different species, there is only one Harvester, so while you may be familiar with woolly aphids on apple trees or ornamental shrubs, the Harvester associates primarily with those that

OPPOSITE: Fuller's teasel is an invasive nonnative plant that is commonly seen growing in wild or abandoned fields. While it can crowd out native plants and is certainly not recommended for propagation, it often attracts crowds of nectaring butterflies. These two Orange Sulphurs display both the dorsal (upperside) view (visible when the wings are held open) and the ventral (underside) view (visible when the wings are folded above the body), allowing for a nice comparison of the wing colors that might be seen when watching this common garden butterfly.

infest alders and hawthorns (which take the form of large shrubs or small trees), as well as beech and ash trees.

Although the members of this small group of shrubs and trees are common and widespread, Harvesters are most commonly found in association with them when the shrubs or trees are growing near streams, ditches, swamps, or creeks. Even though the plants are common and their associated woolly aphids somewhat so, Harvesters are not—they are considered "local," meaning they do not occur in all areas of apparently suitable habitat. Harvesters, with their specific habitat needs, illustrate how difficult (or nearly impossible!) it is to attract certain butterflies to a garden environment.

When watching for Harvesters, look both on leaves, where they may bask in filtered sunlight, and on damp or muddy areas, where they may puddle for minerals. Ask local butterfly enthusiasts whether they know of a Harvester colony you can visit. It is truly magical to watch Harvesters basking in a sunlit opening along a trail in the shaded woods.

The black dot surrounded by bright orange markings on the hindwings of Gray Hairstreaks appears to be a false eye, and the filaments that make up the "tails" on the hindwings mimic antennae, allowing Gray Hairstreaks to pull off a pretty good impression of a head at the back of their body. More than just a jazzy decoration, the false head confuses predatory birds into reaching for the back of the butterfly, thus (it is hoped) coming away with a mouthful of filament tails and a few wing scales rather than a nice butterfly body, and allowing the Gray Hairstreak a chance at escape. Many of the gossamer-wing butterflies have false eyespots, filament tails, or both. When watching Gray Hairstreaks nectar, it is fascinating to see the sawing motion of the wings that makes the false head move back and forth, looking all the more convincingly like the head rather than the tail. Get some close-focusing binoculars and have a look.

Gray Hairstreak

Start closely observing the visitors that come to your flowers and soon you will be familiar with Gray Hairstreak, a Gossamer-wing Family butterfly that is widespread across the United States. Small and slow flying, Gray Hairstreaks are found in gardens as well as in disturbed or weedy areas. Mountainmints are among the best garden plants to watch for Gray Hairstreaks—or any local hairstreaks for that matter— although they will nectar at a large number of other plants as well. Gray Hairstreak caterpillars also feed on a large variety of plants, so to attract this butterfly you need only a pesticide-free garden plus a wide variety of garden plants. While Gray Hairstreak is a common butterfly across the country, its abundance does vary by region. East Coast gardens will, on average, see fewer Gray Hairstreaks than many other parts of the United States.

Metalmark Family

This family receives the "least likely to visit your garden" award among all the butterfly families north of Mexico. In the tropics of Central and South America, metalmarks are much more diverse, much more common, and much more colorful, than the 22 species in the United States.

The metalmarks of the United States are small butterflies, recognized by their green eyes and metallic wing marks. This nectaring Northern Metalmark in New Jersey is oblivious of the fact that its population is threatened—both its caterpillar food plant and its specialized habitat are under pressure from humans and from other plants.

The habitat requirements for Northern Metalmark are so exacting that this butterfly occurs only in small, isolated populations. Roundleaf ragwort is its preferred—and perhaps sole—caterpillar food plant, but Japanese stiltgrass, Japanese barberry, and other invasive nonnative plants threaten to crowd out the ragwort in our wild lands where Northern Metalmarks remain. Even where roundleaf ragwort is abundant, Northern Metalmarks utilize it only under very specific conditions—the plants must be growing within open stands of eastern redcedar on calcareous (limestone-derived) soils. Northern Metalmarks also require that nectar plants (preferably blackeyed Susan and butterfly milkweed) must be available within 150 feet. They won't travel far! As these limited sites become overgrown with invasive plants or are disturbed or ill managed, Northern Metalmark populations remain precariously small and under increasing threat.

Trying to attract butterflies to a garden is not nearly as difficult as helping to save threatened butterflies in the wild, like Northern Metalmarks—theirs is a complex and changing situation that does not have a simple solution. Butterfly gardening at home starts to give gardeners a sense of how hard it is to walk the fine line between human activity and its impact on nature, which it is hoped results in a greater sensitivity to the plight of butterflies that do have exacting habitat demands and an appreciation of how pressure from peoples' activities trickles down to even the smallest creatures.

The Brushfoot Family

The Brushfoot Family includes a dazzlingly wide array of butterflies, many of which are common to gardens and suburbs. Do not let the large size and variability of this family intimidate you when paging through a field guide! Some butterflies, like Monarchs, will be known to just about everyone, while others, like the crescents, may not be as familiar. None of the Brushfoot Family butterflies are as large as swallowtails, but many are brightly colored and large enough to be noticeable from a distance without binoculars.

Crescents—Pearl Crescent, Field Crescent, and Northern Crescent

Commonly seen in many habitats, these three crescents are separated by geography. Pearl Crescent's flight range is throughout the eastern United States up to the Continental Divide. Field Crescent's range extends across the western United States from where the Pearl Crescent's range ends. Northern Crescent's range is, as the name says, the northern part of the United States, with some range overlap with both Pearl and Field crescents. Despite their different locations, all three crescent species share asters as their caterpillar food plants;

This Common Buckeye and Pearl Crescent look like they are lined up on an airport runway, queuing for takeoff. The photographer most likely caught them basking in the morning sun, too cold for flight. But whatever their intent, the proximity of these two butterflies gives a good idea of their relative sizes. Common Buckeye is another Brushfoot Family member that visits gardens; it is a year- round resident in the southern states. Each spring the first brood migrates northward, laying eggs as they go. Over the course of the summer, the population can reach as far north as southern Canada, although the extent of their northward movement varies each year. Accommodating Common Buckeye caterpillars in a garden is straightforward, as they will feed on nonnative but colorful and easy-to-grow garden snapdragons. Willing to accept a number of different food plants, Common Buckeye caterpillars will also readily use the lawn weed common plantain.

however, all asters are not the same and certain asters are more attractive to the crescents than others. Like many things in nature, many specific details about butterfly behavior are not known, and the list of all caterpillar food plants is one of those areas where we are still learning. When it comes to the crescent butterflies, sources differ on which asters are preferred by each species.

Butterfly field guides and other publications often indicate the plant family rather than a particular plant species as the caterpillar food source. Does this mean that caterpillars of these three crescent butterflies will readily consume all plants in the Aster Family? Considering the very large number of aster species, it is likely that some will be more attractive than others to the various crescent species. Additionally, each aster species is suited to certain regions and cultural conditions, so if planting for these butterflies—or for any specific butterfly for that matter—it is best to look for a specific recommended plant species that is known to feed the caterpillar. Lists of specific recommended caterpillar food plants are included in this book. Communicating with other butterfly gardeners to find out which specific plants have worked for them is another tried and true method of selecting plants that will feed and sustain caterpillars. Try the recommended plant first and then branch out to closely related plants if you wish to experiment with caterpillar food plants.

New England aster is often recommended as a caterpillar food plant for Pearl Crescent, as is Pacific aster for Field Crescent. Northern Crescent poses a problem, however, perhaps partly because of the uncertainty surrounding its classification as a species; Northern Crescent and Pearl Crescent were considered the same species as recently as 25 years ago. Even though the two butterflies are currently listed by NABA as separate species, this is not without controversy. Most gardeners will not want to wade into butterfly taxonomy and the battle between the lumping and splitting of Northerns and Pearls, so for now, plant New England asters for Northern Crescent; it is a documented caterpillar food plant that is a good addition to gardens and is an easy to find plant.

New England aster is a large perennial covered with many small flowers—it provides nectar for many fall-flying butterflies as well as caterpillar food for Pearl and Northern crescents.

Question Mark

Butterfly guides describe Question Mark as a butterfly found in and at the edges of woodlands, and specifically moist woodlands. Even if your garden does not happen to be ideally situated next to a bucolic, damp, woody wonderland, Question Marks can still be drawn to parks and yards if their caterpillar foods—elms, hackberries, or nettles—are readily available. Since nettles are renowned for stinging, and elms (still susceptible to Dutch elm disease) are not commercially available, you will probably want to check native-plant nurseries for one of the many species of hackberry tree. As a bonus, if you live within their range, a hackberry may also reward you by attracting the less-common butterflies Hackberry and Tawny emperors, Empress Leilia, or American Snout.

QUESTION MARKS rarely visit flowers for nectar; instead, they gain energy by drinking liquids from rotting fruit, tree sap, and even animal droppings. An interesting way to see Question Marks in a garden setting is to set up a butterfly feeder, which can be as simple as a slice of watermelon set out on a plate where animals and people will not disturb it. Other gardeners create more elaborate arrangements for butterfly feeding.

A Question Mark and a two Hackberry Emperors share a juicy watermelon slice.

Eastern Comma and Hoary Comma

Very similar in appearance to Question Marks, Eastern Commas (east of the Rocky Mountains) are smaller and show a silvery, comma-shaped mark on their closed hindwings, while Question Marks display a crescent mark next to a dot. Hoary Commas (west of the Rocky Mountains in the United States) also display a comma-shaped wing mark but their range does not overlap with Eastern Comma or Question Mark, eliminating possible punctuation problems in the West. There are other commas in the West (Satryr, Green, Gray, and Oreas) but none of them are common or likely to visit gardens.

This American Lady has made an exploratory stop at what appears to be a particularly desirable piece of animal scat. Sharing this morsel is an Eastern Comma, known to prefer non-nectar sources of nourishment, while American Ladies more commonly prefer flower nectar. The silvery comma mark is clearly visible on the Eastern Comma's hind wing.

Mourning Cloak

Widely seen across the United States, although rare in the Gulf States and peninsular Florida, Mourning Cloaks may either overwinter in northern locations or migrate south for the winter. They are large, strong-flying butterflies often seen on the first warm days of spring and the occasional warm day late in fall. The deep blackish-brown color of their wings allows Mourning Cloaks to more easily absorb sunlight to warm themselves.

Another way Mourning Cloaks, as well as other butterflies, warm up is through short bursts of intense shivering. Although this severe shaking might look like a behavior that indicates a problem, butterflies are simply warming themselves by rapidly vibrating their wings in place rather than flapping them up and down. This odd-looking spectacle warms their flight muscles and body and may be observed even on warm days if butterflies have cooled down because of shade, wetness, or other environmental factors. Shivering behavior is something to watch for in butterflies like Mourning Cloaks that fly during relatively changeable cool spring and fall days.

Basking on gravel in the bright sunlight helps this Mourning Cloak absorb the sun's warmth. Mourning Cloaks do not commonly nectar on flowers but are attracted to tree sap, rotting fruit, and animal dung. Watch these sources for hungry Mourning Cloaks.

American Lady

Some American Ladies overwinter as adults in northern climates, so sightings of this wide-ranging butterfly often begin early in spring. The actual northern limit of American Lady overwintering has not been firmly established, and questions persist regarding the life stage in which they overwinter. Some reports suggest that only adults overwinter, while others indicate that both adults and chrysalides overwinter. Additionally, American Ladies are migrants, so as the weather warms each spring, butterflies from the south move northward, laying eggs as they progress. However, one fact *is* clear; American Ladies are widespread and common in gardens!

To the nascent butterfly watcher, American Ladies look quite similar to Painted Ladies, or in the western United States, to West Coast Ladies as well. Painted Lady, with more than 100 recorded host plants, needs no special planting plans, and West Coast Lady caterpillars accept a variety of plant, some of which are weeds, but if you wish to watch the life cycle of American Lady, you will need to provide its caterpillar food plants. These are native plants that are lovely to include in gardens—western pearly everlasting, some of the species of pussytoes, and the similar but rather unattractively named cudweed.

Pussytoes are a group of plants that are easy to incorporate into gardens or wild plantings—their cultural needs are not great, and in fact they can be used as a ground cover in dry areas with poor soil. Approximately 40 different species of pussytoes are native in the United States, although many are not commonly for sale. Native-plant nurseries usually carry at least one species, with shale barren pussytoes, rosy pussytoes, and the oddly named woman's tobacco being fairly common.

ABOVE: This patch of Parlin's pussytoes had only recently been planted before an American Lady stopped by to lay eggs. The butterfly abdomen curved under with the tip of the abdomen touching the pussytoes indicates that she is depositing eggs on the caterpillar food plant.

American Lady caterpillars can skeletonize pussytoe leaves but the plants are resilient and will grow new foliage once the caterpillars become chrysalides. Caterpillars use both the fuzzy plant hairs and the flowerheads from the pussytoes to form downy shelters where they hide and munch the leaves in privacy.

Many butterfly gardeners have reported to NABA that pussytoes has been the plant that most exemplifies the saying "plant it and they will come." Since American Ladies are found in most of the United States and pussytoes are as well, often just planting the caterpillar food plant is enough attract the butterfly to your garden.

Painted Lady

Here is a "bug" that is found everywhere and whose caterpillars eat a multitude of different plants. Sounds like a pest-control nightmare scenario to most people, but in this case it is just the Painted Lady, often called "the planet's most cosmopolitan butterfly." Very common as garden visitors, Painted Ladies nectar at many flowers and their caterpillars feed on at least 100 different plants, so you need no elaborate garden-planting scheme in order to attract this butterfly.

Just grow a plain old flower garden, do not apply pesticides, and the Painted Lady will visit at some point in time. Painted Ladies seen each summer in U.S. gardens have migrated from Mexico. The population expands as temperatures warm, and the vagaries of each year's weather deeply influence the size of each summer's population. Some years bring spectacular numbers, while in other years the lack of Painted Ladies will seem mysterious.

Red Admiral

Painted Lady and American Lady, as well as the less widely distributed West Coast Lady, all belong to the genus *Vanessa*, and their resemblance to each other makes it a little tricky for beginning butterfliers to quickly tell them apart. Red Admiral also belongs to this genus and is similar in size to the three ladies but far easier to identify. On its open, dark wings, prominent white spots decorate the forewing tips and striking reddish-orange bands cross the mid-forewings—no other North American butterfly has similar markings.

Like Painted Ladies, Red Admirals stage large migrations in some years. While you may not actually see hordes of butterflies streaming across the sky,

With wings closed, American Lady (opposite), Painted Lady (below left), and Red Admiral (below) are similar, yet identifiable.

you will know that Red Admirals are passing through when out of nowhere, you suddenly see 20 individuals flitting around your garden. They tend to be very active garden butterflies, and male Red Admirals will stake out a perch while waiting for a female Red Admiral to happen by. The males will perch until something, even you (!), come into their range. Once a moving object has been spotted, the Red Admiral will leave his perch to investigate. Whether the males are defending a territory from other potential suitors or merely passing the time on the perch until a suitable female comes in range is unclear but is a behavior to watch for when Red Admirals are around.

Monarch

Monarchs need milkweed—a commonly known fact even among people who do not garden. For those who wish to plant milkweed, many gardenworthy species are available to encourage Monarch egg-laying. Some, like common milkweed, might irritate (or delight) gardeners when they start to claim the entire

Although all are called milkweeds, each species has different cultural requirements and can fill a different niche in a garden design. Here, swamp milkweed (left) with its purplish-pink flowers will tolerate moist soils and even a bit of shade while orange flowered butterfly milkweed (right) requires soils with excellent drainage and full sun in order to thrive.

neighborhood with their colonizing underground stems. Another, tropical milkweed, may sow apprehension because in some areas it has been implicated in the spread of a deadly Monarch parasite. Making an informed choice about which milkweed to plant can seem daunting, but the basic fact is that planting milkweed is an important steppingstone in helping to boost Monarch population numbers high enough that their migration across much of the United States can continue for generations to come.

If the cultural needs of the milkweed and the gardening needs of the gardener are matched properly, no uncertainty should result about which milkweed to choose. When beginning to plant for Monarchs, select from a small group of readily available milkweeds — swamp milkweed for richer, moister soils; butterfly milkweed for dry, very well drained soils; showy milkweed and Mexican whorled milkweed for California and many parts of the West.

If a particular milkweed is readily available in your area, check its native status and range, find out whether you can provide its soil and moisture requirements, and if so, try it. The range of each plant considered native to the United States can be researched at www.plants.usda.gov. Just be aware that some milkweeds are quite expansive in their habits and can crowd out neighboring plants in just a few years, so plan accordingly by either giving a large space to milkweed or planning to divide the plant colony every few years. Also, be aware that since some milkweeds are rather short-lived perennials, you may have to replenish your colony occasionally if self-seeding does not suffice.

OPPOSITE: A Monarch lays eggs on fresh tropical milkweed growth—when caterpillars hatch from the eggs, they will not have to travel far to eat the tender leaves and flowers.

TROPICAL MILKWEED is not native to the United States or Canada yet it is commonly grown in gardens for Monarchs. It is a perennial plant in southern Florida, southern Texas, and other southern portions of the United States. Tropical milkweed is used throughout the colder portions of the country as an annual plant for use in garden borders as well as container plantings. And Monarchs love it!

In recent years, Monarch researchers have suggested that the use of tropical milkweed in the southern United States may be disrupting the Monarch migration by providing milkweed foliage on a year-round basis, which encourages Monarchs to overwinter in the southern states rather than complete their fall migration to Mexico. Research also suggests that the likelihood of the protozoan Monarch parasite *Ophryocystis elektroscirrha* (or OE for short) is more prevalent on Monarchs that visit tropical milkweed in areas where the plant does not die back in the fall. An increase in OE infections will have a serious impact on the health of the Monarch population, and the idea that Monarchs are being "trapped" and interrupting their migration by nonnative tropical milkweed in the southern United States is still being researched.

Showy milkweed is native to the western portion of the United States and a good choice for California gardens.

Should you avoid tropical milkweed? Not necessarily. Of course, one solution is to plant other, native varieties of milkweed, all of which die back to the ground in the fall, thus eliminating the two primary concerns associated with tropical milkweed. If you choose, however, to plant tropical milkweed, the recommendation is to start with fresh tropical milkweed plants each year and treat it as an annual. This will prevent the buildup of OE spores on the plants. For southern locations where tropical milkweed grows as a perennial plant, it is advisable to cut tropical milkweed plants back to the ground in the fall, thus encouraging fresh, uninfected growth.

The Skipper Family

Skippers are small, fast-flying butterflies that many people initially think are moths. Skippers have relatively thick bodies and short wings and their flight is often characterized as fast, darting, or jerky—obviously thought by some to be a "skipping" motion.

The vast majority of the skippers in the United States lack colorful scales and so tend to be orange, white, brown, black, or gray. Many skippers are smaller than the familiar and colorful garden visitors that initially come to mind when thinking "butterfly," but once you notice skippers, you will appreciate the motion and activity they add to the garden.

Two subfamilies of skippers visit gardens in the United States: spreadwing skippers and grass-skippers. The spreadwing skippers generally perch with both forewings and hindwings open flat, while grass-skippers sit perkily with all wings closed or with the forewings open at a 45-degree angle to the flat hindwings. It is possible to get a peek at the open wings of a grass-skipper when it basks in the sun, a common behavior. Grass-skippers are also equipped with exceedingly long tongues, allowing them to nectar at many types of flowers.

Common Checkered-Skipper in a typical spread-wing stance.

CHECKERED CONFUSION! Common Checkered-Skipper is likely the most widespread skipper in the United States, yet in some areas exact identification of this common garden butterfly may be impossible. The flight range of the visually identical White Checkered-Skipper overlaps with Common Checkered-Skipper throughout the far southern United States from California to Florida, making identification of the two species indistinguishable in the field. In areas where both species occur, it is best to designate the butterfly as Common/White Checkered-Skipper.

Common Checkered-Skipper

Common Checkered-Skipper is likely the most widespread skipper in the United States, and its caterpillars feed on plants in the Mallow Family. This spreadwing skipper inhabits many different settings, from prairies and meadows to yards and pastures. Open, sunny, often disturbed places are what Common Checkered-Skippers prefer.

When gazing in dreamy anticipation through garden plant catalogs, you'll never find a section designated "caterpillar food plants," but it would make things easier, since most butterfly guides list caterpillar food plants by plant family, such as the Mallow Family, which can be vague and confusing. A specific plant listed by genus and species, rather than by an entire plant family, would take the guesswork out of plant selection and entice more people to garden for butterflies. Monarch caterpillars need milkweed, but some milkweed species are more attractive to

Old-fashioned but with plenty of charm, hollyhocks can provide caterpillar food for a few common garden butterflies.

caterpillars than others, and Pipevine Swallowtail will eat only pipevine, yet some of the exotic pipevines, such as pelicanflower, are toxic to their caterpillars; butterflies will lay eggs on pelicanflower, but the caterpillars will not thrive long, the leaves are too toxic. On the other end of the spectrum, there are caterpillars whose behavior is so specialized that they will feed on only one plant, such as the caterpillars of Harris' Checkerspot, which will feed only on parasol whitetop, but these specialized feeders are not common garden butterflies.

The Mallow Family includes more than 4,000 plant species, but are they all suitable for Common Checkered-Skipper? Probably not, or the world would be overrun with very well-fed Common Checkered-Skippers! Hollyhock is among the Mallow Family plants used by this skipper, as are a large number of weeds such as common mallow and cheeseweed mallow. All these plants will sustain the caterpillars of Common Checkered-Skipper as well as those of West Coast Lady, Painted Lady, and Gray Hairstreak—but rather than relying on the weeds, consider choosing hollyhock, an old-fashioned, nonnative biennial.

Checkerblooms are also good decorative garden plants from the Mallow Family and native to many western states, including Colorado, Utah, Nevada, California, and the Pacific Northwest. A variable group of plants, checkerbloom species are difficult to tell apart. Providing nectar and caterpillar food, the checkerblooms are good choices to include in a butterfly garden or wild area. In the West, native-plant nurseries in your particular state are the best places to look for the various species (and subspecies) best adapted to your local conditions.

Henderson's checkerbloom, one of many native checkerblooms suitable for butterfly gardens.

Another widespread skipper that is very common in gardens is Silver-spotted Skipper. Traits common among skippers, such as a short, stout body and large faceted eyes, are evident as this individual nectars on lantana.

For those not from the West, checkerbloom hybrids are available in the nursery trade. *Sidalcea* 'Party Girl' is one of the most common hybrids and goes by the name prairie mallow 'Party Girl'. Both this plant and many of the other hybrids result from a cross between two natives, dwarf checkerbloom and white checkerbloom, both of which are sold as garden plants in their own right. Whether hybrid or species, all the checkerblooms will thrive in areas that pair warm summer days with cool nights. The upper Midwest and New England states can enjoy these plants as nonnative butterfly attractors that will also often self-seed.

TYPES OF GARDENS: METHODS OR STYLE?

Common garden butterflies will come to weed patches, roadsides, and vacant lots. They do not care if your flowerbeds are tidy and carefully thought out, so the way your butterfly haven actually looks is entirely up to you.

The style of a butterfly garden refers to how plants are arranged and the overall feeling that the garden is able to evoke. Style involves choices based on personal preference, resources, and geographic location. Choosing plants that will sustain butterflies in the garden, and maintaining the garden so that butterfly life cycles can be completed, are methods that work within any garden, regardless of style. A garden can serve dual purposes; it can present whatever style of color, shape, and feeling the gardener desires while adding a layer of ecological relevance that complements the style by drawing in butterflies and other living things.

Garden styles have historical as well as cultural and regional foundations. The style choices available to gardeners are limited only by imagination: formal gardens incorporate a balanced design that might include clipped hedges and plants placed in a symmetrical fashion, English country style encompasses a riot of shrubs and perennials jostling for space in a long border, while modern or contemporary garden styles emphasize color, shape, and strong lines. Mediterranean gardens, herb gardens, wildlife gardens, and perhaps most importantly, family gardens—all are styles that can include an emphasis on butterflies while encompassing a variety of functions from play-spaces to meditation areas.

TYPES OF GARDENS

At the National Butterfly Center's native-plant nursery, staff personnel have noticed that many people purchase new butterfly garden plants based on flower colors that will coordinate with their already existing home garden. Planting a garden full of flowers of a particular color is a popular garden style, and introducing butterfly-friendly plants into this scheme is easy.

This wildly colorful garden is located in Kansas at the edge of what was once the Tallgrass Prairie. Although the original prairie did not include a riot of colorful flowers in such tight quarters, at the height of the growing season, the prairie was a mixture of very tall grasses and bright flowering plants. This garden pays homage to its location while adding dense swaths of nectar plants to feed butterflies. Native limestone rocks edge the path and hold back the profusion of plants. Colorful annuals and perennials line the walkways while grasses, trees, and shrubs provide year-round structure and winter interest.

The native plant nursery at the National Butterfly Center may not look like a typical garden center but then, the plants it raises are not typical plants!

For red flower gardens, the National Butterfly Center propagates wax mallow, sixangle foldwing, heartleaf rosemallow, West Indian shrubverbena (also known as Texas lantana), and Wright's desert honeysuckle (also known as flame acanthus). These regionally native plants can thrive and produce nectar in the extreme heat of South Texas while gracefully fitting into many different styles of gardens.

Whatever your style preference, it is better to treat butterfly gardening as a *method* of gardening rather than a *style*. Gardening methods usually concentrate on a particular aspect of gardening that can be incorporated into many different garden styles. The following are some gardening methods that help butterflies:

- **Planting nectar plants in single-species clusters—or even better, in masses.** Butterflies visit flowers to sip nectar as a food source. The less work butterflies have to do in moving from flower to flower while nectaring, the more productive their foraging. Creating a group of plants in one spot in the garden that are all in bloom at the same time lets butterflies obtain their nutrition most efficiently and thus have more energy available for their main goal—reproduction. It is also easier for passing butterflies to detect masses of flowers.
- **Limiting garden cleanup in the fall.** Just because the flowers are gone in winter, gardeners should not forget about butterflies. Some butterflies remain in the garden over the winter as eggs, caterpillars, chrysalides, or even as adults. Many common garden butterflies, like Mourning Cloak, overwinter as adults. Others, like Eastern and Western Tiger Swallowtails, spend the winter as chrysalides. Great Spangled Fritillaries spend the winter as tiny caterpillars on the ground near their food plant, violets. Vigorous raking and removal of all garden debris is harmful to these overwintering forms.
- **Assiduously avoiding pesticides.** Even garden products considered environmentally friendly and acceptable in organic gardening should be carefully evaluated before use. *Bacillus thuringiensis*, commonly called *Bt*, is a bacterium found in pesticides sold to homeowners for the control of such pests as Gypsy Moths, Bagworms, Armyworms, Cabbage Looper, and Tent Caterpillar, among others. What is not specifically stated is that this strain of *Bt* kills *all* caterpillars that ingest it, not just the pesky ones; it is essentially caterpillar poison.

Additionally, many plants in garden centers have been treated with the systemic insecticides called neonicotinoids, sometimes abbreviated to neonics, and should be avoided by butterfly gardeners. If plants at a garden center are not labeled, ask about neonic application before you purchase any plants.

By maintaining a garden for the promotion and protection of butterflies, the choice of plants within any garden design will impact the activity of life within the garden—transforming the garden from a static landscape for passive viewing to a dynamic experience that can be lived in as it changes day to day. A garden that attracts butterflies also helps maximize relationships involving birds, bees, moths, and a huge array of less obvious pollinators. An ecosystem of animal life flourishes when you employ butterfly gardening methods.

BUTTERFLY BASICS

WHAT A BUTTERFLY GARDEN IS NOT

Residential gardens that push the boundaries of design, that turns home gardens into barely curated suburban fields rather than spaces that read as a "garden" are often in the news. While people and municipalities grapple over what looks right and feels right in their communities, the debates are indicative of a shift in priorities that many people are experiencing. Interest in creating habitat for more native wildlife while at the same time lessening the inputs needed to maintain a suburban landscape (such as water, fertilizer, and pesticides) is a worthy goal and one that will continue to evolve. The issue of how to reimagine our landscapes needs be negotiated on a local basis as to what level of wildness is appropriate in each community.

While the renewal of habitat on a large scale is a complex process, the improvement of our local fragmented and degraded habitats is something that just about everyone can work toward. Simple actions, like asking local nurseries to carry a selection of native plants for butterflies, or replacing a section of lawn with nectar flowers and caterpillar food plants, are a start, as is looking around your neighborhood to see what butterfly habitat exists and where more can be added.

CHECKLIST OF ACTIONS FOR GETTING STARTED

- **Decide whether your butterfly garden is going to have a distinct style.** It does not *need* to have a style but it can be useful to work within a style framework as a way to expand how you think about gardening. Gardens are always changing and a garden's style can be changed as desired. Beyond the traditional garden styles, styles that are more modern include no-lawn gardens, water-saving gardens, rain gardens, and wildlife gardens. No matter what your *style*, remember to utilize the three most important butterfly gardening *methods*: plant significant masses of nectar plants, avoid pesticides, and limit fall cleanup.
- **Obtain a good butterfly field guide.** Examine the guide's range maps for the common garden butterflies listed below to learn which butterflies are likely or possible garden visitors to your area, and plant caterpillar food plants accordingly. Use the field guide to determine the flight times of each common garden butterfly in your location, so you know when to look for each species. Consider how likely each butterfly is to overwinter in your garden, and plan your cleanup activities accordingly.

COMMON GARDEN BUTTERFLIES

- **Consider the purchase of close-range focus binoculars.** Observing the fine details of all butterflies can be appreciated by magnification with binoculars. Field marks become clearer and the inherent beauty of each butterfly is easier to see. Small butterflies are easier to identify when using binoculars.

The range maps in the following table are based on historical data. The large irregular colored areas on the maps indicate where the butterfly's range occurs and how many generations per year a species will produce (in this case, orange areas indicate three generations, purple areas indicate two generations, and turquoise areas indicate one generation) while the pink circles mark where a butterfly has been sighted beyond its traditional range. The size of the pink circles do not indicate the number of sightings but remind us that "range" is a moving target and sightings are influenced by chance.

COMMON GARDEN BUTTERFLY	RANGE MAP	OVERWINTERING LIFE STAGE	SOME COMMON CATERPILLAR FOOD PLANTS
Eastern Tiger Swallowtail	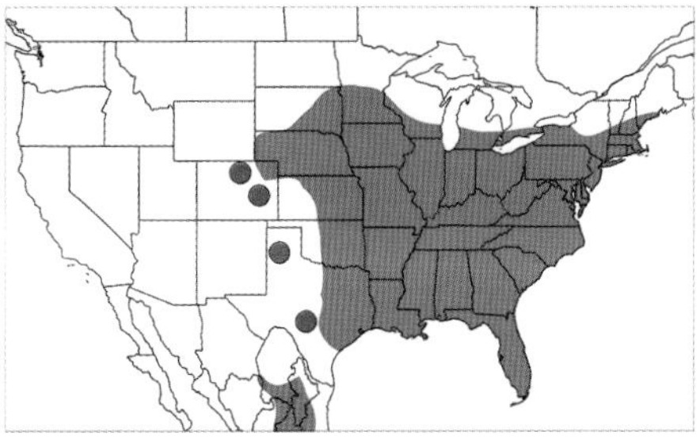	Chrysalis	Black cherry, tuliptree, sweetbay magnolia, and sassafras
Western Tiger Swallowtail	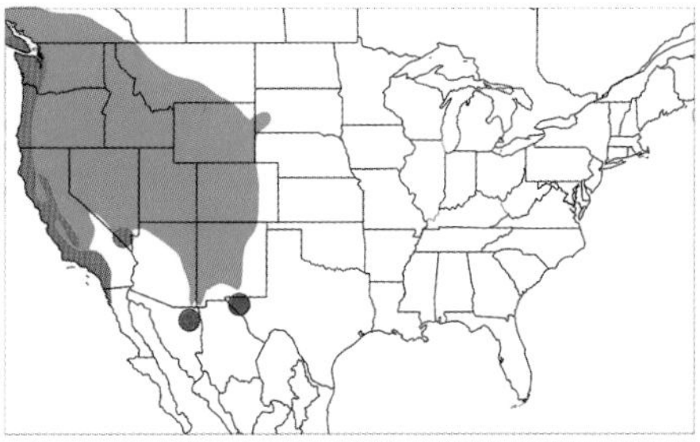	Chrysalis	California sycamore, Fremont cottonwood, willow species
Spicebush Swallowtail	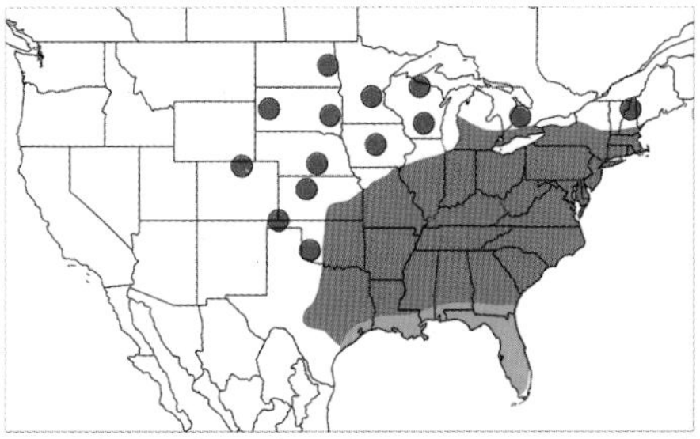	Chrysalis	Northern spicebush

continued overleaf

Table continued

COMMON GARDEN BUTTERFLY	RANGE MAP	OVERWINTERING LIFE STAGE	SOME COMMON CATERPILLAR FOOD PLANTS
Pipevine Swallowtail	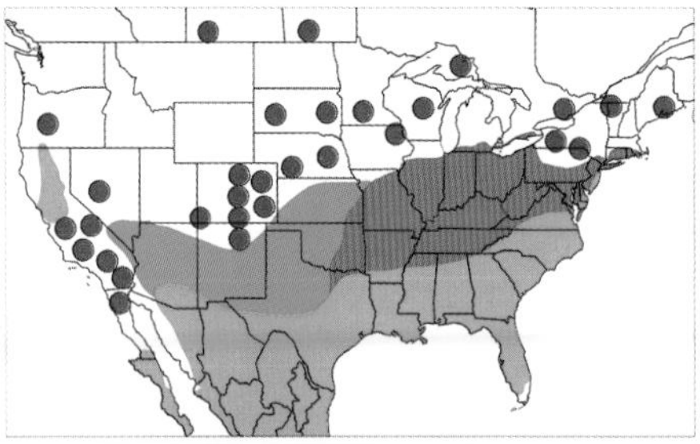	Chrysalis; adults may fly all year in areas without freezing temperatures.	Pipevine, woolly Dutchman's pipe, Virginia snakeroot, and California Dutchman's pipe
Cabbage White	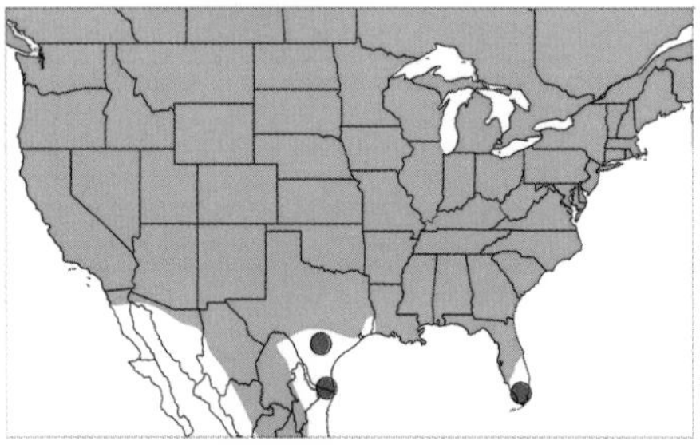	Chrysalis	Many favorite vegetable garden plants such as kale, cabbage, and broccoli. Also a number of weeds.
Orange Sulphur	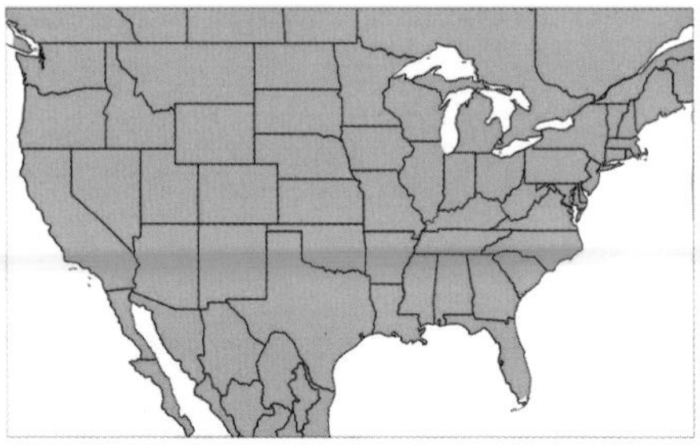	Chrysalis	White clover, alfalfa, crownvetch
Clouded Sulphur	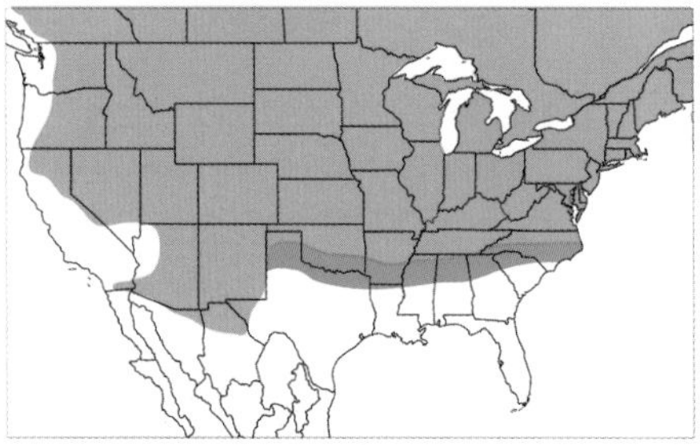	Chrysalis (possibly caterpillar)	White clover, alfalfa
Gray Hairstreak	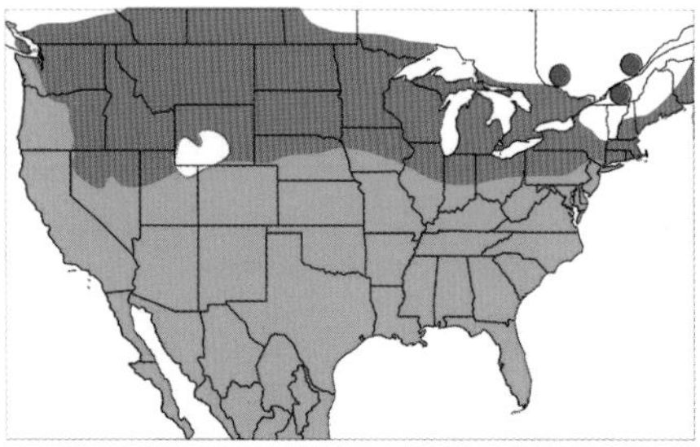	Chrysalis	White clover, hollyhock, alfalfa

COMMON GARDEN BUTTERFLIES

COMMON GARDEN BUTTERFLY	RANGE MAP	OVERWINTERING LIFE STAGE	SOME COMMON CATERPILLAR FOOD PLANTS
Pearl Crescent	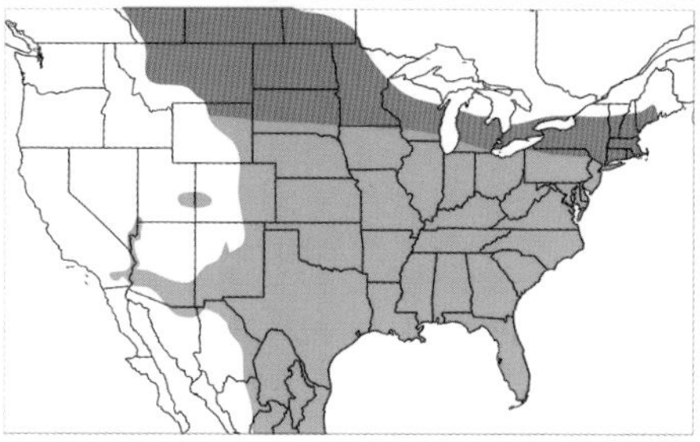	As caterpillar in the north; flies year-round in Deep South	New England aster
Field Crescent	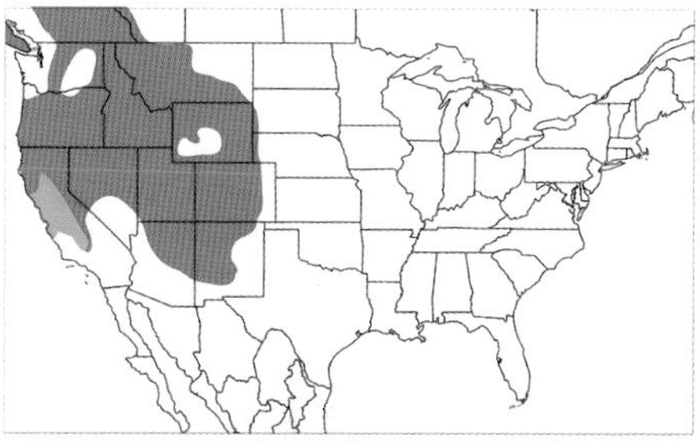	Caterpillar	Pacific aster
Northern Crescent	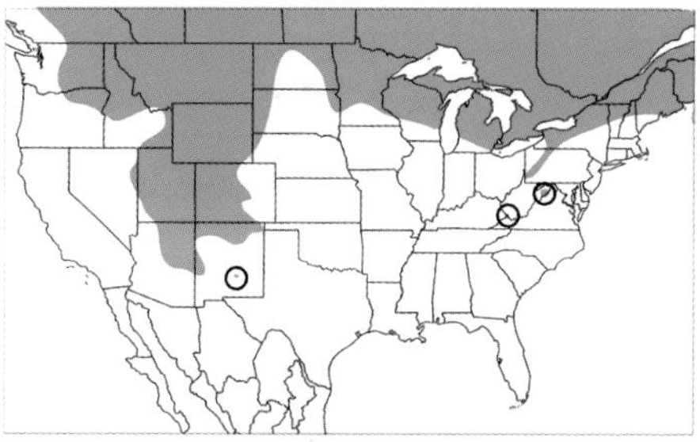	Caterpillar	New England aster
Common Buckeye	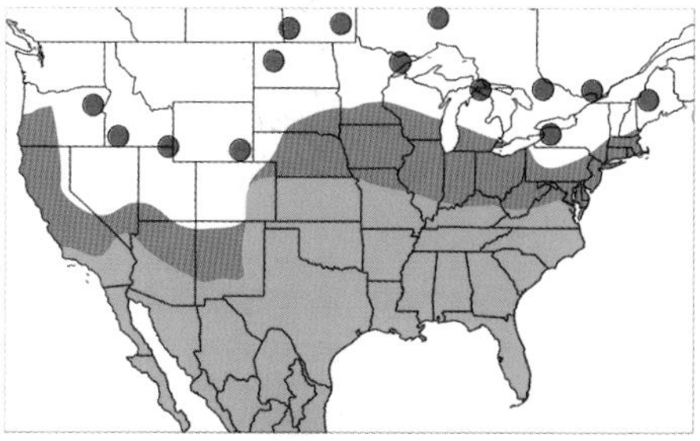	Caterpillars and adults overwinter in the south.	Garden snapdragon and common plantain
Question Mark	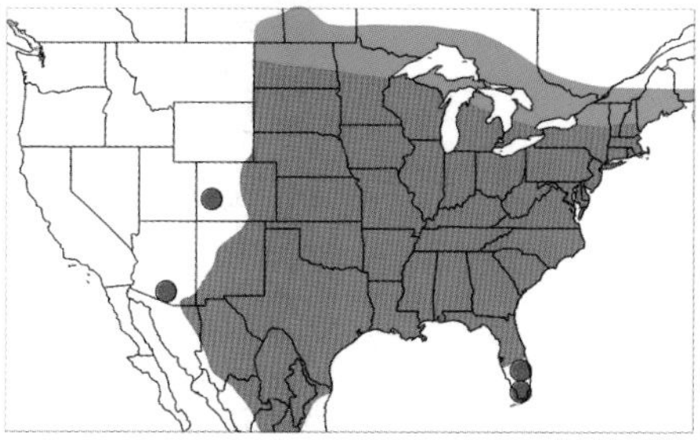	Adults overwinter and some migrate south	Hackberry species and stinging nettle

continued overleaf

Table continued

COMMON GARDEN BUTTERFLY	RANGE MAP	OVERWINTERING LIFE STAGE	SOME COMMON CATERPILLAR FOOD PLANTS
Eastern Comma	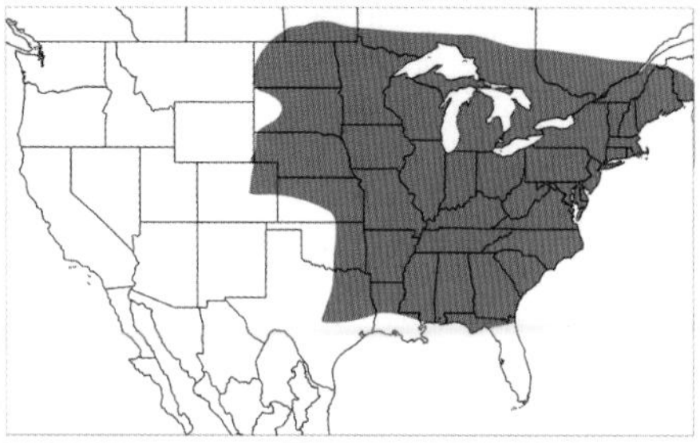	Adult	Stinging nettle, smallspike false nettle, common hop
Hoary Comma	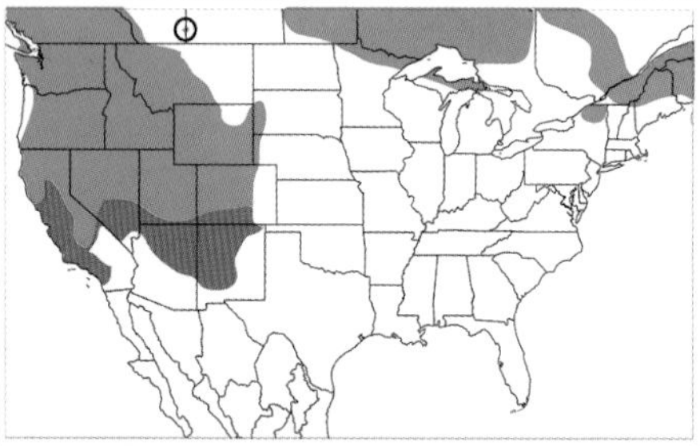	Adult	Western azalea, Sierra currant
Mourning Cloak	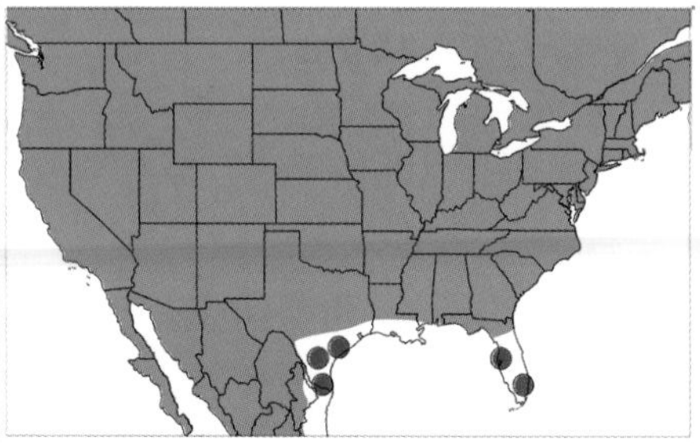	Adults overwinter and some migrate south	Willow species
American Lady	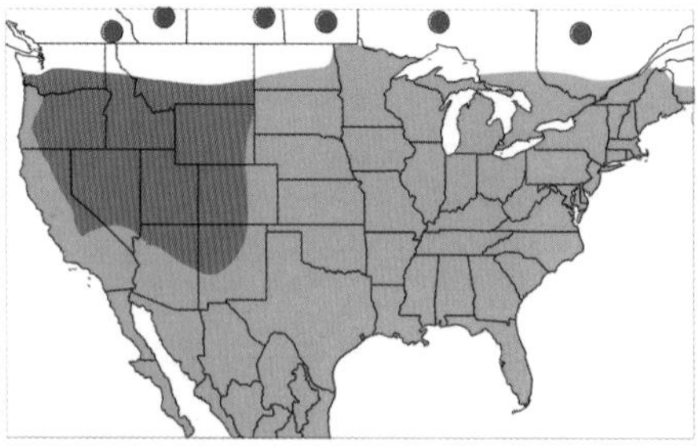	Overwinters as adult; flies year-round in South Texas and Deep South.	Pussytoes, many species to choose from, and western pearly everlasting
West Coast Lady	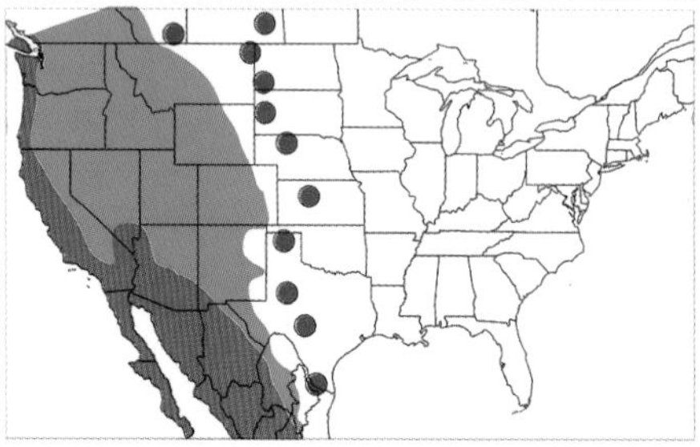	Adult	Checkerbloom species

COMMON GARDEN BUTTERFLIES

COMMON GARDEN BUTTERFLY	RANGE MAP	OVERWINTERING LIFE STAGE	SOME COMMON CATERPILLAR FOOD PLANTS
Painted Lady	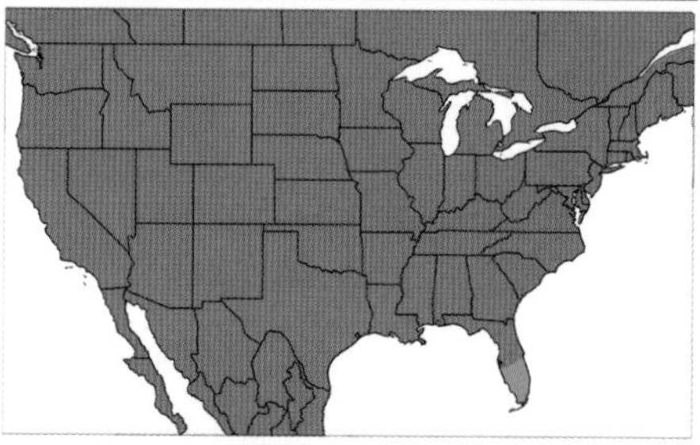	Overwinters as adult in the South and in Mexico	Thistles and many others
Red Admiral	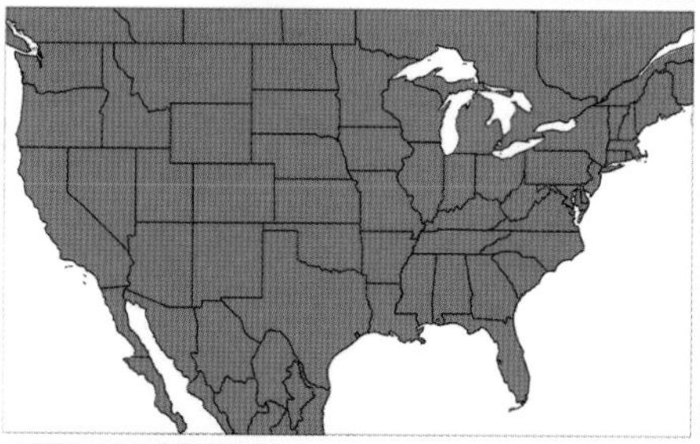	Adult (possibly chrysalis)	Stinging nettle, smallspike false nettle, common hop
Monarch	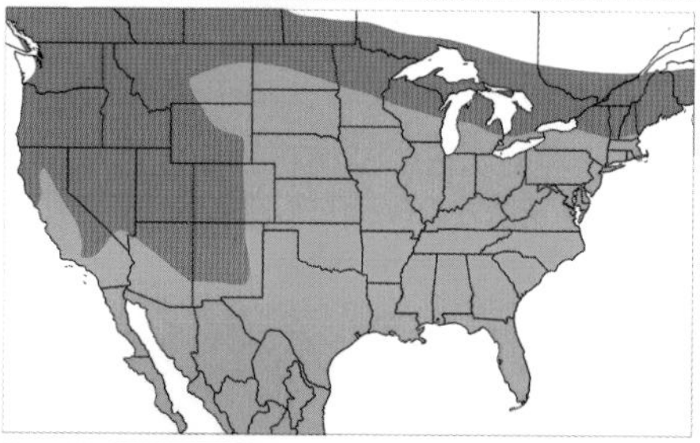	Spectacular migration each fall to Mexico; some adults overwinter in Florida and the West Coast.	Milkweed species
Common Checkered-Skipper	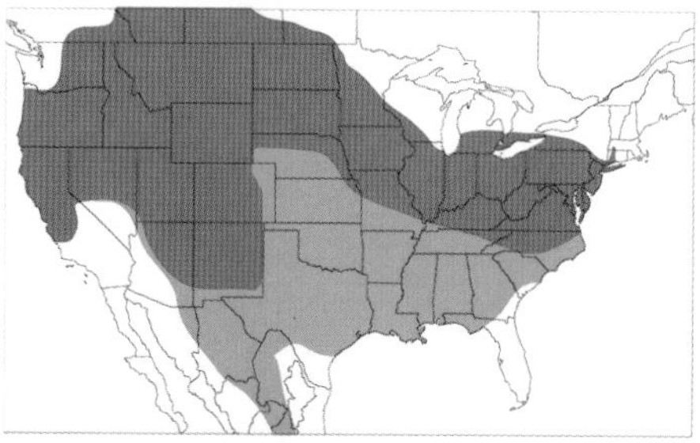	Caterpillar	Checkerbloom species
Silver-spotted Skipper	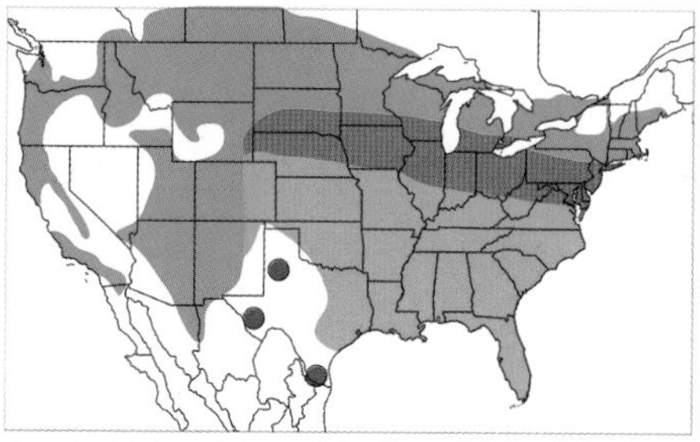	Chrysalis	Black locust

CHAPTER THREE CATERPILLAR CUISINE

When gardening for butterflies, you need to think about more than simply which nursery or garden-catalog flowers will attract adult butterflies. It's important to consider the entire insect life cycle, which involves two active phases—the butterfly and the caterpillar—and two phases that are sedentary—the egg and the chrysalis. The gardener must plan to accommodate all stages of a butterfly's life cycle if the goal is to maintain or increase local butterfly populations. However, while most people love butterflies and the flowers they visit, many aren't so appreciative of the caterpillar phase.

Wormlike, and sometimes squishy to touch, caterpillars are low on many peoples' list of garden friends—so much so, that a goodly number of broad-spectrum pesticides are readily available for the eradication of any alarming caterpillar. Even gardeners whose feelings lean toward caterpillar-phobic can change their perception once they understand the role of caterpillars in the environment. From the perspective of butterfly gardening, we cannot have one without the other; caterpillars become butterflies, and enticing butterflies to visit and remain in gardens is one of the primary reasons that draw people to butterfly gardening.

Each butterfly species has a strategy for caterpillar survival; this brown and white Giant Swallowtail caterpillar effectively mimics a bird dropping in order to avoid being eaten by birds.

Vibrant green Eastern Tiger Swallowtail caterpillars have large false eyespots on their upper side to appear frightening to predators. Yet, when the caterpillar is frightened, it rears up and shows its actual head from underneath the false eyespot–covered hood. Learning the survival strategies of caterpillars increases our engagement with butterflies.

From a larger ecological perspective, caterpillars, whether destined to become moths or butterflies, serve as important sources of food for birds, reptiles, amphibians, other insects, and small mammals; if there were a printed menu in the food web, caterpillars would be listed as high-protein, high-fat snacks. By planting specific foods for caterpillars, gardeners are not only creating habitat for butterflies but also helping to nurture a wide variety of wildlife.

By refocusing your view of butterfly caterpillars from one of icky, amorphous blobs of barely formed pulp to one of interesting and benign wildlife that does not sting, bite, or in any way pose a threat to humans, it is also possible to reorient your response to them from "eradicate" to "protect." Start this change in orientation by planting the caterpillar food plants for your favorite garden butterflies and learning what their caterpillars look like. The growing interest in butterfly gardening already reflects this mainstream shift in thinking. Butterfly gardening is, in its most stripped-down form, a method of protecting and promoting one particular category of insect by managing how we treat the land. To protect butterflies, their caterpillars must be protected as well.

Many people have embraced this ideological shift to protect caterpillars and now garden on the other end of the spectrum by actively looking for

While butterfly caterpillars do not have stinging hairs or the ability to bite people, be aware that a number of moth caterpillars that can be found in gardens, like this Saddleback Moth caterpillar, do sting. Do not handle any caterpillar that you have not accurately identified as safe. Even then, remember that the primary function of a caterpillar is to eat. Moving caterpillars from the plant where they are found to other food sources can be detrimental to the caterpillar, and may even cause it to stop eating and die. So, like butterflies, caterpillars are best observed where they are found.

caterpillars in the garden and then taking measures to protect them. Rearing caterpillars inside a protective enclosure until they mature into butterflies is a passion for many people. Whether or not you feel the urge to actually raise caterpillars, once you decide that attracting butterflies is a desirable garden project, their caterpillars become essential. You need not touch caterpillars—there is no reason to do so—but knowing how to provide food for caterpillars and how to protect the chrysalides that result, is essential for helping butterflies that arrive in your garden to produce future generations.

HOW DO BUTTERFLIES FIND CATERPILLAR FOOD PLANTS?

All the behaviors that butterflies exhibit are hardwired into their very being—they do not have to be taught what to do, including where to lay their eggs. Fortunately for the tiny and relatively immobile newly hatched caterpillar, one of the innate behaviors exhibited by butterflies is the ability to almost always lay eggs on or near caterpillar foods plants that will sustain their progeny. How they accomplish this feat and where they lay their eggs varies by butterfly species, but all butterflies have some basic tricks of the trade.

FINDING CATERPILLAR FOOD PLANTS

Gravid female butterflies search for their specific caterpillar food by using visual cues while flying. The shape of plant leaves or buds can indicate an acceptable food plant from afar. In addition to finding a specific plant, many butterflies lay eggs on particular vegetative plant parts that differ from the rest of the plant; for example, Zebra Heliconians search for new, young, unfurling leaves of passionflowers for their eggs and avoid older, tougher plant materials. Once butterflies locate a possible plant for their eggs, they can also visually assess whether other eggs or caterpillars are already on the plant—and thereby avoid laying eggs where there will be competition from other caterpillars.

In addition to visual clues, female butterflies respond to chemical signals produced by plants. Butterflies do not sense odors through a nose as we do, but they do have nerve cells that function in much the same way. Highly sensitive nerve cells called chemoreceptors are found on the surface of the butterfly's body as well as on the legs, feet, and antennae. These nerve cells allow butterflies both to taste and to detect odors, including volatile chemicals emitted from the food plants needed for their caterpillars.

Zebra Heliconians are the state butterfly of Florida. Commonly found in gardens throughout the year in South Florida and South Texas, they may also visit gardens farther north during warm weather but will be killed by frost.

CATERPILLAR CUISINE

REARING CATERPILLARS in a school setting is one of the primary ways most Americans learn about and actually experience the butterfly life cycle. Observing metamorphosis, from small caterpillar to beautiful butterfly, is an event to share and teach about, and commercial kits are widely available and commonly utilized in schools. Kits include a plastic tub filled with enough artificial caterpillar food to sustain a few caterpillars so children can watch the caterpillars transition through their stages of growth, from egg to adult butterfly.

Conscientious kit users should not release the kit-reared butterflies—it is recommended that the resulting butterflies be euthanized since they are not part of the local butterfly population. When releasing kit-reared butterflies into the wild, genetically distinct, nonlocal individual butterflies are introduced into the population that can include the introduction of disease. It is generally suggested that placing the butterflies in a freezer until they are frozen is a humane method for ending the project. By the completion of this study, metamorphosis has been observed, but what has really been learned about butterflies, caterpillars, and their long-term needs?

Black Swallowtail caterpillars are easy to rear on potted parsley plants. Caterpillars have a voracious appetite, and it is fascinating to watch their activity as they eat. When raising swallowtails in captivity, it is possible to observe one of their defense mechanisms by touching the back of the caterpillar. Swallowtails have a fork-shaped organ called an osmeterium. When threatened (which includes having a human touch its back), swallowtail caterpillars often thrash their bodies back and forth while extending the osmeterium. At the same time, a strong, foul-smelling chemical is released as the osmeterium extends. Some have suggested that the osmeterium shape mimics a snake's tongue, further indicating to predators to "back off!"

Feeding captive caterpillars artificial food and sugar solutions need not be the only way to demonstrate metamorphosis. In regions where Black Swallowtails are common, potted herbs, such as dill, parsley, fennel, and common rue will attract butterflies to lay eggs. Once eggs have been found on a plant, placing netting over the plant or moving the eggs and plant to a protected indoor area allows the entire life cycle to be observed with no concerns about the impact that releasing the resulting butterflies would have on local populations. In the fall, Black Swallowtails form chrysalides that overwinter, making this species appropriate for classroom observation. After the chrysalides have been kept cold for the winter, the butterflies will emerge in the spring as the days lengthen, but well before the end of the school year.

If Black Swallowtails are going to be raised often, attracting the butterflies with herbs is a fine way to start, but consider planting one food plant outside or in a large pot as a reserve food source. Golden zizia, also known as golden Alexander, is a native caterpillar food plant with strong stems that hold-up well when cut and placed in water. Many gardeners who raise caterpillars transition tiny Black Swallowtail caterpillars to an enclosure containing cut golden Alexander leaves. In general, it is not suggested to switch caterpillars from their original food source, but when moved at a very early stage of development, Black Swallowtails can transition to one of their other caterpillar foods. Dill, parsley, and fennel all tend to wilt if picked and placed in a water-filled vase to feed caterpillars. In addition to remaining fresh and water-filled when cut, golden Alexander plants produce a lot of greenery for hungry caterpillars, and you will need a lot of vegetation if feeding very many caterpillars!

Black Swallowtails are certainly not the only caterpillars that can be raised indoors, but this species is a common butterfly that is easy to attract. Depending on your location and the season, other common caterpillars, such as Monarchs (which eat milkweed), American Ladies (which eat pussytoes), and Cabbage Whites (which eat a variety of plants in the Cabbage Family), can be easy to find in the garden once their caterpillar food plants are available.

Over the course of 24 hours, this Black Swallowtail caterpillar (top) went from securing itself to a twig with a silk thread and pad, to shedding its skin (visible at the lower right side of the chrysalis). The chrysalis then changed over many hours from a plump, wriggling chrysalis to a more darkly colored, motionless one (middle and bottom).

The clusters of chemoreceptors on the antennae allow butterflies to sense, or essentially "smell," specific caterpillar food plants from a distance. As a female butterfly searching for suitable egg-laying sites approaches a potential caterpillar food plant, she flutters slowly, circling an area, often alighting on a plant, attracted by the chemicals she has detected in the breeze. Landing on the plant allows the butterfly to evaluate, or "taste," the chemical mixture with her feet and legs, which are lined with chemoreceptors. Butterflies often drum their feet on the potential caterpillar food plant, releasing more volatile chemicals that will tell the butterfly whether the plant is suitable for egg laying.

The behavior of a female butterfly searching for a plant on which to lay eggs is worth noting, both because it offers insight into butterfly life cycles and because a butterfly methodically searching for a specific plant becomes more easily observable. Planting as large an area as possible with any one particular food plant will increase the likelihood that female butterflies will linger long enough to for you to identify them and appreciate their beauty.

If you do notice a butterfly searching your garden and not intently visiting flowers, watch carefully as it alights on leaves or stems. A quick tuck of the butterfly's abdomen is all it takes to deposit an egg. Once you become aware of this egg-laying movement, your butterfly watching shifts to a new level, as you can now monitor whether your garden plantings are achieving your desired goal.

Look carefully at the tip of the Monarch's abdomen to see a pale yellow egg that has just been laid on emerging milkweed. Female butterflies curve their abdomen under to touch the caterpillar food plant when laying eggs.

PLANTING IN MASSES AND PLANTING FOR MASSES

One of the prime strategies when planting for butterflies or caterpillars is to "plant in masses." Masses of flowers blooming all at the same time serve to attract butterflies in search of nectar, while planting in masses for caterpillars presents fertile butterflies with a wide selection of egg- laying opportunities and also ensures a large supply of food for hungry caterpillars. Buying or propagating many plants of the same species is one way to quickly achieve a mass planting, and when first starting a garden, this may be an option to explore.

Another option that is particularly worth considering when planning for a large amount of caterpillar food, is to choose plants that have a tendency to spread or to grow very large. Since caterpillars are essentially eating machines that require a constant supply of fresh food in order to grow and develop, selecting plants that naturally spread to create large stands is an easy way to put out the welcome mat. For those with limited space or who do not relish the idea of constantly editing colonial growth in their gardens, choosing plants that produce a large volume of caterpillar food per plant may be a better alternative.

This mature garden in southern New Jersey demonstrates how planting in masses can create a vibrant, exciting garden that begs to be explored. Composed entirely of native plant species, the garden plants have been allowed to spread and mingle, giving butterflies ample opportunities for nectaring, laying eggs, and finding shelter. A circular path through the garden provides room for observing butterflies and their caterpillars.

Unruly, *aggressive*, and possibly *invasive* are descriptions applied to plants that spread rapidly, either by underground stems or through prolific seed production. Their reproductive strategies can make them problematic for gardeners. Despite their downbeat labels, many of these plants will feed caterpillars, so for some of the plants, it seems more positive to relabel them as "exuberant." They are not going to suit all gardeners or all types of gardens, but plants on the following list will grow luxuriantly and produce a lot of caterpillar food when their growing conditions are optimal.

PLANTS THAT PRODUCE ABUNDANT CATERPILLAR FOOD

CATERPILLAR FOOD	POSSIBLE CATERPILLARS ATTRACTED
Northern spicebush is a small tree or large shrub. It is suitable for a small area and can be kept manageable by pruning. Prefers at least part shade and moist soil.	Spicebush Swallowtail
Common milkweed spreads by underground stems and can be aggressive if left unchecked. Each milkweed plant is large and produces a lot of caterpillar food per plant.	Monarch
Dutchman's pipe species need to be grown on a trellis. They spread by underground stems and can be aggressive, but once the vines are established, a lot of caterpillar food is produced.	Pipevine Swallowtail
Pawpaw is a small understory tree that will tolerate shade. Each tree produces an ample supply of large leaves for caterpillars.	Zebra Swallowtail
Passionflowers need a trellis or support to grow on. They spread by underground stems and have exuberant twisting vines that are relished by caterpillars.	Zebra Heliconian, Gulf Fritillary, Variegated Fritillary
Stinging nettle spreads by both underground stems as well as prolific seed production. It also has stinging hairs as a defense against humans!	Red Admiral, Eastern Comma, Question Mark, West Coast Lady, Milbert's Tortoiseshell, and Eastern Comma.

TERMS SPECIFIC TO INSECT DEVELOPMENT are useful when learning how to garden for butterflies. Learning just a few terms will allow you to talk to other butterfly gardeners in a clear and concise way.

- **Exoskeleton**: an external skeleton. Butterflies and their caterpillars have exoskeletons; they do not have bones. The exoskeleton is a hard casing that supports and protects the insects' internal structures. In order to grow larger, caterpillars must periodically shed this exoskeleton.
- **Molting**: the process whereby a caterpillar sheds its "skin" (actually an exoskeleton, not skin as we know it). In order to shed this protective layer, a new exoskeleton develops underneath the existing one. When the caterpillar becomes large enough, the outer skin splits to reveal a new exoskeleton underneath. The old covering is shed and is sometimes consumed by the caterpillar.

An 8-day-old Monarch has just shed its skin.

A Monarch in its final molt reveals a chrysalis as it wriggles out of its caterpillar exoskeleton.

- **Instar**: a stage of development in a caterpillar's life that occurs between molts. On average, caterpillars pass through four instars although the number of molts varies by species.
- **Chrysalis**: When a caterpillar reaches its ultimate size, the last molt reveals a chrysalis rather than a caterpillar exoskeleton. In the chrysalis stage the insect undergoes the transformation from caterpillar to butterfly.
- **Eclose**: emerge from the chrysalis or egg.

This first-year butterfly garden is composed of garden beds and uses wide swaths of lawn for paths. Over time, plants will fill in and spread so that in coming years, less and less soil will be visible in the beds. A path at the back left side of the garden leads to a wilder, less managed meadow, giving a nice contrast to the carefully edged lawn area and providing garden visitors two separate spaces to observe butterflies and flowers.

EAT, EAT A LOT, AND TRY NOT TO BE EATEN

While most adult garden butterflies imbibe nectar or tree sap, their caterpillars eat very specific plants. The relationship between a particular butterfly species and the food required by its caterpillars has developed over millions of years and reflects adaptations by both butterfly and plant. Evolutionary biologists have yet to agree on exactly how this plant-caterpillar relationship came into being and how it is shifting even in the present. One prevalent idea is that plants and butterflies coevolved over time in a process whereby plants evolved defenses (such as strong, repellent chemicals in their plant tissues) in response to caterpillar foraging, and caterpillars in turn evolved new methods to overcome the plant defenses. Other theories suggest that plants diversified independently of caterpillars, with the food plant–caterpillar relationship developing after plants had branched out into numerous species.

For gardeners, it does not matter that scientists disagree about how caterpillars came to choose their food plants, but it is interesting to realize that even basic information about butterflies is still being developed, so that even butterfly gardeners have a role to play in shaping our understanding of butterflies. By closely observing the insects in our gardens, we butterfly gardeners have a chance to make new observations about butterfly and caterpillar behaviors and food plant choices. By recording what caterpillars do in our gardens, as

YOU ARE WHAT YOU EAT! Caterpillars eat specific foods during their lives but what *exactly* are the foods? NABA's photodocumentation program is working to tease out the details of caterpillar feeding through a simple premise: First, find an egg or a caterpillar on a single plant, then photograph both the plant and the egg or caterpillar, being careful to capture any features that will clearly identify the plant. Protect the egg or caterpillar by either netting the plant or removing the insect to rear in a protected enclosure, feeding it the same species of plant on which it was found. Keep photographing—be sure to photograph the caterpillar as it grows and changes into a chrysalis, and of course, photograph the butterfly after it emerges from the chrysalis. Photodocumentation is one way that everyone can participate in expanding the knowledge base of caterpillar behavior.

opposed to how they behave in a laboratory, we can aid other gardeners, as well as scientists, in better understanding one small area of insect ecology, as well as garden ecology.

CONSIDER THE CATERPILLAR'S NEEDS

From the time they hatch from their eggs, caterpillars are programmed to eat. Often a caterpillar's first meal is its own egg case, and then it moves on to the plant where its egg was laid or a nearby plant. A caterpillar's simple goals in life are to eat, eat a lot, and try not to be eaten.

The caterpillar stage is a very vulnerable time in the life cycle of a butterfly—not only are caterpillars slow-moving creatures with poor eyesight, but they are also prime menu items for an array of highly mobile, hungry predators. To minimize this vulnerable time, caterpillars eat as much as possible, which results in fast and furious growth. For most caterpillars, growing from tiny hatchling to plump final instar (increasing its weight by 1,000 times or more!) takes just a few weeks. So when providing for caterpillars in your garden, make sure to include a lot of each particular food plant—you do not want to run out once the caterpillars start their feeding frenzy (and at the same time, a large stand of any particular caterpillar plant will look less ragged and disheveled if there is more than enough to go around). It is not hard for gardeners to plant enough caterpillar food as there are many common, easy-to-grow plants. Wildflowers and herbs that are widespread have the potential to produce a lot of foliage and will serve a variety of different caterpillars.

WHAT ARE WE TALKING ABOUT?

Before jumping feet-first into choosing and purchasing plants, all butterfly watchers and gardeners should be able to talk with each other about their interests and, to do so, they need a common language, which starts with understanding how things are classified. Without a general idea of how other people view the natural world, the number of butterflies and their associated plants can seem like a foreign language, particularly for the beginner. The number of different butterflies—some of which look confusingly alike—is seemingly endless, and the names given to plants are often unwieldy and esoteric.

CLASSIFICATION of plants and animals has many levels. The following "family tree" for Variegated Fritillary shows many higher-level classes that are not used in everyday discussions of butterflies (or plants for that matter!). Butterfly watchers, gardeners, and scientists primarily use the genus and species classifications when speaking of specific insects and plants. It can be helpful, however, to use the family tree for reference. In the case of Variegated Fritillary, it is interesting to note that it is placed in a subfamily: Heliconians and Fritillaries. Within the subfamily, there are different genera that share traits. Greater fritillaries (those in the genus *Speyeria*) use only violets as caterpillar food, lesser fritillaries (those in the genus *Boloria*) use a variety of caterpillar foods, some of which may be violets, and the remaining heliconians (which includes six different genera) use passionflowers as caterpillar food. The final genus, *Euptoieta*, includes two species found in the United States—Variegated Fritillary and Mexican Fritillary, which share traits with other genera in the subfamily by using both violets and passionflowers as caterpillar food.

- Kingdom: Animals (Animalia)
  - Phylum: Arthropods (Arthropoda)
    - Subphylum: Hexapods (Hexapoda)
      - Class: Insects (Insecta)
        - Order: Butterflies and Moths (Lepidoptera)
          - Superfamily: Butterflies and Skippers (Papilionoidea)
            - Family: Brushfooted Butterflies (Nymphalidae)
              - Subfamily: Heliconians and Fritillaries (Heliconiinae)
                - Genus: *Euptoieta*
                  - Species: *claudia* (Variegated Fritillary)

Additionally, once gardeners start to plant specifically for butterflies, the need to definitively tell one plant from another similar plant becomes vitally important. Butterflies have definite preferences about nectar plants, and their caterpillars certainly will not feed on just any old plant in your garden. To communicate clearly about butterflies and their food plants, you'll find it tremendously helpful to learn a little about how animals and plants are classified and named.

Taxonomy is the system of classification that places all living creatures into groups based on their presumed relationships. Plants and animals are separated into different groups, with—in our case—butterflies placed in the animal kingdom and garden plants placed in the plant kingdom. Despite their being relegated to different kingdoms, the language used to describe the categories within the kingdoms is the same whether talking about butterflies, such as Variegated Fritillary, or garden plants, like eastern purple coneflower. Family, genus, and species are the taxonomic distinctions that matter most to butterfly gardeners who wish to communicate with others about butterflies or to be certain about the identity of plants they purchase.

The family classification informs us that all the organisms in the group are in some way similar and share some distinct features. For example, eastern purple coneflower is placed in the family Asteraceae, commonly called the Aster or Daisy Family. (The scientific name of every plant family ends in "-aceae," pronounced "ā-cee-ee.") At the family level of classification, relationships are commonly determined by features involved in reproduction, which in plants include flowers, fruits, and seeds. Members of the Aster Family have complex flower structures but include many familiar plants such as sunflowers, common dandelions, and thistles. The family classification for Variegated Fritillary is Nymphalidae, a very large group of butterflies that contains some of the most commonly recognized large, colorful butterflies such as Monarch, Mourning Cloak, and Zebra Heliconian. (All butterfly family names end in "-idae," pronounced "ih-dee.")

Variegated Fritillary nectaring on eastern purple coneflower.

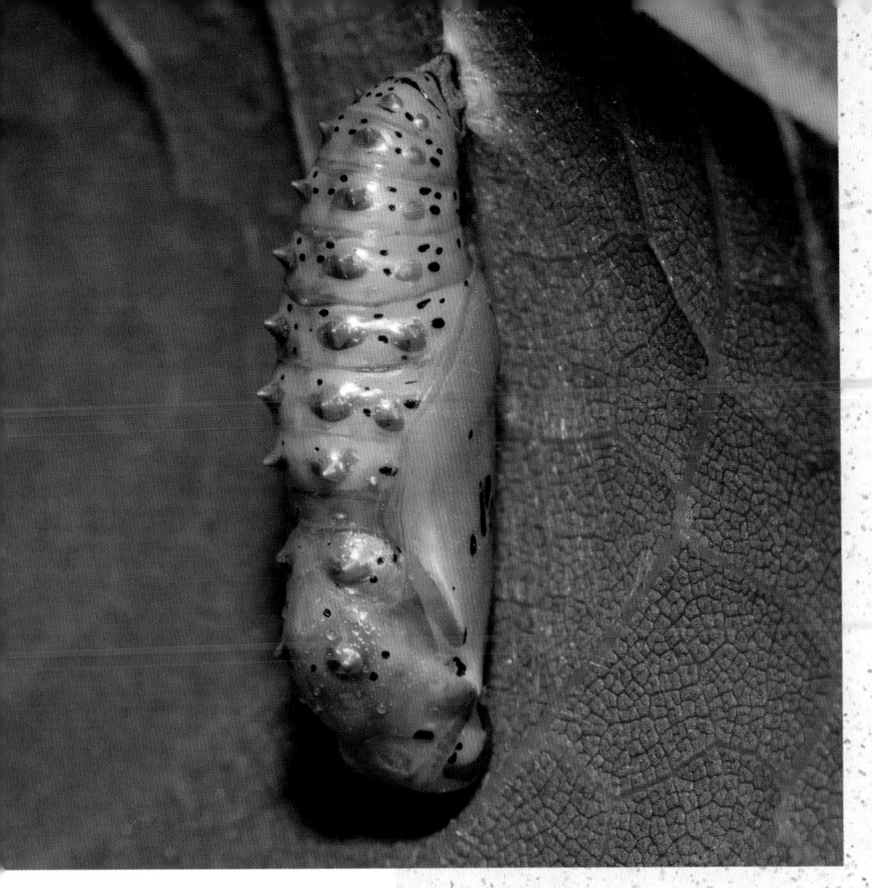

Variegated Fritillary is a garden butterfly in the Family Nymphalidae that is found throughout most of the United States, except the Pacific Northwest. Providing the caterpillar food plants for Variegated Fritillary—violets and passionflowers—in abundance is the best way to entice this species to stop, lay eggs, and hopefully produce a stunning chrysalis like this one.

Considering a butterfly or plant family provides a first pass at narrowing down characteristics that butterfly gardeners care about; a plant in the Asteraceae will have a certain type of flower that, in general, is loved by butterflies! The family designation for butterflies has immediate value even if you are just a casual butterfly watcher, as it will help you navigate a butterfly field guide. Butterflies in the family Nymphalidae appear to have four legs rather than the usual six; the front pair of a nymphalid butterfly's legs are reduced, so that the butterfly appears to have four legs plus two small, brushlike front appendages, which can be a helpful indicator when looking at a butterfly and wondering where to start looking in a field guide. Are you looking at a butterfly that appears to walk on four legs? It is in the Nymphalidae, which goes by the much more easily remembered common name of Brushfoot Family. Not mentioned in most field guides, but nice features of many brushfoot butterflies, are their spectacular chrysalides, some of which have shiny spots like the familiar Monarch chrysalis with its golden spots and line.

For plants the next level of classification below family is genus. Comparing plants at the genus level can be informative since all the plants in a particular genus will be more similar to each other than to relatives at the family level, often in ways that are quickly obvious to gardeners. Flower shape and color as well as plant growth habit all become more similar at the genus level. If one plant in a particular genus is known to be a stellar nectar plant for butterflies, other plants in the same genus might also be worth considering. Eastern purple coneflower is in the genus *Echinacea* (ek-ih-NAY-see-uh), characterized by the easily recognizable coneflower-style flower head surrounded by drooping rose-purple (or sometimes yellow or white) petals. These flower heads are actually made up of many individual flowers, called florets, which in the case of *Echinacea* can range from 200 to 300 per flower head! Each of the individual florets opens and produces nectar, but not all the florets open at the same time, which explains the magical attraction of coneflowers for butterflies and other pollinators—nectar is produced from many flowers over a long time frame. While eastern purple coneflower is the best-known plant in the genus, other plants in *Echinacea* have this same nectar-producing attraction to butterflies and may fit into gardens that have cultural requirements not filled by eastern purple coneflower..

A butterfly genus can represent a large number of species worldwide but not all those species may be found in the United States. Variegated Fritillary is in the genus *Euptoieta* (yoop-toy-EE-tah), which includes about eight species native mainly to the Neotropics. Of these only Variegated Fritillary and Mexican Fritillary are found in the United States, and only Variegated Fritillary is wide ranging here.

The last and perhaps easiest classification to grasp is species. Whether we are contemplating butterflies or plants, a species can be considered to comprise all individuals that can successfully reproduce with each other. In other words, if two individual butterflies can mate and the female can produce eggs that hatch into live caterpillars that in turn develop into sexually fertile butterflies, they belong to the same species. Likewise plants that "mate" with each other through cross-pollination and produce fertile offspring belong to the same species (although plants can successfully hybridize much more easily than animals, so the species concept for them is somewhat more flexible!). In butterfly gardening discussions, plants and butterflies are usually referred to as particular species. When writing the scientific name of an organism both the genus and species are given because the reason for using taxonomy in general, as well as when gardening for butterflies, is to be as informative as possible. In fact, native plants that have not been bred or altered in any way are called "straight species" to indicate that the plant is considered to be in its most native form.

Plant purchasers should be aware of the finer distinctions beyond species. Cultivars, nativars, subspecies, hybrids, selections, and varieties are all possible finer tunings beyond the species-level classification. A great many of these kinds of plants are produced through direct human involvement dependent on a variety of plant breeding methods, so while plants that are listed only at the genus and species level are naturally occurring species, ones that have further distinctions, such as echibeckia™ summerina™ yellow, for example, have been altered in some way from the naturally occurring straight species. As a man-made cross between two straight species, *Echinacea* and *Rudbeckia*, echibeckia summerina is an intergeneric cross (i.e., between two genera), and the ™ symbols in its name indicate that propagation is not permitted.

Resembling flowers in the genus *Rudbeckia*, this cross between two genera advertises large flower size, fast growth, disease resistance, and flowers that last longer than a month. But what will butterflies think?

When a plant is bred to be different from the straight species, it may become less useful to butterflies and their caterpillars. Double flowers may produce less nectar or make getting to the nectar more difficult; breeding and selecting a different-colored or different-textured foliage may render a plant inedible by caterpillars, or a hybrid flower's bloom period may not overlap with a butterfly brood's flight period. Given the wide number of variables that altered plants introduce, it is easy to summarily dismiss garden plants that have been bred to differ from the straight species as harmful to the garden food web. However, these plants are a fact of life and are promoted by a large, thriving, retail nursery industry—cultivars, nativars, and all their man-made kin are not going away anytime soon and so the plant buyer should be aware of both their virtues and their shortcomings. Therefore, it is wisest to learn the straight species of plants that are known to best feed butterflies and caterpillars before branching out to explore their cultivated relatives.

WILDFLOWERS, WEEDS, AND HERBS

Common plants abound that will attract female butterflies to your garden; some plants you can purchase, others are weeds or wildflowers that are already nearby and may be available for the digging or the seed collecting. The distinction between wildflowers and weeds is a narrow one; a plant may be a weed in one situation but a wildflower in another, although most people would consider all nonnative, invasive plants to be weeds. Each gardener must decide personally whether a plant seems "too weedy" for their garden scheme. Plants that spread easily, grow too large, or have stinging leaves may not appeal to all gardeners; it is a personal choice and there are plenty of plants that feed caterpillars to choose from. Although many people would argue that a butterfly garden is not complete without milkweeds, in reality there are no "required plants" for a butterfly garden. Starting with common plants for common butterflies is the fastest way to shift from garden to habitat—you need to make some choices only about which plants to use.

VIOLETS, PASSIONFLOWERS, AND FRITILLARIES

Great Spangled Fritillary is a large, showy butterfly found throughout a large section of the United States from southern Canada down to northern California on the western half of the continent, with the range extending down across the country to North Carolina on the East Coast. Within its range, Great Spangled Fritillary can be considered a common garden butterfly that is on the wing during the summer months and through the early fall.

When coupled in mating, butterflies attach to each other at the abdomen. The facing-away-from-each-other stance during mating is typical among all butterflies, not just Great Spangled Fritillaries as seen here. Even though butterflies can fly while attached to each other during mating, coupled butterflies are often not flying, making them easier to spot and can be a regularly observable occurrence in a well-stocked butterfly garden.

Great Spangled Fritillary caterpillars hatch from their eggs in the fall and overwinter near violet plants. The early caterpillars are so small that it is doubtful you will see one in your garden. In the fall and early spring it is important to not clean up leaf debris around violets or you risk removing the tiny, secretive caterpillars.

Violets are the only plant that Great Spangled Fritillary caterpillars will eat. Great Spangled Fritillaries do not care whether the violet flowers are blue, yellow, or white, though it does matter to egg-laying butterflies that the violets are native. African "violets," which are grown as houseplants, and pansies, which are sold at garden centers as outdoor bedding plants, are not suitable for Great Spangled Fritillary caterpillars. Since most violets spread enthusiastically, you may regard them as weeds or wildflowers, but native violets are the kind needed to feed Great Spangled Fritillaries as well as a number of other fritillary species that have smaller ranges.

In addition to the Great Spangled Fritillary, 17 other species of violet-eating fritillaries occur in the United States. Each fritillary has a range over which it is likely to be found, and quite honestly, many of the North American fritillaries have very specific habitat requirements that make them unlikely garden visitors. Although Great Spangled Fritillary is the most common and widespread of this group, depending on your location you could see a few of its violet-eating relatives visiting your garden.

Meadow Fritillary is not as common in many parts of the country as it once was; violets used to be more widespread but as more habitat is urbanized or placed under intensive cultivation, the abundance of wild violets, along with the meadows where they grow, has declined. Meadow Fritillary is common in some parts of the East and Upper Midwest, where multiple broods are possible, but has a very restricted range in the West, where it has just one brood.

Despite its name, Meadow Fritillary is common to edges of woods and moist areas and is not restricted to meadows. You can nurture weeds and wildflowers such as common dandelions, oxeye daisy, mountainmints, and blackeyed Susan as nectar plants for this butterfly if it occurs in natural habitats near your location.

VIOLETS, PASSIONFLOWERS, AND FRITILLARIES

Variegated Fritillary is another potential butterfly visitor to gardens with abundant stands of violets and a possible garden butterfly in almost the entire United States, with the exception of the Pacific Northwest. Variegated Fritillary is a year-round resident of south Texas and parts of Florida as well points farther south. Each year, butterflies from the southern states migrate northward on a simple mission: they are searching for nectar and appropriate caterpillar food plants. As they migrate, Variegated Fritillaries lay eggs along the way, and unlike Meadow and Great Spangled fritillaries, Variegated Fritillary uses leaves and shoots of passionflowers as caterpillar food in addition to violets.

Butterflies bearing the common name "fritillary" can be confusing; since they all share a name, one could conclude that they all belong to the same genus, and therefore share similar characteristics. But things are not that tidy in the butterfly world, or in the gardening world either, and the fritillaries mentioned so far are actually all a bit different. The CliffsNotes-style version on likely garden fritillaries is this:

- Great Spangled Fritillary belongs to the genus *Speyeria*. They have one brood per year and their caterpillars eat only violets. Hosting Great Spangled Fritillaries requires gardeners to hold off on vigorous flowerbed cleaning in the fall. By leaving leaf litter undisturbed surrounding violets, gardeners preserve caterpillar overwintering habitat, ensuring that any unseen caterpillars are able to remain near violets and complete their life cycle. Since Great Spangled Fritillary produces only one generation per year, if your yard is cleared each fall and spring by landscape crews, or by overenthusiastic family members sent outside on a fine fall day, the potential to lose overwintering caterpillars is high.
- Variegated Fritillary is related to the *Speyeria* fritillaries (although they are in a different genus) but has three lifestyle differences gardeners should be aware of. Variegated Fritillaries

Worn and tattered, this Great Spangled Fritillary is laying eggs near a violet in a planting bed along a building foundation in early fall.

have multiple broods per year. They migrate as the weather warms in spring to colonize northern gardens, and their caterpillar foods include passionflowers, flax, and a few other plants in addition to violets. In order to attract Variegated Fritillaries in northern areas where the butterfly does not overwinter, gardeners usually stick with violets, which are fast growing and hardy in colder climates. Passionflowers can grow quickly and produce a lot of plant material for caterpillars to eat, but the hardiest passionflower, purple passionflower, is hardy only into parts of USDA Zone 5. In the colder sections of this zone, it may require a microclimate such as a large, sheltered, south-facing brick wall if it is to survive winter temperatures. Perhaps the best strategy for northern gardeners would be to plant passionflowers on a trellis with violets around the base. Add some nectar plants and garden seating for a fritillary-viewing garden within a garden!

VIOLETS, PASSIONFLOWERS, AND FRITILLARIES

■ Adding to the fritillary fuss is a third garden butterfly, Gulf Fritillary, the sole occupant of the genus *Agraulis*. Although as a large, orange butterfly with silver spangles it somewhat resembles a Great Spangled Fritillary, it is not technically classified as a fritillary. It is actually a heliconian, showing that common names can be tricky and emphasizing the need for at least an acquaintance with taxonomy. There is no trick, though, about what to plant for Gulf Fritillaries, because their caterpillar food plant is straightforward: within their range they are easily attracted to the garden by passionflowers.

Variegated Fritillary, (opposite page), and Gulf Fritillary, (below), nectaring on blazing star.

FOOD FOR FRITILLARIES

Common blue violet is native east of the Rockies. Those who love uniform lawns dislike its purple flowers and aggressive attitude. In addition to lawns, common blue violet prefers moist woods and damp fields. Common and quick-spreading under the right conditions, common blue violet can be used as a ground cover for moist, semishaded areas.

Birdfoot violet, also native to most of the country east of the Rockies, will thrive on dry or sandy soil and can be found in open woodlands. Easily crowded out by more aggressive plants, birdfoot violet is a good choice for the front row of a sunny border or a rock garden where it can be protected from crowded conditions. Consider it a short-lived perennial that will reseed.

Hookedspur violet is regarded as a wildflower rather than a weed. Native to areas primarily west of the Rockies, this violet is adaptable to many soil and moisture conditions.

Two native passionflowers are available for gardeners that are more northern, and whether you consider them weeds or wildflowers depends on your location. A wetland species, yellow passionflower is considered hardy to

Birdfoot violet (below left), and common blue violet (below right), are two violets that will feed fritillaries.

Purple passionflower produces many eye-catching flowers over the course of a growing season.

USDA Hardiness Zone 5, reaching the northern limit of its range in Pennsylvania and the western limit in Kansas. Its flowers are small and not as showy as those of other passionflowers. Purple passionflower, on the other hand, has a showy flower and produces an edible fruit if grown where the season is long enough. All passionflowers, native or not, can be weedy or downright aggressive given the right mixture of heat, moisture, and time.

Fetid passionflower is native to only a tiny section of the southern parts of the United States. It is more common south of the U.S. border and has naturalized in many tropical regions across the planet. Fetid passionflower is a good choice for gardens in hot, dry locations such as Arizona, Texas, and southern California. In Florida this species is considered an invasive exotic that disrupts native plant communities, so Floridians can choose the native corkystem passionflower instead.

BELOW: In southern states, Gulf Fritillary may be in flight all year and will produce many broods. Gulf Fritillary caterpillars will feed on all parts of passionflowers and can defoliate entire plants.

WHITE CLOVER WILL FEED A CROWD

While violets and passionflowers straddle the weed-wildflower divide and tend to land closer to the wildflower side, white clover is most often considered a weed by lawn lovers or a pasture component by farmers. White clover is not native to North America and the butterflies that use it as caterpillar food will also use a number of other Pea Family plants. But this easy-to-grow plant has the potential to feed many caterpillars as well as provide nectar for adult butterflies. It grows over a long season, producing a lot of caterpillar food per plant and so provides fresh caterpillar food and nectar for multitudes.

White clover is certainly not the first plant that comes to mind as a "garden plant" but with some forethought, it can fit into many garden spaces. For those who love an expansive, uniform lawn, white clover has no place, but for many lawn areas, some white clover is not problematic, as low-growing varieties often mingle with lawn grasses. Small lawns can be given over to white clover entirely with just stepping stones wading through the green expanse for a low-maintenance, butterfly-friendly yard. As with many caterpillar food plants, white clover is also suitable for locations that are visually less prominent, or as part of a wildscape area. Red clover can also support butterflies and their caterpillars but is less "lawnlike" and may be used in wildscapes or less manicured situations.

The butterflies that will thank you for a clover patch are the following:

- Eastern Tailed-Blues lay their eggs on the flower buds of white clover. Their caterpillars hatch and eat the buds, flowers, and even the seeds. Caterpillars hibernate over the winter and go on to form their chrysalides in early spring. Overzealous garden cleaning in the fall and spring will interrupt this butterfly's life cycle.
- Gray Hairstreak caterpillars often choose the white clover flowers as their food. Older caterpillars may eat the leaves as well. Gray Hairstreaks overwinter as chrysalides.
- Orange Sulphur eggs are laid on white clover leaves and the caterpillars remain on the leaves. Orange Sulphurs form chrysalides for the winter.
- Clouded Sulphur caterpillars also eat white clover leaves and will accept other plants in the Pea Family as caterpillar food. This butterfly overwinters as a caterpillar.
- Northern Cloudywing caterpillars eat the leaves of white clover and other Pea Family plants. This skipper overwinters as a fully grown caterpillar.
- Reakirt's Blue caterpillars eat white clover flowers and seedpods, as well as other Pea Family plants.

An Eastern Tailed-Blue perched on a white clover flower. Both the flower and the butterfly are relatively small

All these butterflies eat various parts of the white clover as caterpillars and, with the exception of Reakirt's Blue (which flies year-round in South Texas and migrates northward in the warmer months), overwinter as either caterpillars or chrysalides. When planting white clover, or any other plant in the Pea Family, think about how it can be managed within your particular garden. Will it be interspersed with lawn grasses that need to be mowed weekly? Choosing to grow white clover where it will not need regular mowing and not be exposed to lawn chemicals is an important consideration.

In addition to serving as caterpillar food, white clover provides nectar for many small and medium-sized butterflies, including Least Skipper, European Skipper, Common Sootywing, and American Copper.

Common Checkered-Skipper nectaring on white clover.

White Clover Choices

White clover has been bred for a variety of uses and performs best east of the Rockies and along the West Coast. It is considered a widely adaptable plant, so feel free to experiment with its placement. Taller varieties, such as ladino, may be useful in wilder areas, letting it compete with other grasses. Ladino is commonly used in hay mixtures, an indicator of its height and coarseness. Middle-height varieties, called Dutch white clover, are suitable to include in lawns. A low-growing variety, wild white, grows 3–5 inches and is suggested for areas with heavy foot traffic, although frequently traveled paths are not ideal for caterpillars, chrysalides, or butterflies.

PLANTING FOR MONARCHS

The plight of Monarchs and the efforts to save their migration have introduced butterfly gardening to gardeners and nongardeners alike. The overall number of Monarchs has decreased over the last few decades to a point where their spectacular annual migration, from Mexico to Canada and back each year (in the course of several generations), is threatened. It is worth noting that at this time, the Monarch population itself is not threatened with extinction, but its migration routes have been stripped of milkweed, the Monarchs' only caterpillar food plant. Their overwintering sites in Mexico are also dwindling and are expected to remain threatened as a result of illegal logging and the impact of climate change. These factors have combined to reduce the population to a level where scientists fear that eventually there will not be enough individual butterflies to maintain the species' migratory lifestyle.

With their migration in jeopardy, Monarchs have become media stars. "Plant Milkweed for Monarchs" is the battle cry and the campaign is underway to increase the plant that Monarch caterpillars eat exclusively—milkweed. But not just any milkweed will do, since like most caterpillars, Monarch

Butterfly milkweed lives up to its name!

caterpillars are particular in their food choices and find some milkweed species much more palatable than others.

Many species of milkweed are native to the United States and their names hint at their uses and histories; there are milkweeds named after states (Arizona, California, and Carolina are a few of the state names attached to "milkweed"), people (*Asclepias sullivantii* named after William Starling Sullivant, an American botanist of the nineteenth century), and habitat preferences (swamp milkweed's name suggests its affinity for wet soil). Each milkweed species is unique and has its own habitat requirements, which gardeners must take into consideration in order to cultivate a successful milkweed patch. Since many of these species are not commercially available and many would not be considered stellar garden plants, it is best to start with a handful of milkweeds that are fairly easy to find either at garden centers or through mail-order catalogs or websites.

Monarch Joint Venture is an umbrella group of government and nongovernment agencies and academic programs. Their website provides abundant information about Monarchs and their conservation, and how planting milkweeds can positively impact the Monarch migration. An important feature of Monarch Joint Venture is its vision to promote "[M]onarchs as a flagship species whose conservation will sustain habitats for pollinators and other plants and animals." To apply this simple strategy specifically to butterflies it reads like this: Start with Monarch conservation, identify what other butterflies come to visit, and plant their respective caterpillar food plants.

Milkweeds for Monarchs

When planting milkweeds for home gardens, choosing more than one species will ensure that fresh caterpillar food is available over the longest possible period. Each milkweed species has its own growth rate, flowering period, and cultural needs. Planting multiple milkweed species around the garden to utilize the various soil, sun, and moisture conditions is a great way to sustain Monarchs throughout their flight season.

Swamp milkweed is a good choice for gardens with rich soil or even soil that contains some clay. As its name indicates, swamp milkweed prefers damp and even wet soils, making it a good candidate for rain gardens.

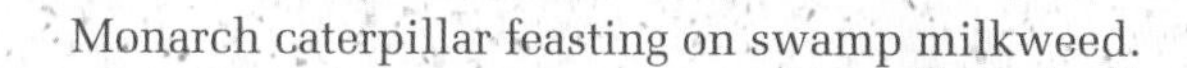

Monarch caterpillar feasting on swamp milkweed.

Great Spangled Fritillaries nectaring on butterfly milkweed.

BELOW: Purple milkweed flowers.

Butterfly milkweed prefers soils that are very well drained. Too much moisture will cause butterfly milkweed roots to rot.

Purple milkweed (*Asclepias purpurascens*) is well liked by Monarchs and is native to a large section of the Midwest and eastern United States. It can tolerate a small amount of shade.

Green antelopehorn milkweed has a strong following among Monarch enthusiasts, particularly in the south-central states of Texas and Oklahoma. Native to a large area that encompasses the Monarch migration route, green antelopehorn milkweed may not be easy to find at retail outlets and will need to be sourced from native-plant nurseries or seed catalogs.

Milkweed is considered an agricultural weed and is still not welcome in large-scale farm fields. A number of factors, including changing farming systems and the use of glyphosate-resistant crop plants, have been blamed for the overall decline in milkweed plants along the

The greenish-colored flowers of green antelopehorn milkweed may not fit into every garden's color scheme; but these Gray Hairstreaks indicate that nectar is flowing.

Monarch migration path. While no one factor can be definitively called out as the reason for the Midwest's missing milkweed, one thing has certainly happened—public perception of milkweed has shifted from one of a pernicious weed to something of a wildflower darling. Weeds can be agricultural pests and are often the bane of a gardener's existence, though in the world of butterfly gardening, there are a surprising number of weeds that feed caterpillars.

CATERPILLAR FOOD PLANTS FOR THE ADVENTURESOME: NETTLES AND OTHER EXUBERANT PLANTS

Violets, white clover, and some species of milkweeds are all common plants, ones that are available at garden centers or observable growing naturally in your lawn. Other caterpillar food plants fall far outside the domain of garden-center popularity but have a place in the realm of feeding caterpillars. These are plants for intrepid gardeners who can withstand a bit of chiding from fellow gardeners over their plant choices as well as for those gardeners willing to experiment with plants that can be aggressive in their growth habits.

Milbert's Tortoiseshell may be found in gardens within its flight range. It is not considered a "common" garden butterfly, but plant stinging nettle (or watch a patch in the wild) and you may be graced with a visit by this beautiful, bright butterfly.

Stinging nettle best exemplifies the type of butterfly garden plant that will cause your loved ones to scratch their heads and wonder whether gardening for butterflies is a euphemism for poor judgment. Make no mistake, stinging nettle is a widespread, potentially weedy plant; one that is best recognized by sight rather than brushed up against, as the stinging hairs can leave quite a painful welt. But stinging nettle and a few other plants in the Nettle Family are the only food on which Red Admiral caterpillars will feed. While some of the other Nettle Family plants, such as smallspike false nettle and Pennsylvania pellitory, do not have stinging hairs, gardeners with an empty, moist, secluded spot might consider planting stinging nettle rather than a less threatening, stingless nettle. Not only does stinging nettle feed Red Admirals, but other very common garden butterflies such as Eastern Comma, Question Mark, and West Coast Lady will also use the plant as caterpillar food. Slightly less widespread garden butterflies, such as Milbert's Tortoiseshell and Satyr Comma, also find nettles suitable for their caterpillars. Then, of course, do not forget that in addition to caterpillars, many humans consider young springtime nettles to be a tasty cooking green. Once people start to share food plants with caterpillars, some level of competition may arise for the choicest parts of the plants, so try to plant plenty and check carefully for caterpillars before harvesting!

Recommending stinging nettle for a butterfly garden brings up an important, seldom-addressed question—namely, where can one obtain plants or seeds of these weedy or less popular species? Many plants, like stinging nettle, will never be sold at the majority of plant nurseries, and some other very interesting butterfly garden plants can also be very difficult to find! It will certainly feel odd to many, purchasing seeds to grow weeds, but it can be done. Stinging nettle seeds are listed in some vegetable seed catalogs under the section for different types of cooking greens. Seed catalogs and plant nurseries that specialize in herbs are another possible source for stinging nettle seeds or plants. Should you choose to search out smallspike false nettle and Pennsylvania pellitory, two stingless alternatives to stinging nettles, it will be even harder to find a plant or seed source, as these plants are not showy plants that most gardeners seek out and they have no herbal or culinary use for humans.

Stinging nettle.

Stinging nettle plants are not much to look at. Their flowers are wind pollinated so they do not have showy, colorful petals. The plants can spread aggressively by underground stems when grown under optimal conditions of full sun and adequate moisture. No one would consider a tall, aggressively spreading, coarsely textured plant with stinging hairs to be anything other than a weed. But if feeding caterpillars is of interest, consider stinging nettle.

Expanding your plant palette away from highly cultivated plants to the more ragged edges of the gardening world will change the population of insects that visit your garden, draw new and varied wildlife to your plantings, and expand the definition of "garden," all while providing large amounts of caterpillar food for some lively and brightly colored butterflies.

EXUBERANT PLANTS FOR CATERPILLAR FOOD

CATERPILLAR FOOD PLANT	POSSIBLE CATERPILLARS ATTRACTED
Stinging nettle spreads by both seed and underground stem.	Red Admiral, Eastern Comma, Question Mark, West Coast Lady, Milbert's Tortoiseshell, Satyr Comma.
Common milkweed is a vigorous milkweed that spreads by underground stem as well as by seed.	Monarch
Dutchman's pipe species grow as vines that can spread by underground stems	Pipevine Swallowtail
Passionflower species are vines that can spread by underground stems.	Zebra Heliconian, Variegated Fritillary, Gulf Fritillary
Common pricklyash is a tall shrub that can form colonies by underground stems. Numerous thorns line the branches, making it a plant to keep in check unless you have unlimited room to let it roam.	Giant Swallowtail

A HOME FOR EXUBERANT PLANTS

If you choose to try some exuberant caterpillar food plants, plan ahead! Consider a special garden bed that will contain the roots of nettles and other plants that spread underground. For more visual interest over a long period of time, plan to add tall, annual, nectar-producing flowers such as zinnias to the bed. Choose a spot in full sun if possible and mark out the shape of the bed; it can be as large as you wish. The smallest size for a bed of robust plants depends on how long you hope to continue the bed; a small space—one less than 3 feet by 3 feet—will fill up quite quickly once the plants start to spread, crowding the soil in the bed with rhizomes.

Place a root barrier around the perimeter of the bed to prevent the plants from spreading beyond their designated area. Traditionally, root barriers are used to keep tree roots from infiltrating garden beds or areas next to structures such as sidewalks, where the roots can damage hardscape or foundations. The barriers are often thick plastic or metal and come in a variety of depths. For herbaceous plants with robust underground growth, the barrier is to keep the colonizing roots inside the planting area. Barriers in this situation should be as deep as possible, since the traveling underground stems of stinging nettle and some milkweeds can explore quite deeply under the soil surface. Surround this bed with a decorative fence to keep out the unwary, and your "weed garden" has become a garden for caterpillars.

Adding a sign to let visitors know the importance of your garden bed adds to the charm of trying unusual plants. This sign at National Butterfly Center lets garden visitors know they are at the "Monarch Nursery."

A less backbreaking containment approach is to install a raised bed that has a layer of weed-barrier fabric attached to the bottom of the frame. No digging is needed to install the raised bed, although the initial cost of the bed, weed-barrier fabric, and soil to fill the bed will most likely be higher than for simply purchasing root-barrier materials.

Whether you install a raised bed or opt for root barriers, when growing any plant that is known to spread, there is one other management strategy beyond containing the roots with barriers—place the garden bed where the perimeter of the bed can be mowed or cultivated. Any plants that sprout outside the containment bed can be run over with a mower or attacked with a string trimmer. Although the initial effort of creating a containment bed can be high, trimming around the bed during the growing season is relatively easy.

Once you move from purchasing whatever plants are available at the store and begin selecting specific plants for specific purposes, you will need to seek many desirable garden plants through less common avenues. Native-plant societies and native-plant nurseries should always be the starting point when looking for new plants. Not only are these sources likely to have seeds or plants that are commonly unavailable at big-box stores, they also often source their seeds and plants from regional stock that is not harvested from the wild.

HERB GARDENS

A traditional herb garden conjures up images of geometric, boxwood-edged garden beds filled with aromatic plants. The herbs contained in the beds usually follow a theme—the plants can be medicinal, fragrant, culinary, or just about any group of plants that gives pleasure to the gardener. The culinary herb garden is particularly suited to beginning butterfly gardeners—plants are easy to obtain, the garden layout is adjustable depending on how much space is available, and many culinary herbs serve as caterpillar food plants. After starting with some basic culinary species, adding in just a few other, more unusual plants will create an herb garden that provides food for caterpillars as well as a functional area to harvest from and to relax in.

Black and Anise Swallowtail caterpillars eat plants that are eminently suited to a traditional culinary herb garden. Parsley, dill, garden lovage, fennel, and parsnip all belong to the Parsley Family of plants and will feed the caterpillars of these two swallowtails. Perhaps with the exception of fennel and parsnip (because of their size), all these plants can be included in a traditional, small, culinary herb garden. Most of these plants are also sold at garden centers as small plants, making it easy to begin an herb garden.

Pipevine Swallowtail.

The Citrus [aka Rue] Family also provides caterpillar food for Black and Anise Swallowtails, with common rue the most widely utilized food plant (these two swallowtails do *not* use the species that produce citrus fruits). Giant Swallowtail, however, utilizes both common rue and citrus. So as you can see, the topic of caterpillar food plants sometimes gets a bit complicated. It would be so simple for gardeners if it were possible to state that a certain butterfly

CHEMISTRY plays a large role in plant selection by all female butterflies looking for an egg-laying site: volatile oils in plants attract fertile butterflies and, in fact, induce them to lay eggs. In the case of Black and Anise Swallowtails, plants in the Parsley Family and the Citrus Family produce volatile oils that are very similar in chemical structure and that will induce egg-laying behavior.

When presented with a garden offering parsley, dill, fennel, and common rue, how does a butterfly decide which is most desirable for egg-laying? It depends on a tremendous number of factors, many of which we can only speculate about. The growth stage of a plant matters, since leaves of a certain age will produce the right texture or chemical composition needed by young caterpillars. The size of the plant plays a role since a large, robust, healthy plant can produce more of the butterfly-attracting volatile oils. The number of plants of a given species may be important, since a large number of caterpillar food plants will have the potential to produce more butterfly-attracting volatile compounds in the air. The interactions in nature that result in a butterfly laying an egg on a specific plant are beyond our control, so we can best help butterflies in this regard by planting known caterpillar food plants, planting a lot of them, and keeping them as healthy as possible.

would use only certain plants from certain plant families. If we could further dictate our preferences, it would also be nice to know exactly when butterflies would show up in a garden, but butterflies don't pay attention to plant taxonomists or gardeners and fly by their own rules.

Common rue is a nonnative plant that is easy to grow and can be started from seed. It has a history as a medicinal herb and is used in a few cuisines; it is a component of grappa in Italy and is featured in the Ethiopian spice mixture called berbere. Adding other Citrus Family plants, such as a potted orange tree, to an herb garden will entice another dramatic butterfly to explore herb gardens east of the Rockies and in the desert Southwest—Giant Swallowtail. The largest of the naturally occurring butterflies in the United States, Giant Swallowtails are strong fliers and exciting to see in a garden.

Common hoptree is another Citrus Family plant that is suitable for some herb gardens. It has a history of medicinal uses, and its one culinary use is in beer making, where its small, tan, wafer-shaped seeds have been used to replace common hop, although the seeds more commonly serve as food for wildlife. Common hoptree is a North American native tree that grows well in dry soils and will tolerate shade. As it can grow to 25 feet if left unpruned, common hoptree may not suit every herb garden. Plant it at the back of an herb garden as an accent plant or consider placing it in a shrub border.

Herb gardens that feature an arbor or sturdy trellis could include Dutchman's pipe to supply Pipevine Swallowtails a place in the herb garden. Although steeped in herbalist lore, Dutchman's pipe are carcinogenic for human consumption so their inclusion is thematic rather than medicinal or culinary. Occupying much the same range as Giant Swallowtail, Pipevine Swallowtail is considered locally distributed, meaning that although its range is extensive it does not occur in all seemingly suitable habitat—so gardeners who plant Dutchman's pipe may be rewarded with a visit from this black-and-iridescent-blue butterfly right away, or it may never appear. Dutchman's pipe is a large-leaved, decorative vine, so it is worth planting even if the swallowtails fail to show. If including Dutchman's pipe in a herb garden, or any garden that has obvious boundaries, consider a root containment method.

It is a matter of opinion as to which is more beautiful—Pipevine Swallowtails with their iridescent blue hindwings, or Pipevine Swallowtail caterpillars with their chocolate brown bodies and orange tubercles. This caterpillar's coloration is called "red form," while the "purple form," with a dark purplish-black body, is more common.

Common hoptree seeds are plentiful and are eaten by birds as well as mammals. The flattened round seeds are wafer-shaped, giving this tree a second common name of "wafer ash".

To feed a fifth swallowtail in this herb garden, choose a tree for the background. Black cherry, sweetbay, or a willow will provide shelter for all butterflies while adding the caterpillar food plant for Eastern or Western Tiger Swallowtail, depending on your location.

Although these five swallowtails require five different food plants, their caterpillars can be accommodated in a small garden, which could even include a space for a garden bench. Add in some butterfly milkweed as an accent plant plus a few other flowers for season-long nectar. Swallowtails will be happy.

WILDFLOWERS, WEEDS, AND HERBS DETAILS

CATERPILLAR FOOD PLANT	POSSIBLE CATERPILLARS	PROPAGATION NOTES	CULTURAL NOTES
Violets	Great Spangled Fritillary, Meadow Fritillary, Variegated Fritillary, and possibly other fritillaries based on your location	Violets are resilient plants that spread easily.	
White clover	Eastern Tailed-Blue, Gray Hairstreak, Orange Sulphur, Clouded Sulphur, Reakirt's Blue	Seed is available through some garden catalogs/websites. Many garden centers sell seed for lawns. Seed is easy to start and germinates quickly.	Consider growing white clover where it will not need to be mowed or choose a low-growing variety.
Milkweed	Monarch	Milkweed started from seed will usually not bloom the first season.	Choose a few different milkweeds if space allows so bloom periods will be staggered over the growing season.
Stinging nettle	Red Admiral, Eastern Comma, Question Mark, West Coast Lady, Milbert's Tortoiseshell, and Satyr Comma.	Seeds for stinging nettle may be gathered in the fall from the plants. For the less intrepid, seeds can be purchased from catalogs/websites that sell garden seeds or herb seeds.	While it can reproduce by seed, stinging nettle forms colonies primarily by underground stems. To manage unwanted spread, select a location where it is possible to cultivate around the plant thereby eliminating the plant's enthusiastic spreading nature.

continued overleaf

WILDFLOWERS, WEEDS, AND HERBS DETAILS *continued*

CATERPILLAR FOOD PLANT	POSSIBLE CATERPILLARS	PROPAGATION NOTES	CULTURAL NOTES
Parsley Family plants: parsley, dill, garden lovage, fennel, golden Alexander, and parsnip	Black, Anise, Indra, and Ozark swallowtails	Easily started from seed and may self-seed in many instances	Golden Alexander and fennel can spread by seed to overwhelm small spaces. Consider deadheading these plants.
Common rue	Giant and Black swallowtails	An easy plant to start from seed but will take a year or two to achieve a size large enough to feed hungry caterpillars.	Phytophotoder-matitis is a skin condition that can occur when skin is exposed to sunlight after brushing against the foliage of common rue. In sensitive individuals, oils from the plant are activated by sunlight to cause rashes and/or blistering. So handle rue with gloves!
Common hoptree	Giant Swallowtail	Can be grown as a small tree or cut back to perform as a shrub.	
Dutchman's pipe species	Pipevine Swallowtail		Can grow into a very large, woody vine (like wisteria), so requires a large, sturdy support. Plant where spreading stems can be mowed or trimmed to keep plant in check.

CATERPILLAR FOOD PLANT	POSSIBLE CATERPILLARS	PROPAGATION NOTES	CULTURAL NOTES
Black cherry, sweetbay, or willow species	Eastern Tiger Swallowtail or Western Tiger Swallowtail depending on location. Spicebush Swallowtail may also eat sweetbay.		All three of these tree species can be grown as small trees or large shrubs by judicious pruning.

SHRUBS, TREES, AND VINES

Woody plants are an essential component of butterfly gardens —in addition to providing food for many caterpillars, shrubs and trees create refuge from adverse weather, a hiding place from predators, and shelter from the wind. With their large expanse of leaves and buds, trees and shrubs can provide a lot of caterpillar food where the evidence of munching caterpillars will not be noticed. Many of the commonest garden butterflies do not use trees or shrubs as caterpillar food, but a host of other widespread butterflies do require woody plants for their caterpillars. Add trees and shrubs to your plant list in order to attract a wider variety of butterflies to your garden!

WHEN SIZE MATTERS

When planning a butterfly garden, woody plants may seem too large to consider. Fortunately, the size of many trees and shrubs favored by caterpillars can be managed in a dramatic way by trimming them back to the ground in a process called coppicing. Many experienced butterfly gardeners routinely coppice their trees and shrubs—this both allows woody plants to grow where space is tight, and also produces leaves and buds at eye level, allowing for easy caterpillar viewing.

Coppicing involves cutting a tree down to just above ground level, which stimulates the plant to regrow into a multistemmed, shrublike plant rather than a tall tree with a single trunk. The same technique works for shrubs and can be used to rejuvenate a tall, overgrown shrub into something more manageable. For some large trees, the first year after the initial coppicing may not

TREES AND SHRUBS TO COPPICE FOR CATERPILLAR FOOD

CATERPILLAR FOOD TREE	POSSIBLE WIDESPREAD GARDEN CATERPILLARS ATTRACTED
Northern spicebush	Spicebush Swallowtail
Black cherry	Eastern Tiger Swallowtail, Coral Hairstreak, Red-spotted Purple
Hackberry species	Question Mark, Mourning Cloak, Hackberry Emperor, Tawny Emperor, American Snout
Tuliptree	Eastern Tiger Swallowtail
Willow species	Western Tiger Swallowtail, Mourning Cloak, Compton Tortoiseshell, Red-spotted Purple, White Admiral, Lorquin's Admiral, Weidemeyer's Admiral, Viceroy, Dreamy Duskywing,
Common pricklyash	Giant Swallowtail
Common hoptree	Giant Swallowtail

produce much growth but usually by the second year the shoots become more vigorous, and with regular coppicing, annual regrowth will be strong.

The flush of stems that arise from the live stump, which once cut is called a stool, may need to be thinned, although many stems will die out over the first few years. Depending on the space available and the species of tree or shrub, most coppiced plants will need to be recut every one to five years. Fast-growing willows may need annual trimming while a northern spicebush may not outgrow its space for four or five years.

WHEN SIZE MATTERS

The checklist of strategies to employ when gardening to attract egg-laying butterflies and provide for their caterpillars:

- Plant as many different species as possible of known caterpillar food plants, and plant each species in groups throughout the garden. This strategy enhances the butterflies' ability to recognize the caterpillar food and find plenty of egg-laying opportunities, all while minimizing the energy needed to search.
- Know what parts of plants are eaten by caterpillars and keep caterpillar food material as fresh as possible. Young Black Swallowtail caterpillars start eating parsley leaves, then proceed to eat the parsley stems after no leaves remain. By growing a number of parsley plants and trimming each plant at a different time over the course of the growing season (checking for caterpillars first before trimming of course!), fresh caterpillar food will be ready should a Black or Anise Swallowtail stop by. Caterpillars that eat white clover flower buds will need consideration when a patch of white clover is to be mowed. Monarch caterpillars prefer fresh leaves and buds, so planting a few different milkweeds that grow at different rates will cater to them. Common milkweed can also be cut back in order to provide fresh foliage for late-season egg-laying and caterpillar munching.
- Keep shelter and nectar nearby. Butterflies need to recognize a space as "habitat" if they are to linger. Providing shelter with shrubs and trees (many of which can also provide caterpillar food) allows butterflies to find safe spots to rest and shelter from the weather. Nectar-producing flowers will provide the fuel that butterflies need in order to mate and lay eggs.
- Consider trees and shrubs even if your space is limited. By including woody plant species, a garden can feed many more caterpillars as well as many more species of butterflies. Coppicing trees and shrubs can keep them down to a manageable size.

CHAPTER FOUR

BUTTERFLY BANQUET

BUTTERFLY BANQUET

When creating a flower garden, one's plant choices depend on climate, budget, design, and expected maintenance. However, when planting specifically for butterflies, a few other considerations come into play. Many butterflies feed on nectar (a high-energy liquid produced by flowers) and for these, choosing flowering plants that butterflies prefer—and keeping those plants healthy so that they produce flowers over the longest possible period—are the cornerstones of butterfly gardening.

Other butterflies find sustenance from nonfloral resources; they choose overripe fruit, mud puddles, animal scat, and even pollen for their meals! Butterflies will land on people to drink sweat and salt from skin, or will imbibe salts and nutrients from puddles or damp, sandy spots. Supplying all the different sources of butterfly nutrition in one garden is a challenge, and most gardeners start by providing carefully selected nectar-producing flowers. Choose to add different types of butterfly foods over time and you will create a banquet line for butterflies that rivals any Golden Buffet along the interstate highway.

HOW BUTTERFLIES EAT

Unlike caterpillars, which feed by chewing plant materials, adult butterflies eat by imbibing liquids through long, strawlike tongues. Technically called a *proboscis*, the butterfly tongue is made up of two slender tubes that are held together by microscopic scalelike structures. The scales interlock, connecting the two tubes like puzzle pieces fitting together. The tiny opening that remains between the two tubes forms a feeding canal through which the butterfly sucks nectar or other liquid food. If sticky or thick material enters the feeding canal, the scales can be adjusted to allow the tubes to separate for cleaning. When not in use, the long tongue is coiled into a tight spiral that rests beneath the head.

Scientists have determined that different species of butterflies have small variations in the structure of their tongues, which allows them to eat different types of foods. Butterflies that feed primarily on sap have a brushlike tip on their proboscis, while in nectar-feeding butterflies the brushlike tip is reduced or entirely absent.

TWO BUTTERFLIES from the genus *Heliconius* occur in the United States—Erato and Zebra heliconians. While Eratos are considered strays from Mexico and only rarely seen in south Texas, Zebra Heliconians can be seen all year by butterfly gardeners in south Texas and peninsular Florida. The diet of Zebras is unique among U.S. butterflies, for in addition to nectar, they also eat pollen.

Grains of pollen collect on the tongue of Zebra butterflies as they visit flowers. Their tongues are specially adapted to secrete enzymes that dissolve the pollen, turning it into a protein-rich fluid the butterfly can drink. The amino acids in the protein provide enhanced nutrition that allows Zebra Heliconians to live longer than most butterflies—up to several months—during which time they lay eggs and produce multiple generations. Within its range, the beautiful Zebra Heliconian may be locally common in gardens. North of its core range this species may visit flower gardens but eventually will be killed by frost

In general, tongue length is proportional to body size in butterflies. These Zabulon Skippers (female below left, male below right,) have extended their tongues to reach nectar found deep at the base of tubular flowers, demonstrating that with tongue length there are exceptions to every rule.

COMMON BUTTERFLIES AND THEIR FOOD PREFERENCES

- ~ Tiger Swallowtails: Nectar from a wide variety of flowers
- ~ Cabbage White: Nectar from a wide variety of flowers
- ~ Orange Sulphur: Nectar from a wide variety of flowers
- ~ Gray Hairstreak: Nectar from a wide variety of flowers
- ~ Pearl Crescent, Field Crescent, Northern Crescent: Nectar from a wide variety of flowers
- ~ Question Mark: Overripe fruit, tree sap, animal scat, carrion. Will imbibe floral nectar when other sources are not available.
- ~ Eastern Comma: Tree sap or overripe fruit
- ~ Hoary Comma: Tree sap and some nectar
- ~ Mourning Cloak: Tree sap is preferred but will also feed on overripe fruit. Occasionally visits flowers.
- ~ American Lady: Nectar from a wide variety of flowers
- ~ Painted Lady: Nectar from a wide variety of flowers
- ~ Red Admiral: Will nectar but prefers overripe fruit, tree sap, and bird droppings.
- ~ Monarch: Nectar from a wide variety of flowers
- ~ Common Checkered-Skipper: Nectar from a wide variety of flowers

Butterfly tongue lengths vary by butterfly species and influence the types of foods they eat. In general, the larger the butterfly, the longer the tongue, although many skippers have very long tongues in comparison to their body size. For butterflies that visit flowers, a larger butterfly such as a Western Tiger Swallowtail will have a long tongue that can drink nectar from large, tubular flowers like lilies and agapanthus, while a much smaller butterfly, such as a Pearl Crescent, will have a much shorter tongue and prefer nectaring on smaller, shallower flowers. Life is short for a butterfly and its energy reserves are small. Regardless of tongue length or structure, butterflies strive for feeding efficiency in order to achieve their ultimate goal—reproduction. In the garden, two primary types of butterfly feeding—flowers for nectar and butterfly feeders for non-nectar feeders—provide many options based on garden location and gardeners' interests.

SKIPPERS are currently not considered "true" butterflies; their current limb on the taxonomic family tree relegates them to the status of close relatives of butterflies. The classification of skippers and true butterflies may change in the future; a reappraisal has been suggested to add skippers into the same "superfamily" that currently houses true butterflies. Despite these classification issues, two obvious physical differences separate butterflies and skippers—their wing size relative to body size, and their antennae.

Butterflies have wings that are large in relation to their bodies and when in flight, they move their wings in a flapping motion. The wings of skippers tend to be smaller in relation to their body size and their bodies are stockier than those of true butterflies. When in flight, skippers beat their wings in a very fast flutter.

Another prominent difference between true butterflies and skippers is the shape of their antennae. The tips of butterfly antennae are rounded knobs, while the tips of skipper antennae have a hook at the end that may or may not be quite obvious depending on how close a view one can get.

Not all flowers produce nectar. Some, like this spiderwort, produce only pollen. Bees love spiderwort! Butterflies may investigate nectarless flowers but they move on quickly. This spiderwort is growing next to a very large blue giant hyssop, which produces a multitude of nectar-filled flowers. Perhaps this Least Skipper was on its way to drink at the hyssop and paused for a moment for a photo opportunity.

NECTAR-FILLED FLOWERS

Butterflies are pollinators, along with bees, flies, moths, ants, and other insects; hummingbirds; and bats. While butterflies do aid in the transfer of pollen between flowering plants, nectar is what draws butterflies to flowers. A liquid produced by flowers in special glands called *nectaries*, nectar contains sugar, water, fats, resins, and amino acids, all of which are important for butterfly nutrition, health, and reproduction.

Tongue length and structure are just two of the many factors that influence which flowers are visited by butterflies and other nectar-seeking insects. The thickness, or viscosity, of a plant's nectar also affects how easily butterflies are able to imbibe it. Honey bees have shorter tongues with a different structure that allows them to lap nectar, while butterflies drink nectar through suction. With shorter tongues and different feeding mechanics, honey bees prefer nectar with a sugar concentration of around 50 percent. Butterflies, on the other hand, seek nectar with around 35–40 percent sugar, which is less sticky and more fluid.

The nutrient content and availability of a flower's nectar for butterflies varies widely. Over the course of a flower's life, the makeup of its nectar will depend on a surprising number of factors: the species (the flowers of different plant species produce different amounts of nectar), the time of day (the metabolic processes of each plant fluctuate over the course of a day), the weather (nectar may become less dilute as the heat of the day causes evaporation), the status of the flower (once pollination occurs, flowers stop producing nectar), the health of the plant (water or nutrient stress can influence the quality or quantity of nectar produced), and whether it has recently been visited by a pollinator for a drink (and is therefore depleted of nectar), to name just a few variables that can directly affect the quality and quantity of nectar at any given time.

WHICH FLOWERS ATTRACT BUTTERFLIES?

Just observing flowers in a garden on a warm, sunny summer day will show you which flowers attract butterflies. Since different species of butterflies are in flight at varying times over the course of the warmer months, a single visit to a garden or garden center will not give you the knowledge needed to plan an effective butterfly garden, but it can be a valuable exercise in fine-tuning your plant choices once you have established a basic garden.

Think like a butterfly and consider the following features of flower morphology when considering a nectar plant for your garden:

- **Flower shape and arrangement:** Some flowers are shaped in a way that allows butterflies to reach their nectar, but not all. Butterflies with long tongues, such as swallowtails and many skippers, can access nectar from deep flowers. Smaller butterflies tend to have shorter tongues and will seek out shorter flowers. Flower heads that comprise many smaller flowers allow butterflies to land and drink without having to expend energy to fly to adjacent flowers. When planning a garden for butterflies, start by choosing plants that among them have a variety of different-shaped flowers, so

OPPOSITE: The action of a butterfly drinking nectar at a flower is called *nectaring*. Watch as a butterfly lands on a flower, unfurls its tongue, and stands still. The butterfly may not move its feet or fly to another flower but merely move its tongue from flower to flower if the flowers are small and close together, and if the nectar flow is sufficient. This Eastern Tiger Swallowtail is nectaring on a summer-blooming ornamental onion. Gardeners can choose from a number of such onions; some bloom in spring, others in summer or fall, and all will attract butterflies.

that different-sized butterflies will be able to find nectar. Some of the most widespread and popular butterfly nectar plants include the following:

- Plants in the Aster Family such as purple coneflowers, blazing stars, goldenrods, and sunflowers. Plants in the huge Aster Family feature many small, nectar-producing flowers in each flower head. The small flowers, called *florets,* open in sequence so that any one flower head includes nectar-producing flowers at various stages from unopened (and not yet producing nectar) to beginning to open (and maybe not producing abundant nectar) to fully open, ready-to-pollinate florets (an irresistible feast of nectar), and finally to a pollinated floret (exhibiting an "expired sell-by date" to pollinators). When a butterfly lands on an Aster Family flower, it may be able to drink from many florets without having to move anything other than its tongue.
- Plants in the Mint Family, such as beebalms, giant hyssops, and mountainmints, are butterfly magnets. Unlike culinary mint, which can spread vigorously by underground stems, beebalms and mountainmints tend to be slower in their colonization and are easy to pull out if they spread beyond their designated spots. Giant hyssops may spread by seed if conditions are right, but do not spread by underground stems. All three of these Mint Family plants bloom over a long period and produce many flowers per plant. Mountainmint flowers tend to be small and are a favorite with small butterflies such as hairstreaks.

■ **Landing stage:** Flowers that provide a stable landing platform where a butterfly can perch and sip nectar with minimum expenditure of energy are important to include in gardens. Observe butterflies nectaring on zinnias or purple coneflowers: to access nectar they merely move their tongues from floret to floret while having a stable base of petals on which to stand. Many butterflies will flutter their wings as they nectar but they are not flying while feeding; they have come to a stop, and this makes them vulnerable to predation.

■ **Flower scent and condition:** Fresh flowers that have recently opened are visually attractive to humans and often attractive to butterflies as well. But after a flower has been pollinated, various signals serve to decrease its attractiveness to butterflies and other pollinators: the flower's color may become less vibrant, its scent may change or decrease, and its orientation can shift (by drooping or crumpling). These changes indicate to pollinators that they will earn no reward for visiting the already-pollinated flower.

Two Eastern Tiger Swallowtails are slowly circling the perimeter of this sunflower, nectaring along the outer edge of the flower head where some of the sunflower's nectar-filled florets are open. Florets on the very edge of the flower head may have already yielded their nectar, while florets toward the center of the head have not yet opened (and may not open for many days). A single *inflorescence* (the name given to the assemblage of florets that make up the sunflower "flower") may comprise up to 2,000 individual florets, each of which can supply nectar for pollinators.

It should be noted that floral scent for butterflies is not necessarily the same as an intense flower fragrance that gardeners might covet. Roses, for example, are completely ignored by butterflies! Some flowering plants, such as fall phlox, are both attractive to butterflies and have a very pleasant scent that will be noticeable in gardens, but floral scents that draw butterflies to nectar sources are more than pleasant smells. These scents

Fall phlox is native to half the United States and a staple in many butterfly gardens. It produces many flowers that are densely arranged in a manner that provides a landing platform for butterflies. The flowers in this photo show several stages of development that are visible upon close inspection of the flower head. Crumpled, bluish blossoms are no longer producing pollen or nectar and would not be accessible by butterflies, while wide-open flowers provide easy access to nectar at their centers. Tightly curled pink buds have yet to open, so nectar is not yet available. A large stand of fall phlox may offer bright, nectar-filled flowers over a 3-week time frame, although not all flowers open at the same time.

communicate information from plants to butterflies—they can attract butterflies to flowers that are ready to be pollinated, but they can also be produced to repel egg-laying by butterflies whose caterpillars will harm the plant. The interrelationships between plants and butterflies are extensive and highly complex and provide a variety of levels of study and observation for those who are curious.

- **Nectar guides:** Butterfly vision differs greatly from our own. When looking for flowers, flying butterflies recognize blocks of color, so massing one particular species of plant in a group increases the likelihood that passing butterflies will be attracted to your welcoming garden. Butterflies also see in the ultraviolet portion of the light spectrum (which is not detectable by human eyesight), allowing them to view flowers in a way that we cannot. Once butterflies get close to flowers, certain details in the light reflected in the ultraviolet range provide them with important clues about the availability of nectar.

  Many flowers have patterns on their petals that are visible only in the ultraviolet range. These patterns, which can consist of lines, dots, or differently colored petals, are called *nectar guides* and serve to direct butterflies toward the center of the flower where they can quickly access the flower's nectar. These guides are obvious on fully open flowers that are producing nectar, while on flowers that have not yet fully opened or have started to wilt the nectar guides will not be visible, allowing butterflies to direct their foraging efforts as efficiently as possible.

Butterflies in the wild generally live from a few days to a few weeks (although a few live considerably longer). The length of a butterfly's life span varies from species to species, and weather impacts a butterfly's life span as well. During their short lives, butterflies must mate and, if female, find an appropriate egg-laying location. During all this activity, they must also find and drink enough nectar to sustain their energy levels. It seems unlikely that butterflies are nectar connoisseurs with the luxury of selecting only the perfect vintage of nectar. The constant whirl of activity we so enjoy as butterfly watchers is in fact just part of a race for survival from the butterfly's point of view.

Many garden flowers display lines, speckles, and color blotches that are visible to humans. When you examine the flowers in your garden, notice if there are color variations or markings that direct your eye to the center of the flower. Fringeleaf wild petunia is a low-growing perennial that serves as a nectar plant for many butterflies as well as caterpillar food for the wide-ranging Common Buckeye. The dark purple veins serve as nectar guides to draw pollinators toward the lighter purple center of the flower. Fringeleaf wild petunia is easy to grow in a variety of soils and locations but does spread, although slowly at first. When seeds mature on the plant in the fall, they explode out of their seedpods, launching them many feet away from the mother plant.

ORNAMENTAL PLANTS developed for home gardens are often grown out in trial gardens where they are tested for overall gardenworthiness. Depending on the plant and location, a trial in Colorado might test blue giant hyssop for its length of bloom in the dry climate found in the state, while a trial in Illinois might evaluate the performance of asters for the Upper Midwest, which would include tolerance of bone-chilling winter temperatures.

A plant trial is simply a way to evaluate plants for specific traits by growing a group of similar plants over many years and monitoring their responses to the environment. It is a time-honored way of weeding out the weak, the floppy, and the powdery-mildew prone of the horticultural world. Plant trials are run by arboreta, botanical gardens, universities, and commercial plant breeders and can be valuable for helping to select plants on a regional basis. Traditionally, plant trials have not included tests for nectar quality or quantity, but as the interest in pollinator gardens and environmentally beneficial gardening continues to grow, some trials are starting to investigate which pollinators (including butterflies) are visiting what flowers and when.

Mt. Cuba Center in Delaware runs plant trials on native plants and their cultivars. The beebalm trial, pictured here, ran from 2014 to 2016 to evaluate the most disease-resistant and top-performing (e.g., with regard to growth habit and floral display) beebalm selections for the mid-Atlantic states. Powdery mildew is a pervasive problem with beebalm in humid locations, and the trials at Mt. Cuba carefully evaluated cultivars that were resistant to this difficult-to-control foliar disease.

Using the results from their trial gardens, Mt. Cuba has planted their top-rated perennial plants in a mixed perennial border in a formal-style garden. While not specifically designed as a butterfly garden, the borders contain exclusively native plants, many of which are beloved by butterflies. In this summer view (upper photo) of the border, eastern purple coneflower, blazing star, rattlesnake master, and turk's-cap lily are all in bloom and will supply butterfly nectar. As the season progresses, asters and goldenrods come into their glory (lower photo), demonstrating that a native-plant garden (and butterfly garden) can fit any style desired.

Once confined to exotic or highly bred garden varieties, a few plant trials, run primarily by graduate students, have also been started that evaluate native plants and their cultivars. The evaluation methods vary—some trials make only visual observations, while others measure nectar quality, quantity, and replenishment rates. Regardless of the method, the handful of trials that evaluate native plants and their attractiveness to pollinators are a beginning to creating vital information that will allow gardeners to fine-tune their nectar plant choices for butterflies—it is hoped more trials will be held in the future!

BUTTERFLIES AND PLANTS: MORE THAN A ONE-NIGHT STAND

Habitat gardening, ecosystem gardening, and natural landscaping are all styles of gardening that emphasize the use of native plants when creating gardens or home landscapes. The role of exclusively native plants in butterfly gardening is a hotly debated topic, and one that needs to be considered when starting a butterfly garden.

Native plants are uniquely suited to butterfly gardening because the relationships between butterflies, caterpillars, and the plants they use for food are not casual ones. They have developed over millions of years as flowering plants coevolved with insects. Because of this long association, today's caterpillars will accept only certain plants for food, and therefore butterflies must be equally fussy about what plants they select to lay their eggs on. Moreover, plants, in turn, have developed over time to entice butterflies to visit their flowers. Certain native plants are highly desired and necessary for butterfly reproduction.

Insisting that new plant materials be chosen only from those plants considered native eliminates a large number of potential butterfly gardeners who do not have the resources or inclination to find and purchase native plants from specialty growers. Additionally, the idea of "native plants" is a bit of a moving target. How do we discern whether a plant is native to our locale? How much does the history of a plant's origin (also known as *provenance*) matter as the land continues to be irrevocably changed by human creations and introductions? The most highly recognizable native plant is probably the eastern purple coneflower, which is native to barely half the United States but widely marketed as a native plant. Without refining the definition of "native plants" or addressing the limited propagation and distribution of the straight species, designating certain plants as more suitable than others can thwart the goal of making butterfly gardening accessible and enjoyable to as many people as possible.

NATIVE PLANTS. Plants that occur in a particular region and that have been historically traced to that region before European settlement of the United States are considered *native* plants. They have developed in their specific locality along with a community of other plants, insects, animals, and fungi. It is this long association of the plants and animals, and their side-by-side evolution over millions of years, that makes native plants particularly attractive to insects.

The majority of butterfly gardeners who certify their gardens with NABA grow a mixture of native and nonnative plants. Each gardener decides what he or she considers native in their area; there are websites and books to help, but trends in which native plants are chosen specifically for butterflies are noticeable among the certified gardeners. Plant lists shared with NABA show a decided preference for planting native plants for butterflies, yet most gardeners admit to a weak spot in their hearts for a few plants that draw butterflies in masses and are not only nonnative, but even banned in some locations.

Get any group of enthusiastic butterfly watchers and gardeners together and start the discussion about garden plants. What always transpires is a lively and heated exchange about the pros and cons of orange eye butterflybush. NABA has not taken a firm stance either for or against orange eye butterflybush for butterfly gardens, but a review of the pros and cons of this particular plant highlights just about all the primary decisions a gardener will need to make when considering nectar plants for a garden, be they native or nonnative.

LONG SEASON OF NECTAR

Butterflies choose to nectar at plants that suit their needs—nectar quality and quantity, as well as flower shape and condition, all play a part in what constitutes a desirable nectar plant to a butterfly. Even with the constraint that not all flowers are equally attractive to butterflies, gardeners have a wide choice available. One of your critical tasks is to find out which of these many plants are best suited to provide a long season of nectar for the butterflies likely to be visiting your particular garden location. Flowers that produce nectar over a long period help drive success at bringing butterflies to plantings, so always consider the length of a plant's blooming period.

Butterfly populations vary from year to year and the timing of their arrival each year varies. "Long season of nectar" simply refers to having nectar-producing plants available throughout the entire warm season when butterflies might be in flight. You cannot control when the butterflies might show up—Great Spangled Fritillaries may be abundant in your garden one year and rare the next, but despite this high degree of variability, you can be ready with a "welcome mat" of nectar plants that are in bloom for the entire season!

The most common long-season "butterfly-friendly" plant marketed to gardeners is orange eye butterflybush. In popular books and Internet articles, orange eye butterflybush is not a neutral topic. An ocean of people at a butterfly gardening meeting can be parted like the Red Sea by the mention of this one plant. Very few people will be standing in the dry ground between the two groups. Gardeners are generally divided between "butterflybush haters" and "butterflybush lovers." Both groups can make good arguments for their point of view. One point that no one can dispute, though, is that orange eye butterfly-bush—the species most commonly sold in the United States—provides a lot of nectar over a very long period. Certainly, other plants can provide nectar and lots of it, but for one shrub to be able to sustain nectar flow over months rather than weeks is a boon for people with small gardens or people who do not wish to take care of a lot of plants.

INVASIVENESS

Some butterflybushes are native to the United States, but these plants are local to the Southwest and not readily available across the country, and are unlikely to thrive in other climates. The species that gets some people so agitated is *Buddleja davidii,* also known as orange eye butterflybush. Native to China, this butterflybush is listed as a Class B noxious weed in Washington State (which means that it is illegal to plant and grow it in that state) and is listed as a class B designated weed in Oregon.

The Oregon State Department of Agriculture states, "If you planted your butterfly bush before it was listed (2004), you do not have to remove it, but you are required to prevent it from propagating. You must deadhead the plant after blooming to prevent the seeds from spreading." However, some types of butterflybush may be transported and sold in the state, including sterile cultivars—butterflybushes that have been bred to not produce viable seeds—and interspecific hybrids—plants that have been bred from two different species of *Buddleja* and are assumed to be seed sterile.

For those not botanically inclined, two of the terms in Oregon's restrictive language merit further exploration when considering nectar plants of all types: *sterile cultivars* (technically, sterile-seeded cultivars) and *interspecific hybrids.* Although both are usually produced through deliberate breeding techniques, these plant types do occasionally occur naturally. No matter how they come into existence, these plants are maintained and propagated by the nursery industry and are promoted for their noninvasiveness.

The debate between the use of native and nonnative plants centers on how each creature in our environment eats within the interconnected food chains that sustain all of us (including butterflies), with nonnative plants often cast as aggressive bullies that displace our native flora and are unpalatable to our fauna. This central argument is overlaid with concerns about each particular nonnative plant's possible invasiveness—complicated by the fact that information on invasiveness is not often provided on a local basis. Orange eye butterflybush has not proven to be invasive in parts of Texas (where many gardeners report that it struggles to survive); in Kansas it is reported to be well behaved (staying in the confines of gardens), in New Jersey concern about invasiveness is variable, and of course along the Pacific Coast, orange eye butterflybush is so wildly invasive that it merits severe restrictions on propagation and sale.

Understanding a few plant-breeding terms will help gardeners make more informed choices about what they wish to plant for butterflies, and allows all of us to consider how to support our native food chains and local habitats. Since our landscapes are no longer in their native state and the plants we purchase are not either, the more quickly gardeners become informed consumers, the faster they can get down to the important business of gardening.

TOO MUCH OF A GOOD THING AND STERILITY

Some plants provide too much of a good thing. Their growth patterns allow them to spread (by seed or underground roots) to such an extent that they crowd out other plants. In a garden setting, such a plant might be called spreading, aggressive, or perhaps exuberant. When a plant reproduces to the extent that it spreads beyond the garden and is able to crowd out native species in the general area, then it is truly invasive. A spreading or aggressive plant is something for the gardener to note and manage within the confines of a garden, while a plant with the potential to invasively move beyond the garden is something that should not be brought home in the first place.

Orange eye butterflybush spreads by seed: each plant produces a copious volume of lightweight seeds that are easily spread by wind or water. The germination rate of these seeds is very high, and when the seeds germinate on bare soil they can achieve flowering size in just one growing season. Roadsides, waterways, and disturbed areas (such as manmade clearcuts in forests or lands recently impacted by fire) are prime areas for orange eye butterflybush to colonize. Other native and nonnative plants use the same strategy for infiltrating new territory, but orange eye butterflybush stands out as a plant that, on the one hand, is heavily promoted by the plant nursery industry as highly desirable in the garden, but, on the other hand, is potentially invasive as many gardeners have discovered to their cost.

CONFUSING PLANT NAMES

Choosing specific plants for specific uses is one of the enjoyable aspects of designing your own garden. Since butterflies prefer certain flowering plants over others, the first step in planning a butterfly garden is to know exactly what plant you are looking for, confident that the plant you eventually place in your shopping cart or order online is the one that you want.

An annual nectar plant used by many butterfly gardeners across the country is purpletop vervain. Every garden plant has at least two names, a common name, like purpletop vervain, and a botanical name, which in this case is *Verbena bonariensis*. Often a plant will have many different common names—in this example, tall vervain, tall verbena, or Argentinian verbena—but any one plant has only one botanical name, so it makes sense when purchasing a plant to double-check the botanical name!

Many gardeners are put off by the botanical names of plants, and that is understandable. At first glance, botanical names appear hard to pronounce and seem nonsensical. They might even bring an aura of snobbery to the garden world for some, while others appreciate the exact knowledge they provide—but whatever your personal preference, when purchasing plants for a butterfly garden, check the botanical name so that the plant you bring home will in fact be a plant that feeds butterflies and behaves in the garden as you expect it to.

To further confuse the issue, a plant very similar to purpletop vervain is commonly called Brazilian vervain and goes by the botanical name *Verbena brasiliensis*. Brazilian vervain has a coarse, weedy growth habit and is invasive in many southern states. Unfortunately, because of the similar names and somewhat similar flowers, it is easily confused with purpletop vervain and the common names are often interchanged. Yet, like most things, even pretty garden plants require the buyer to beware—but it is worth doing a little research since what is really invested in growing great gardens is time, so starting with the correct plant material is a must.

By looking at the genus name, *Verbena*, it is clear that the two plants share some common features, but if you mistakenly brought home Brazilian vervain, you would wonder why a coarse, gangly plant with dull-colored blossoms was recommended for your garden—where exactly were the advertised hordes of butterflies? Then there is the problem that both these plants, in the right locations, become invasive. Poor purpletop vervain, loved by butterflies, flowers in the first season when planted from seed and is effective for gardeners who wish to provide a long season of nectar, but has thuggish relatives and may promiscuously jump the fence and make a run for the neighbor's (flower) bed.

Comparing the two flower heads side by side shows how purpletop vervain, (opposite left), outshines Brazilian vervain, (below), in the number of flowers open.

Invasive plants and seeds of possibly invasive plants are sold at garden centers and through catalogs with no mention of their wanton habits. In a few cases, state regulations restrict the sale of certain garden plants (each state has lists of prohibited plants or noxious weeds), but in general, it is up to the buyer to do the homework. The situation is muddied by the fact that any particular plant, like purpletop vervain or orange eye butterflybush, might be invasive in only certain locations and or even certain situations. Invasiveness varies from state to state and even within a state.

MORE OPTIONS IF YOU LOOK DEEPER

Flowering garden plants that are potentially invasive spread primarily either through prolific seed production or by creeping underground stems or roots. A few plants, like some of the native goldenrods, will spread aggressively by vigorous underground growth as well as abundant seed dispersal; forethought on how they will be controlled in a garden setting is essential! Underground growth can be managed by containment methods or by mowing—or avoided by carefully selecting plants that do not have spreading traits.

If you choose to grow aggressively self-seeding plants for butterflies (and you might because some of them are great nectar plants), one way to keep those plants in check is to deadhead the flowers. Although grisly sounding, *deadheading* merely refers to removing the flowers from a plant after they start to fade but before they have produced seed. Aside from preventing the plant from spreading by seed, deadheading also often has the added benefit of encouraging new flowers to emerge in the same growing season.

For a flowering plant, setting seed is the way for the plant to create the next generation—it is the reason for flowers in the first place. If their flowers are removed before they go to seed, many plants will go on to produce more flowers in the same growing season, hoping to still win the race to produce the next generation before cold weather ends the contest. The unsuspecting plant has no way of knowing that the gardener will always be there with clippers in hand, ready to thwart its reproductive goals.

An additional benefit of deadheading is related to plant vigor. As flowers become pollinated, they cease nectar production and turn their energies toward seed production. This shift corresponds with a decreasing robustness in the plant—leaves may start to die back and no new foliage is produced. Deadheading often circumvents this process by causing the plant to "reset" and again direct its energy to nectar production, which is accompanied by overall robust growth of the plant and its foliage. Some plants respond better than

MORE OPTIONS IF YOU LOOK DEEPER

others to deadheading, and in general the quicker you deadhead flowers that have just passed their prime, the greater the chance that the plant will flower longer. In a large planting, deadheading can take a lot of time and this is the main downside to the strategy—while deadheading is a chore that some people enjoy, others would rather not bother with it.

As with most things in gardening, you can find more choices if you dig a bit deeper. Many garden plants that are butterfly magnets because of prolific flowering—but unpopular with gardeners who dislike the resulting aggressive seedlings—are available in selections whose flowers produce few seeds, or sterile seeds. Selections that produce few seeds or sterile seeds might be bred from two closely related species, or they might derive from a naturally occurring mutation that was noticed in the field and propagated vegetatively. However the plants came into cultivation, the results are twofold: more flowers are produced over a longer period of time, and few if any seeds are produced.

This Painted Lady sips nectar on *Buddleja* 'Blue Heaven', a sterile butterflybush in the Flutterby series.

SOME BASIC HOUSEKEEPING TERMS that all gardeners should learn before spending their hard-earned cash on nectar plants involves deciphering plant descriptions on labels and in catalogs. When the plant catalogs start arriving in the dead of winter, read them carefully, and research what is really being sold so you get the best bang for your buck in terms of butterfly attractiveness.

- Straight Species: A plant that is described with just its genus and species name (i.e., its botanical name) has not been subjected to breeding, selection, or hybridization, and can be referred to as the "straight species." If you are browsing plants at a nursery that sells exclusively native plants, all the plants will be straight species. The offspring of these plants will be similar looking, which can be a great way to increase the size of your butterfly garden! Straight species are the best choice if you are a beginning butterfly gardener.
- Cultivar: Considered "cultivated varieties," cultivars are plants that are selected or bred to display a specific trait or traits. A cultivar can be selected from a naturally occurring plant, like phlox 'Jeana' (which was found growing naturally in a group of fall phlox), but most cultivars are the result of plant breeding programs. (Note that cultivar names are generally enclosed in single quotes.) If the specific traits of a cultivar are to be maintained throughout all future plant generations, almost all cultivars must be vegetatively reproduced through either division or tissue culture. With a few exceptions, seeds saved from cultivars will not produce a plant similar to the parent plant. Many cultivars are fine nectar plants, but it is wise to research them carefully, through either book

The flowers of phlox 'Jeana' are decidedly smaller than those of the straight species of fall phlox but butterflies do not seem to mind!

or web searches, or ask other butterfly gardeners about their experiences to find out whether the cultivar in question is as attractive to butterflies as the straight species. But in the end, if you are smitten with a beautiful cultivar of a well-known nectar plant, the only way to determine whether butterflies like it may be to grow it yourself and observe how it performs in your own garden.

~ Nativar: Plantsman Allan Armitage suggests "nativar" as a term for cultivars of native plants. If you see this term you will know that the parentage of the plant is traceable to a native species or two. Just to confuse the issue, the same cultivated variety of a native plant could also be referred to simply as a "cultivar." The big take-away from this naming exercise is that whether you call it a "cultivar" or a "nativar," the plant you are talking about was created, or at the very least is being maintained, through human intervention.

Is a plant's breeding important to butterflies? In many cases, yes! Many of the traits for which cultivars are specifically developed, such as double flowers or flower color, are significantly different from the straight species and may result in their (a) making it difficult for butterflies to reach their nectar (the former), or (b) not even being recognized by butterflies as nectar-producing flowers (the latter).

Double flowers are a popular feature for plant breeders to work toward; the resulting flowers are showier, fluffier, and just plain old more eye-catching. But the attraction of double flowers is all for the human eye. When changes in breeding result in more petals, other parts of the flower shift as well. Each cultivar will be different, but the addition of more petals can often decrease, or even eliminate, the nectar-producing structures of a flower.

A cultivar of eastern purple coneflower is one of the parents of *Echinacea* 'Secret Affair', while the other parent is Bush's purple coneflower (the native *Echinacea paradox*, which has yellow flowers). The cross has yielded a distinct new *Echinacea*, one that looks entirely different from either of the parent plants. While both the parent plants of *Echinacea* 'Secret Affair' are excellent nectar plants for butterflies, it remains to be seen whether the many coneflowers bred for new flower shapes and colors—of which 'Secret Affair' is just one—are attractive to butterflies or if it transpires that the true secret is that they cannot consummate a nectar love affair with butterflies.

'Meteor Shower'® *Verbena bonariensis* is shorter than the straight species, allowing it to be used in the front of the border. Tolerant of hot, dry situations, 'Meteor Shower'® is growing alongside sweet alyssum in an exposed rock garden. Sweet alyssum is a fragrant, low-growing annual sold across the United States that will attract butterflies as well as other important small pollinators.

STERILE NECTAR PLANTS FOR BUTTERFLIES	CULTURAL NOTES	GROWTH HABIT
Meteor Shower® *Verbena bonariensis*	USDA Hardiness Zones 7a–11b. In colder areas, plant as an annual. Height: 20–30 inches Spread: 8–12 inches Bloom period: Spring through Fall	Displaying a dense, upright growth habit, this plant sets very little seed and should not become invasive over its long bloom period. Will bloom until a hard frost. The flowers of the straight species, *Verbena bonariensis*, are borne on tall stems and often placed throughout a border where its long, slender stems mingle among other tall perennials. Meteor Shower is much shorter and bushier than the straight species and will work in pots or toward the front of a bed.

STERILE NECTAR PLANTS FOR BUTTERFLIES	CULTURAL NOTES	GROWTH HABIT
Phlox paniculata 'Jeana'	USDA Hardiness Zones 3–8 Height: 4–5 feet Spread: 2–3 feet Flower color: pink Bloom period: midsummer	Discovered as a natural mutation, 'Jeana' blooms over a longer time frame than the straight species; the energy that it saves from setting seed is put into a longer bloom period. In addition, 'Jeana' is not as susceptible to powdery mildew, a fungal disease that can race through a stand of fall phlox causing discoloration of the leaves as well as reducing the plant's the vigor and bloom. The pinkish flowers on 'Jeana' are a bit smaller than the straight species but still much loved by butterflies.
Agastache 'Black Adder'	USDA Hardiness Zones 6–10 Height: 2–3 feet Spread: 2–3 feet Flower color: purple Bloom period: late summer	A hybrid between the native *A. foeniculum* (blue giant hyssop) and the nonnative *A. rugosum* (Korean hyssop), 'Black Adder' has showy flowers but does not set seed. The hybrid is reported to be longer lived than the native parents, which are considered short-lived perennials but can spread by seed.
Butterflybush sterile hybrids such as Flutterby® or Low & Behold® series	USDA Hardiness Zones 5–10 Height: varies Spread: varies Flower color: varies Bloom period: summer through fall	Sterile hybrids produce the same amount of nectar-filled flowers as orange eye butterflybush. Many are also bred as smaller plants that are easier to fit into a garden plan.
Lantana 'Miss Huff' and 'New Gold' are just two of the sterile cultivars available	'Miss Huff' has orange and pink flowers; it is evergreen in frost-free zones and established clumps have survived to 0 °F. 'New Gold' has yellow flowers; it is evergreen in frost-free zones and hardy to Zone 10.	Lantana is sold throughout the country as an annual bedding plant but can be invasive in warmer locations where it behaves as a perennial. Sterile lantana varieties curb invasiveness while also having a longer blooming period than the nonsterile lantanas.

The state of Oregon allows interspecific hybrids of *Buddleja* to be propagated and sold within the state. These plants appear very similar to orange eye butterflybush and—most importantly—they feature the abundance of nectar-filled flowers that make these plants desirable, but rather than being cultivars of the orange eye they are in fact the result of crossing two species within the genus. The breeding of interspecific hybrids might best be illustrated with an example from the animal world. Mules are the result of a female horse mating with a male donkey. Horses and donkeys belong to the same genus but are different species, and although the two species are able to mate and produce offspring, the resulting progeny, mules, have a mismatched number of chromosomes that leaves them sterile—unable to produce sperm or eggs. Like mules, which have an appearance somewhere between a horse and a donkey, interspecific hybrids of orange eye butterflybush with another species of butterflybush will look similar to, but not exactly like, the orange eye parent. And as with mules, offspring resulting from the crossing of two different species are usually unable to reproduce.

When looking for a sterile butterflybush, you will seldom find the words "butterflybush" or "interspecific hybrid" on the plant tag or in the catalog description The genus name, *Buddleja* (also sometimes spelled *Buddleia*), is often associated with the sterile hybrids but these plants most often have a trademarked name associated with them, such as the Flutterby® series. One plant in this series that looks very similar to orange eye butterflybush is 'Buddleia Flutterby® Lavender', which is given the common name "nectar bush." Low & Behold® is another commonly found interspecific hybrid series, bred to be more compact than orange eye butterflybush and called "summer lilac."

FLOWER POWER ANNUALS

For those who just want to dive in and get started without making an initial investment in time, money, or long-term commitment, annual flowering plants are the perfect solution and will get any first-year butterfly garden off to a good start. Annuals—flowering plants that finish their life cycle of blooming and setting seed in just one growing season—are easily found at garden centers of all types and can also be started from seed. A butterfly garden consisting entirely of annuals is a great first start. Although it most likely will not feed caterpillars, it will give you an opportunity to learn what butterflies live in your area.

The majority of plants considered the backbones of a butterfly garden are perennials—that is, plants that become dormant during the colder months and regrow each following year (or that grow continuously in warmer climates). Perennial plants can live for many years, so the initial investment is minor when considering the length of time the plant will enhance your garden. One downside to using perennials, though, is that for the first year (or two), while they send down extensive roots and become established, they do not bloom as profusely or reach their full size. Lots of blooming flowers to attract butterflies is the goal, so while perennials take their time to settle in, annuals can jump-start the butterfly garden banquet.

Two of the best annuals for butterfly gardens are zinnia and purpletop vervain; both plants are easy to grow from seed and commonly sold in seed catalogs as well as at garden centers. In addition, zinnias are usually offered for sale as starter plants. Both these annuals bloom throughout the summer, particularly if deadheaded.

A third annual that acts as a butterfly magnet is Clavel de muerto, also known as Mexican sunflower. It is easily started from seed and grows rapidly if given a sunny location. Unlike zinnia and purpletop vervain, Mexican sunflower does not begin to flower until late summer, but once it starts to bloom it will continue to display an abundance of nectar-producing flowers until the plant is killed by frost. Large and branching, this sunflower often appears shrublike by the end of the summer, but it is worth the garden space if a sunny spot is available.

With an open wingspan of approximately 3 inches, the Monarch is fairly large for a U.S. butterfly—but the blooms on Mexican sunflower are large enough to provide it with a stable and ample landing pad for nectaring.

Other annuals are useful in butterfly gardens but more regionally specific—tropical milkweed, Egyptian starcluster (also known as pentas), and lantana are all attractive to butterflies, but their appeal is often limited by location. In more northern climates, where the summer temperatures are more moderate and the growing season shorter, these annuals may not become large enough to produce a large volume of blossoms.

Consider the following when choosing butterfly garden annuals:

- **Zinnias** are among the most commonly used annuals for butterfly gardens. Native to Mexico, zinnias grow in a wide variety of climates and are easy to maintain over an entire growing season. Plants can be purchased at garden centers, or seed is readily available. Since butterflies are attracted to large masses of flowers, the more zinnias planted in one location, the better. If space is limited, zinnias can be grown in pots or planters.

  Red zinnias are often recommended as the best color to attract butterflies, but the number of zinnia plants blooming at any one time is probably just as important as the color of the flowers when trying to draw as many butterflies as possible. Choose single, old-fashioned zinnias (*Zinnia elegans*) rather than double. Many double flowers do not provide as much nectar as those with a single row of petals; the only real way to tell whether this is the case with double zinnias is to grow single and double varieties next to each other and observe the butterfly activity. What is certain, though, is that single-flowered varieties provide a large, stable landing space for butterflies to stand on while nectaring. In double zinnias, this space is taken up with flower petals.

  Aside from single *Zinnia elegans*, the Profusion Series of zinnias is also recommended when a shorter plant is preferred. Growing 12-18 inches tall, the Profusion Series zinnias are interspecific hybrids between *Zinnia elegans* and *Zinnia angustifolia*. The plants have some resistance to powdery mildew and are commonly sold in garden centers as small plants. Seeds can be purchased through most large seed catalogs. Choose single-flowering varieties rather than doubles. Profusion zinnias are bushier than *Zinnia elegans,* which might be more practical for smaller gardens. With their shorter stance and more lateral growth habit, Profusion Series zinnias also cover the soil more fully than tall *Zinnia elegans,* which helps suppress weed growth and gives a more uniform look to flower beds.

  Seeds for either type of zinnia are easy to start outside once the soil has warmed and all threat of frost is past.

- **Purpletop vervain** blooms from midsummer until frost. Each cluster of small flowers sits atop a long, almost leafless stem that is strong yet flexible enough to bow in the wind. It is easily grown from seed, and in fact can become invasive in certain areas by its prolific seed set. In a carefully tended garden where reseeding is a problem, purpletop vervain can be managed by weeding out the volunteer seedlings in the early summer—but be sure to leave a few for the butterflies.

Most annuals are usually planted in blocks or groups so their vibrant colors catch the eye (and butterflies appreciate this!), but purpletop vervain is an annual that can be intermingled among other plants to great advantage. Most of the plant's foliage grows at the base of the plant while the flowers are far above where they can intermingle with taller plants. The sterile cultivar of purpletop vervain, *Verbena bonariensis* 'Meteor Shower', is a shorter plant that is more suitable for the front of the border than weaving throughout a planting of taller species.

Two rows of purpletop vervain line a brick path, creating a dramatic walkway. Planting long, wide rows of purpletop vervain brings butterfly viewing to child height or wheelchair height and will put on a show for the entire summer.

- **Mexican sunflower** is an annual for late-summer butterflies. Plant it where it can stretch out—its height can reach 6 feet, and one plant might spread 4 feet. Planting three Mexican sunflowers in a close triangle, with plants approximately 2 feet apart will yield a group of plants that, by fall, will appear as one large shrub that will attract butterflies as well as the horticulturally curious. A row of Mexican sunflowers at the back of a flower border will act as a hedge, but be warned that at the end of the season, cutting down the frost-killed plants will feel like cutting down a hedge, as the central stems of the plants become very thick and stiff, similar to a small shrub. Although it is drought resistant, Mexican sunflower will look better and flower more profusely with moderate moisture.

FLOWERS EVERY YEAR

Perennial flowers that provide nectar for butterflies are a shopper's delight, there are so many to choose from! Use a list of proven perennial butterfly nectar plants, double-check that their cultural requirements can be met in your garden, and move forward with confidence. Whenever possible, plant several of each chosen species and plant all of them together in a section of the garden.

At the top of your shopping list should be plants that provide caterpillar food for common garden butterflies in addition to nectar. Milkweed, sunflowers, New England or Pacific asters, and black cherry trees are all "double-duty" plants so consider them part of your basic plant palette. After choosing double-duty plants, add in a few annuals to fill in any gaps, and then move on to select perennials that provide a long season of nectar and years of value. Consider some of the following plants to provide a perennial backbone for butterfly gardens:

- **Purple coneflowers** (*Echinacea* spp.) **Eastern purple coneflower** is one of the best known butterfly nectar plants

Blue giant hyssop, foreground, blooms for many weeks starting in summer, orange coneflower (also known as perennial black-eyed Susan) blooms in late summer through fall, and little bluestem, in the background, provides structure and winter interest to a small bed of perennials for butterflies.

because it is beautiful, easy to grow, and adapts to a wide variety of garden conditions. Other purple coneflowers may not be common at garden centers but they can be found at native plant nurseries or in seed catalogs. Consider other plants in the purple coneflower genus, including the following:

- **Pale purple coneflower** should be planted in well-drained soil. In the first few years of growth, it develops a taproot, making it hard to move once established.
- **Blacksamson echinacea**, also known as narrow-leaved coneflower, is native to a large central swath of the United States and will tolerate drier conditions. Its flowers are similar to those of eastern purple coneflower.
- **Bush's purple coneflower** is the only plant in this genus that (despite its name) produces yellow flowers. Butterflies love the fragrant flowers and the plant grows well in gardens in the Upper Midwest and Northeast.

■ **Blazing Star** (*Liatris* spp.) **Dense blazing star** is the plant most likely to be found at garden centers and through national plant catalogs. It is a hardy, beautiful garden plant that when planted in a group is dramatic and a favorite with butterflies. Native to the eastern United States, dense blazing star requires a moist, somewhat fertile soil. Other blazing stars that will attract butterflies but that have different cultural requirements include the following:

- **Prairie blazing star** is native to the central United States and will grow in poorer soils than dense blazing star; it will even tolerate clay soils. Growing up to 5 feet, prairie blazing star can be used as a dramatic accent plant.
- **Dotted blazing star** forms a deep root system, making it quite drought resistant once established. Shorter than most blazing stars at around 2 feet, dotted blazing star is a good choice for xeriscapes or plantings that will not receive regular watering.
- **Rocky Mountain blazing star** has a reputation for its magnetic pull on Monarchs. With a blooming period that coincides with the Monarch migration, Rocky Mountain blazing star's tall spikes of vibrant purple flowers bloom over many weeks to draw in and feed passing Monarchs.

■ **Goldenrods** (*Solidago* spp.) Goldenrods are a large genus of flowering plants but many of them are not considered gardenworthy. They provide invaluable nectar for migrating and late-season butterflies as well as a

Rocky Mountain blazing star attracts Monarchs but will also serve nectar to a wide variety of other butterflies as well.

brilliant splash of color in the fall garden. Butterfly gardeners across the country all agree that goldenrods are essential for butterfly gardens, but there is very little consensus on which one to plant! Many can be very weedy, throwing volumes of seed on the ground each year, spreading aggressively by rhizomes, or both! Others are quite tall, with a tendency to flop over at the first hint of windy fall weather. It is perhaps best to start with tamed cultivars, which have been selected for their restricted growth and shorter or upright stature. When visiting gardens or plant sales, ask other gardeners about their preferences as there are so many goldenrods to choose from and each has its pros and cons. Consider the following to start:

- **Solidago 'Little Lemon'** is widely available and for good reason. It is petite by goldenrod standards (reaching about 14 inches tall) and is clump-forming rather than spreading. It blooms in summer and if cut back after its initial bloom, a second flush of flowers can be encouraged.
- **Solidago rugosa 'Fireworks'**, a cultivar of *Solidago rugosa*, has none of the fast-spreading underground stems and colonizing nature of the straight species. The plant will increase in size and should be divided every few years but does not form colonies. Fast growing to 4 feet in bloom, 'Fireworks' needs regular watering to perform well.
- ***Solidago sphacelata* 'Golden Fleece'** was selected as a naturally occurring variation of the straight species. 'Golden Fleece' is compact, with flowers held on stiff stems that remain upright. It will spread slowly to form a clump and will occasionally self-seed. The straight species is native to the eastern United States, but 'Golden Fleece' grows well outside its native range.
- **Showy goldenrod** is a straight species that blooms a bit later than the two aforementioned cultivars. Large, bright heads of goldenrod flowers

are held high on 5-foot stems. It can spread by both underground stems and seed, but its beautiful fall display is worth it for gardeners who have room for a larger goldenrod and can tolerate a vigorously spreading plant.

- **Asters** (*Symphyotrichum* spp.) Asters should be a component of all butterfly gardens—not only do they provide vast amounts of nectar in the late summer and early fall, but they also provide caterpillar food for Pearl, Northern, and Field Crescents. All asters benefit from "pinching back" in late spring/early summer. Pinching back sounds a bit dainty when in fact the procedure can remove up to half of each existing shoot, making the activity more like a strong haircut. Pinching back encourages the plant to branch out and grow stockier, making it more resistant to toppling over later in the season as well as promoting more flower buds to form.

The rich flower color of New England Aster shines in the fall sunlight and draws in fall-flying butterflies like this Orange Sulphur.

- **New England Aster** is a beautiful, easy-to-grow choice found at most garden centers. It prefers moist, rich soil and can take up a large space in the garden, growing five feet tall and spreading three feet under optimum conditions. Other asters to choose from include the following:
- **Smooth blue aster** is tolerant of drier soils and can be spaced as close as 12 inches apart, making it a versatile aster for most gardens. It is shorter than New England Aster, around 4 feet, and will slowly increase in size in a garden bed.
- **Pacific aster** is a drought-tolerant plant suited to Pacific Coast states. It can spread vigorously by rhizomes and therefore should be planted in a space where it can be kept in check. Alternatively, it can be used on slopes for butterfly-friendly erosion control.

NON-NECTAR FEEDING: BUTTERFLY FEEDERS

In the wild, some species of butterflies are attracted to rotting fruit, tree and plant sap, and animal feces or urine; butterflies sip the liquids on and in these materials to gain sugars, proteins, or amino acids, all of which are vital for their survival and reproduction. Introducing some of these materials into a garden setting is a practice unique to butterfly gardening. A device that utilizes this non-nectar approach to attracting and feeding butterflies is commonly called a "butterfly feeder," and even though plants are not involved, adding butterfly feeders to your habitat is considered part of gardening for butterflies.

A ruby-throated hummingbird in a South Carolina garden threatens a Gulf Fritillary visiting a hummingbird feeder for a sugary drink. Hummingbird feeders are occasionally visited by butterflies but are not considered the best method for drawing in butterflies for observation.

Time is often overlooked as an element of gardening. It can take many seasons for a garden to settle in and look "just right," making gardening an exercise in patience. Although the butterfly gardening mantra assures us "plant it and they will come," sometimes waiting for butterflies to discover a recently planted garden can tax even the most patient gardener. That is when it may be time to take a break from the flowers and try your hand at placing a butterfly feeder in your garden. Another reason to consider using a butterfly feeder is to attract butterflies that are unlikely to visit flowers because they prefer to feed on non-nectar sources. Finally, attracting butterflies to a location where you can view them up close adds great pleasure to butterfly watching.

FRUIT FEEDING

Butterfly "houses," including both indoor displays, which often feature nonnative butterflies, and outdoor butterfly enclosures, often use feeders or bait to attract butterflies to eye level. Whether a container that can be refilled with sugary nectar, a tray of overripe fruit, or a log smeared with "butterfly brew" (see below), any device that attracts butterflies to stop and feed can be considered a butterfly feeder. The goal is to attract butterflies to a central area where their behavior and beauty can be observed. These nectar alternatives can be simulated in a number of different ways, so gardeners need not resort to drilling holes in trees to drain sap or to piling animal feces on their property in the hopes of attracting butterflies!

Some of the widespread garden butterflies that rarely visit flowers but often visit butterfly feeders are Mourning Cloak, Question Mark, Eastern Comma, Painted Lady, and Red Admiral. Other butterflies that are regional in their ranges but also visit feeders are Goatweed Leafwing, Hackberry and Tawny Emperors, American Snout, Red-spotted Purple, and Viceroy. All these butterflies prefer tree sap, rotten fruit, and animal excrement but can also be attracted to butterfly feeders. Not everyone has success with butterfly feeders—in fact, many gardeners report that no butterflies visit their feeders at all! If this happens, try putting out a feeder at a time when butterflies are flying in and around your garden, thereby trying to lure existing butterflies that are actively feeding. This tactic will allow you to see if the attractant, be it fruit or a constructed "butterfly brew," will work in your garden. If this initial trial draws butterflies (and remember, many butterflies that prefer nectar will come to a feeder as well), you can be confident that your feeder will work and can be placed in the garden under less optimum conditions. If no butterflies are drawn to your feeder, consider a different food (orange slices, watermelon, and overripe bananas are commonly used), move your feeder

Butterflies often hold quite still when sipping at fruit feeders, allowing extended viewing of otherwise fast-flitting species like this Red Admiral.

to a different location (a sunny location might cause the food to dry out, a shady condition may be too cool for butterflies to consider), or try adding some water to your feeder to moisten the food (if the mixture is too thick, butterflies cannot drink it). Experimentation is part of all aspects of butterfly gardening!

BUTTERFLY BREW

Many gardeners have tremendous success with a fermented fruit mixture commonly called *butterfly brew*. When placed on a horizontal surface, such as a log or a plate, butterfly brew will attract nearby butterflies to visit and partake.

The National Butterfly Center uses the following fermented butterfly brew recipe with great success:

1. Blend or mash 8–10 very ripe bananas until fairly smooth; it is fine to have some small chunks of banana in the mixture. Mix the bananas with one pound of brown sugar, and then carefully add one bottle of unpasteurized beer to the mixture.
2. Divide the mixture into jars but do not seal the containers. The yeast in the unpasteurized beer will ferment the fruit-sugar mixture, with gas as a

Butterfly brew is replenished twice a day at the National Butterfly Center in Mission, Texas. Tawny Emperors are the primary species of butterfly gathering on this log smeared with butterfly brew. It is impossible to tell what other butterflies have joined in this feeding frenzy; Hackberry Emperors are the other species that show up in great numbers at the National Butterfly Center's feeders. Many other species feed on the brew but not in such vast numbers.

byproduct. If the containers are sealed at this point, they could explode from a buildup of fermentation gases. You can store the butterfly brew in the refrigerator, which will slow down the fermentation and allow you to keep your brew over a longer period.

Smaller portions of butterfly brew can be made by following a ratio of 1 part mashed, overripe bananas, 1 part brown sugar, and 1 part dark beer. Flat beer works just as well as fresh beer—it's the unpasteurized part that's important.

Butterfly brew is not a magic potion! It will not miraculously draw butterflies to a location where there are none. If weather conditions are not conducive to butterfly activity, butterfly brew will still attract creatures, most likely flies, wasps, or even raccoons! However, if offered when butterflies are actively flying, a butterfly feeding station with butterfly brew can attract butterflies in your area that you may not know are nearby.

DON'T FEED CREATURES OTHER THAN BUTTERFLIES!

Ask anyone who maintains a butterfly feeder and they will tell you that certain measures are needed to prevent the feeder from becoming a sticky, fermenting mess that attracts every yellowjacket (or other hungry creature) in town. Depending on the type of feeder you use, these are some hints for success:

- If using a plate as a feeder, keep a second plate handy to use as a cover if rain threatens. The food should be moist, but not flooded by rain.
- Using nylon fishing line to suspend hanging feeders helps prevent rodents from accessing the feeders. Hanging a feeder from a tree or post helps deter ants.
- Place the feeder where it can be cleaned regularly with a hose and put away when not needed. If the feeder is replenished with fresh food that is not left out overnight, fewer creatures will visit. Remember, butterflies will visit only in daylight when outdoor temperatures rise into the 60s and above; there is no need to leave a feeder out overnight if the temperatures are low or if rain is forecast.
- Embrace the mess! Many people enjoy the variety of creatures and non-butterfly activity that occurs at butterfly feeders. Pat Sutton, one of NABA's directors and coauthor of *How to Spot Butterflies*, notes that humming-birds will feed on fruit flies that hover around the feeder, and by shining a flashlight on the feeder at night, moths can be observed. Pat suggests

Butterfly feeders can draw more than butterflies!

bananas that have been peeled, frozen, and then defrosted for use in butterfly feeders.

NABA member Don Dubois has thought long and hard about how to exclude bees and wasps from his butterfly feeder. His elegant solution involves modifying a plastic hanging bird feeder to allow butterflies to drink butterfly brew while excluding other flying insects. To accomplish this, Don installs a wire screen atop a bird feeder's seed tray, then fills the seed tray with butterfly brew but leaves a gap of at least ¼ inch between the wire mesh and the butterfly brew surface so that butterflies, with their long tongues, can sip the brew while flies, honey bees, and wasps, with their much shorter tongues, cannot reach the mixture.

The type of bird feeder Don uses is widely available but in order to modify it, the feeder must have a slight lip around the edge of the seed holder portion of the feeder. The style of feeder chosen by Don also has a plastic rain shield mounted above the seed holder. Although it was designed to keep birdseed dry, the rain shield works well to protect the butterfly brew from becoming diluted during rainy weather.

The wire mesh used to modify the feeder has ⅛-inch openings and is available from apiary suppliers. Plastic mesh is available from many hardware stores but does not maintain a tight seal when added to the bird feeder and tends to warp. Don also seals any drain holes in the seed tray with silicone sealant so the butterfly brew will not leak out. Once the wire mesh is cut to size (extending just beyond the lip of the seed tray), a small hole is made in the center of the mesh so it can be threaded onto the support rod that holds the rain cover and seed tray together. The wire mesh is held in place by a screw clamp

With a wire mesh circle held tightly against the seed tray by an adjustable screw clamp, this modified bird feeder allows butterflies to sip butterfly brew while discouraging insects such as bees, wasps, and flies that have shorter tongues. Here, three Question Marks and a Goatweed Leafwing sip butterfly brew without interruption.

that came with the feeder and is placed above the mesh to hold it taut against the seed tray.

Additional modifications to the feeder include:

- Plaster of Paris can be added inside the feeder tray so that less butterfly brew needs to be added to fill the feeder. Don filled his feeder with Plaster of Paris to about ½ inch below the lip of the seed tray.
- The modified feeder is easy to fill using a squeeze bottle. The butterfly brew needs to be blended smooth in order not to clog the bottle; freezing and thawing the bananas before mixing the brew helps to make a smoother concoction. Just place the tip of the squeeze bottle under the screen to add more brew.

PUDDLING

Perhaps the trickiest non-nectar feeding method to create in a garden is a puddling station. Puddling behavior involves butterflies—from a single individual to large groups—alighting at (usually) a moist, sandy, or gravelly spot on the ground; probing the surface with their tongues, they suck up the available moisture and the nutrients dissolved in it. It is always a spectacular sight to see a group of butterflies puddling, although the reasons for this activity are not entirely understood.

It is commonly reported that butterflies congregating at puddling stations are predominantly male and seeking nutrients that are rare in flower nectar, such as salt. But female butterflies can also be found puddling, which suggests that many factors are involved in puddling behavior. For example, puddling could be a result of competition between different ages of butterflies. If older, more experienced butterflies are able to outcompete younger, less experienced butterflies for floral nectar, then the younger butterflies might seek puddles for whatever available nutrients they can find. Add in other variables such as weather, the absence or abundance of nearby floral nectar, and the propensity for different species of butterflies to visit puddles at different rates, and it becomes clear that puddling behavior is driven by a complex and ever-changing group of components.

Directions for creating puddling stations usually involve mixing gravel or sand with a concentration of salt that is then kept moist, since it is the moisture that lets butterflies drink. To date, no NABA members have reported long-term success with homemade puddling stations. Therefore, it may be best to just

In a surface depression where the road meets the yard, these Eastern Tiger Swallowtails congregate in early summer to puddle. Salt from winter road treatments has probably accumulated here, providing a "natural" puddling area.

observe puddling behavior in the wild, although the wild can be in your yard or nearby neighborhood.

In neighborhoods that do not have curbing, winter road salts and sands accumulate along the roadside and can create prime locations for puddling parties. Tire ruts form a nice depression that collects moisture and results in a somewhat naturally made puddling spot. The tipoff to finding a roadside puddling spot is the fluttering of butterflies. Most butterflies at the puddle stay close to the puddle on the ground, but some individuals are always coming and going; watch for low-flying butterflies in groups. Just be cautious when dawdling around the roadside that oncoming motorists don't knock you down!

Gardeners who want to design their gardens to attract butterflies in every possible way can try a puddling station even though its success at attracting butterflies will be uncertain. Adding a sandy or gravelly path is a decorative way to add a puddling station that is integrated into the garden. If no butterflies arrive to puddle, you still have a lovely path (and clean shoes). Remember that puddling butterflies seem very interested in salt, and urine is very salty. No one will know if you do not tell!

CHECKLIST OF ACTIONS FOR GETTING STARTED

- **Start planning now!** Today is the best day to start feeding butterflies. If it is winter, plan for the spring by searching for annual flower seeds. Ask at a local garden center or call a local Extension Master Gardener to learn when to start the seeds in your location. Consider whether you have space to fit a few perennials in your yard or even in pots on a patio or balcony. Spring is the best time to find specific plants you may be seeking, so have a shopping list ready. If it is summer, visit a garden center, nearby butterfly garden, or a friend's garden to observe butterflies. Note which plants are attracting butterflies and plan to add those to your garden. Fall (when perennials are often on sale) is a good time to pick up plants for the coming year or to replace plants that did not fare well during the previous seasons.
- **Plant nectar plants in groups.** With existing gardens you can add more plants, divide existing plants, or rearrange their design to add large blocks of each nectar plant. For new gardens you should consider purchasing several of each chosen species or starting many plants from seed—with nectar plants, the more plants the better, and the more of each species in the same area, even better.
- **Explore which nectar plants work best in your location.** More plants are listed in the following section of this book but local native-plant societies or local NABA chapters can also be a valuable source for butterfly garden plant information; for example, they will be able to advise which milkweeds perform well in your area, or what species of coneflower, goldenrod, or aster is best suited to your particular climate.
- **Experiment with butterfly feeders.** Not everyone will have success with butterfly feeders, but if you are interested in seeing what may be flying near your garden, butterfly feeders are worth a try. Be sure to try putting out feeders on different days, in different weather conditions, and in a location where you can watch them, such as outside a window.

Karen N
MEMORIA
BUTTERFLY GA
& Schoolyard Wildlife

BUTTERFLY GARDENING BY REGION

NABA MEMBERS SUGGEST BUTTERFLY GARDENING PLANTS

PART II

NABA is dedicated to promoting nonconsumptive butterflying—strongly discouraging the use of nets for capturing butterflies while enthusiastically promoting the use of binoculars for viewing them and cameras for capturing their images. The core values of NABA are teaching people how to find and identify butterflies, explaining how to create butterfly habitat through gardening, and providing information on the use of binoculars and cameras to view butterflies. With so many ways to enjoy butterflies, just about everyone will find that at least one aspect of NABA's mission resonates with them.

NABA-CHAT is a discussion list forum where NABA members can post questions about any detail of their butterfly experience. In the spring, new

gardeners may ask when to expect milkweed to emerge, and NABA members who travel may ask where good butterfly watching can be found along the route from Houston to Denver. Aside from the exchange of information about any aspect of butterflies, the value that NABA-CHAT most clearly exemplifies is the generous sharing of ideas and experiences among NABA members.

This big-hearted spirit carries throughout NABA's mission but is perhaps most evident in the arena of butterfly gardening. Not only does every NABA-CHAT question about butterfly gardening get a thorough evaluation, but NABA butterfly gardeners also meet in person at NABA chapter meetings and other butterfly-related functions—a group of people representing some of the most

PREVIOUS SPREAD: The Karen Nash Memorial Butterfly Garden in Washington, New Jersey, educates school children as well as the adjacent community on butterflies and wildlife. As an all-volunteer organization, the garden teaches children concern for the environment, conservation, volunteering, and social skills.

A NABA Chapter field trip in early fall provides a relaxing and sociable way to be out in nature.

experienced and welcoming butterfly gardeners across the country. A cross section of these people have shared their knowledge and experiences in the following section of this guide.

To develop NABA's butterfly-garden plant lists, experienced gardeners from across the United States were contacted. Interviews were held, emails exchanged, and photos submitted. It is impossible to glean everything that a gardener of 10, 20, or even 30 years has learned, but the NABA members who shared their stories would have been happy to try! Each garden interview illustrated the uniqueness of that gardener, yet the experiences of all demonstrated three consistent themes; first, butterflies are welcome, and second, pesticides are not. A third theme that came to light during each garden interview was the willingness of each person to share their experiences while at the same time being open to whatever unfolded in the next season of their gardening adventures. Despite their expertise, these butterfly gardeners are constantly learning new things and trying new plants!

SUGGESTED PLANTS, SUGGESTED ADVICE

During every interview, each gardener spoke of their favorite plants—the flowers that draw the most butterflies, the caterpillar food plants that are particularly attractive in a specific location. The plants highlighted in this section are by no means the only plants for butterfly gardens in the United States but they are the ones recommended by NABA butterfly gardeners. The lists of plants included in this section serve as an excellent jumping-off point for beginning gardeners while also giving seasoned gardeners some new ideas.

Since the United States has many different ecoregions, each with its own soils, temperatures, and rainfall, it would be impossible to accurately suggest plants for each reader's specific situation. Therefore the plants suggested represent a basic library of butterfly-gardening plants that can be used in a variety of settings. If you are lucky enough to live within range of a NABA chapter, contact your local members to find out what plants they use most successfully in your particular area.

If you are an adventurous plant explorer, choose a plant to trial in your garden and see how it performs. Careful observation over a season or two will let you know if you should make it a permanent part of your butterfly garden. The more cautious gardener should review the plants suggested and seek specific advice for their location. To determine the suitability of various plants, check with your state's Native Plant Society or a local native-plant nursery. For non-native plants, local nurseries or Extension Master Gardeners (found through each state's Cooperative Extension Service) will have knowledgeable staff that can tell you whether the plant in question is right for your garden's soil, moisture, temperature, and light levels.

NABA BUTTERFLY GARDEN GUIDES

The garden interviews have something for everyone no matter where in the United States they live. Should you read about butterfly gardeners in Seattle even though you live in Texas? It cannot hurt! Many of the strategies that work in Seattle will work in Texas, although the plants and butterflies will likely be different.

The eight butterfly-gardening guides in the following section are based on the plants that NABA gardeners emphasized in their interviews and the gardening strategies they described. Gardeners in the Grasslands region do plant trees, but they uniformly favor flowering plants that can survive bitterly cold winters. In the Eastern Deciduous Forest region, butterfly gardeners may not themselves live in a forest but are well aware that the surrounding woods that are a feature throughout the region support many butterflies, in particular their caterpillars. Western-state gardeners work in a variety of elevations, soils, and temperatures and, as such, have a wide plant palette to choose from—but gardening in a dry climate is also a consistent theme and challenge in that region.

The regions covered by the eight garden guides were determined by recurrent themes that emerged from numerous interviews and other communications with experienced NABA gardeners. These garden guides are loosely based on the underlying ecosystems of the regions. Their design epitomizes the nature of butterfly gardening in general: garden location and probable butterfly visitors form the starting point, but the boundaries of possibilities in any butterfly garden are fluid and expansive given the wealth of plant materials and the ever- increasing amount of information shared by experienced gardeners.

Butterfly gardening is more art than science, which leaves a lot of room for experimentation and individualization. Plants grown in the ground as perennials in Texas might yield excellent results if treated as annuals in patio planters farther north. A south-facing brick wall in Kansas can create a sheltered microclimate where tender plants can thrive or bloom earlier than they would otherwise, perhaps just in time for an early spring butterfly. The most successful butterfly gardeners constantly try new ideas based on observations of their own gardens and communication with other gardeners. The following are some of the experiences reported by NABA butterfly gardeners across the United States.

CHAPTER
FIVE

CHALLENGES OF PACIFIC NORTHWEST

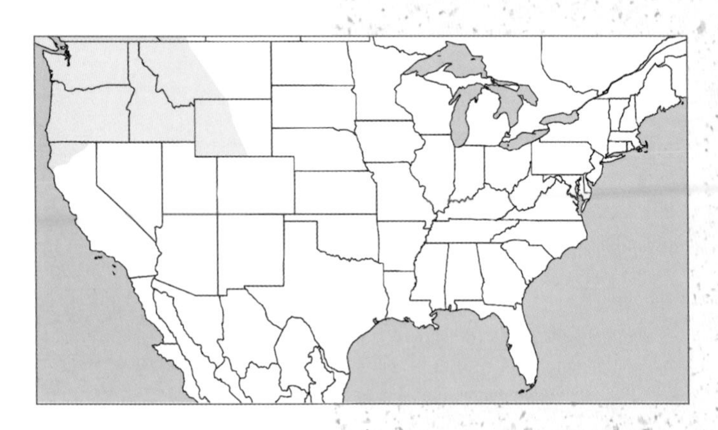

The Pacific Northwest region.

The western boundary of the Pacific Northwest is the Pacific Ocean; its eastern boundary has a less well-defined frontier. Butterfly gardeners who shared information for this garden guide live in the cooler, coastal areas, to the west of the Cascade and Coast ranges. A more expansive definition of the Pacific Northwest region pushes the eastern boundary to the Continental Divide, thereby including the more arid sections of Washington State, Oregon, Idaho, and sections of Montana and Wyoming. Butterfly gardeners in these dry areas east of the Cascade and Coast mountains may find that many of their plant choices might better be made from species listed in the Prairie-Plant Inspired Butterfly Garden Guide in chapter 7, which focuses on plants suited to colder and drier garden conditions.

The cool, rainy weather of the Pacific Northwest makes butterfly gardening a challenge, but one that is not without pleasures. Here, one's approach to attracting butterflies to a home garden will have to take into account many factors specific to the region—elevations can vary widely, full sun might be at a premium, and the makeup of native plant communities shifts depending on proximity to water. Even with all those variables in play, 20–25 butterfly species can be attracted to gardens, although not all at the same time!

Mourning Cloaks are commonly found near woods and have a long flight period in the Pacific Northwest.

A COOL CLIMATE

BUTTERFLY GARDENS

BUTTERFLIES NEAR SEATTLE

Although Julie O'Donald has a full complement of butterfly-friendly plants growing on her property, she knows that butterflies look beyond property lines, therefore, she does too. She gardens outside Seattle in USDA Hardiness Zone 8b, where average annual minimum temperatures range between 15° and 20°F. Julie is fortunate to live in an area of Washington State where "native growth protection areas" can be designated in municipal codes. These protected areas contain riparian areas, steep slopes, or other environmentally sensitive areas that are set aside from development or disturbance. Protection areas near Julie's home contain tall Pacific willows, bitter cherry, Western red cedar, black cottonwood, and bigleaf maple. In addition to preserving tall trees, the native growth protection areas act as habitat corridors, connecting residential areas to nearby riparian habitats. All Julie needs to do is add plants to her yard that will support the butterflies already thriving in the surrounding protected lands.

Colorful beds filled with fall phlox, goldenrod, globethistle, and other nectar plants at the O'Donald garden.

Even though Julie's garden is a riot of colorful flowers, caterpillar food plants play an important role in her planning. Western pearly everlasting and rosy pussytoes attract Painted Ladies to come visit at ground level and lay their eggs, salal acts as a ground cover as well as a food plant for Brown Elfins and Spring Azures, and toward the back of the yard, grasses are allowed to grow tall with minimal disturbance, encouraging Woodland Skippers to complete their life cycle.

While Julie concentrates on plantings at ground level, Western Tiger Swallowtails fly high above and lay eggs in the tall bigleaf maples. Often seen from April until August, this swallowtail has the longest flight season of any butterfly that visits Julie's garden. She feels that part of these swallowtails' success in her garden is due to their choice of caterpillar food plant. Spending the caterpillar portion of their lives high up in the trees allows Western Tiger Swallowtails to avoid the concentrations of yard and garden chemicals that are prevalent in Julie's neighborhood and may account for their robust numbers. The trend toward extensive areas of lawn, and associated reliance on pesticides, is a problem for butterfly gardeners and one that particularly affects Julie's garden even though she maintains a pesticide-free property.

Although their caterpillars live in the trees, Western Tiger Swallowtails nectar at eye level, this one on common milkweed.

Pacific Northwest weather can be cool and not always hospitable for heat-seeking butterflies. Although she cannot control the weather, Julie stays ready for when the temperature is warm and accommodating by keeping a banquet of flowering plants available. Oceanspray is one of her favorites as it is adaptable to growing in sun to part shade and butterflies love its flowers. The plant does not need much maintenance but it does need

Oceanspray teams up with coastal hedgenettle and orange honeysuckle for a native-plant nectar trio.

some growing space in order to reach its mature size of 10–20 feet wide and tall. A smaller version, rockspirea, also known as dwarf oceanspray, reaches 6–15 feet tall but it is not as easy to find at nurseries. And a smaller oceanspray of course has fewer flowers, so Julie suggests that if you have room for it, the larger oceanspray is preferable.

Although not native to the Pacific Northwest, eastern purple coneflower is one of Julie's favorite nectar plants. It blooms over a long season, the flowers withstand rainy weather with aplomb, and each plant produces many blooms. Native eastward through the Great Plains, eastern purple coneflower is included by almost all butterfly gardeners in their plantings regardless of its native status in their local area.

The native spireas are useful for butterflies both as a nectar source and as a caterpillar food plant for Spring Azures. Julie recommends a lovely, small-growing spirea that comes with a confusing array of names: *Spirea betulifolia* is also known as *Spirea lucida* or *Spirea betulifolia* var. *lucida*. It is commonly called shinyleaf spirea or sometimes just white spirea. A small plant that blooms in late May, it is a great starter plant for a small butterfly garden. The larger rose spirea grows 4–5 feet tall and produces large, light pink flowers in the summer months. This plant will spread by suckers so be sure to give it room to roam or otherwise contain it.

Lupines do not produce nectar for butterflies, but their beautiful blue flowers, light scent, and interesting foliage make them garden favorites. As a bonus, lupines also provide caterpillar food for a number of butterflies. While both

Woodland Skipper nectaring on eastern purple coneflower.

Both riverbank lupine and bigleaf lupine provide color to a garden and butterflies appreciate both. This stand of riverbank lupine should be treated as a short-lived perennial.

bigleaf lupine and riverbank lupine are good garden plants, Julie has had more luck growing the former. Although not all of these have visited Julie's garden (yet), the following butterflies fly in the Pacific Northwest, and their caterpillars will treat lupines in your garden as a meal: Orange Sulphur, Clouded Sulphur, Western Tailed-Blue, Painted Lady, West Coast Lady, Gray Hairstreak, Spring Azure, and Silvery Blue.

Julie has tallied 18 butterfly species that have visited her gardens over the years, with one butterfly—Sara Orangetip—appearing only once. Since this orangetip is generally seen at higher elevations, Julie suspects that this single visit resulted from the butterfly being blown off course.

In addition to butterflies, Julie is particularly interested in bees. The cool, damp Pacific Northwest weather has many days when butterflies will not venture out despite the lure of colorful nectar gardens. However, bumble bees and other pollinators will! Over time, Julie has become interested in all the flying (and crawling) creatures that inhabit her small section of Earth. Planting for butterflies can be the first step to opening a world of possibilities for learning about many of the creatures that inhabit the world immediately around us.

BUTTERFLIES NEAR PORTLAND

Bruce Newhouse is a tireless advocate of butterfly gardening with native plants. His carefully researched charts of native butterfly nectar and caterpillar food plants grace the Eugene-Springfield NABA Chapter website and he maintains a home garden that is planted almost exclusively with species native to the Portland, Oregon area.

While many gardeners across the United States rely on nonnative zinnias and purpletop vervain as annuals to provide butterfly nectar, Bruce suggests two native annuals for his area that are easy to grow from seed or small plants. Shortspur seablush blooms in spring and early summer, bearing small pink flowers in profusion. Bruce also grows bluehead gilia, which is in the same plant family as fall phlox. Bluehead gilia's globe-shaped flowers more closely resemble chives or ornamental onions than fall phlox and it produces ample amounts of nectar over its long blooming period of April to July.

Colorful native nectar and caterpillar food plants suitable for small gardens include riverbank lupine, dwarf checkerbloom, and common woolly sunflower.

One nectar plant that Bruce does not grow is orange eye butterflybush, which is banned from sale in Oregon. Native to China, orange eye butterflybush would not fit Bruce's penchant for native plants even if it were available for purchase. This plant is as attractive to gardeners as it is to butterflies, but the objectionable invasive aspect of orange eye butterflybush is borne out by Bruce's own observations in the wilder areas that surround Portland. This butterflybush produces vast volumes of seed that are able to spread far and wide by floating on Oregon's many waterways. Once these seeds germinate, orange eye butterflybush shows aggressive growth that displaces important native caterpillar food plants that inhabit streamsides, such as willows, cottonwoods, and alders. Therefore, what seems like a beautiful, gardenworthy nectar plant in fact ends up decreasing caterpillar food plants in the wild.

Clodius Parnassian ranges throughout the Pacific Northwest, as well as other Western states, and is found in open woodlands, alpine meadows, forest edges, and moist forests, but not usually in a small Portland home garden. Bruce's garden includes Pacific bleeding heart, the Parnassian's caterpillar food plant. It is a tough garden flower that will attract hummingbirds, but Bruce was surprised to see a Clodius Parnassian visit and lay eggs; this species is usually seen at higher altitudes and is decidedly uncommon in the middle of urban Portland. "Plant it and they will come" is clearly a motto to work with when gardening for butterflies, and even if *they* do not come, Pacific bleeding heart is a lovely plant to include in a garden.

Bluehead gilia.

Clodius Parnassian nectaring on monardella, a western native nectar plant.

Bruce's garden-plant selection is native and local. He acknowledges that plenty of nonnative plants are available for butterflies, but locally native plants are his passion. While many organizations (including NABA), offer garden certification signs that proclaim a gardener's intent and purpose, Bruce felt that none of the available signs reflected the inclusive feel of his Portland garden, where all wildlife is catered to and local plants are highlighted, so he made his own sign!

Bruce Newhouse Garden Sign.

Over the years, the design on the sign has changed but it is simply a document created on his home computer. He starts with a photograph and layers text over his chosen image. The resulting sign is printed on photo paper using an inkjet printer. He has the sign laminated at a local print shop to provide weatherproofing, and then posts it in his front yard. Not only does it start conversations with passersby about protecting native plants and animals, but even those who don't stop to engage in conversation can learn something about the protective practices being implemented at one home in Portland. Bruce encourages every butterfly gardener to talk about butterflies and their needs with their neighbors as a simple way to encourage the preservation of more habitat.

Both of these Pacific Northwest gardens represent what can be achieved when gardening in an urban area where the likely number of butterfly species that will visit gardens is relatively low. Both gardeners appreciate all wildlife that visits their gardens while they wait for butterflies, and both have found that emphasizing regionally native plants works well when space is at a premium.

RECOMMENDED BUTTERFLY PLANTS FOR PACIFIC NORTHWEST GARDENS

The table on pages 166–9 highlights plants found by NABA members in the Pacific Northwest to be alluring to butterflies. While highly suited to butterflies in this region, these plants may also thrive and attract butterflies in other locations.

Pacific Northwest gardeners who live west of the Cascade and Coastal mountains may wish to also consult the list of recommended butterfly plants for gardens in the Grasslands in chapter 7, and all Pacific Northwest gardeners can benefit from perusing the water-saving plants suggested in chapter 10 for California gardens.

To determine whether a plant from the list will grow in your area, consult the Native Plant Society or Cooperative Extension Service websites specific to your state. To determine whether a butterfly from the list has a range that includes your garden, consult a butterfly field guide or www.webutterfly.org.

SCIENTIFIC NAME	COMMON NAME	NATIVE RANGE
Annuals		
Gilia capitata	Bluehead gilia	Primarily western US
Plectritis congesta	Shortspur seablush	Washington, Oregon, and California
Perennials		
Anaphalis margaritacea	Western pearly everlasting	Most of the US excluding Oklahoma and southeastern states
Dicentra formosa	Pacific bleeding heart	Washington, Oregon, and California
Echinacea purpurea	Eastern purple coneflower	Eastward from Iowa in the north, Colorado in the west, and Texas in the south
Eriophyllum lanatum	Common woolly sunflower	Primarily Washington, Oregon, California, and Idaho
Lupinus polyphyllus	Bigleaf lupine	Montana, Idaho, Nevada, Washington, Oregon, and California as well as New England, Wisconsin, and Minnesota
Phlox paniculata	Fall phlox	Eastern US
Sidalcea malviflora	Dwarf checkerbloom	California, Oregon, Washington
Solidago canadensis	Canada goldenrod	Entire US excluding Florida, Alabama, Louisiana, Georgia, and South Carolina
Urtica dioca	Stinging nettle	Not native to US

	FLOWER COLOR, FLOWER SEASON, AND NECTAR SOURCE	USDA HARDINESS ZONE	CATERPILLAR FOOD PLANT FREQUENTED BY GARDEN BUTTERFLIES
	Blue flowers in spring with ample nectar	Annual reaching 24 inches tall	Not a caterpillar food plant
	Pink flowers borne in profusion in spring to early summer generate large amounts of nectar	Annual reaching 4–24 inches tall	Not a caterpillar food plant
	White flowers in summer provide nectar to many butterflies	Zones 3–8 perennial plant growing to 2–3 feet	American Lady
	Pink flowers in spring are not used by butterflies but do attract hummingbirds	Zones 4–8 perennial reaching 12 inches tall	Clodius Parnassian (not a common garden butterfly but is possible)
	Purple flowers with orange centers are one of the most popular summer nectar plants	Zones 3–8 perennial growing 1–3 feet	Not a caterpillar food plant
	Yellow flowers in summer provide nectar	Zones 5–10 perennial plants with daisylike flowers reaching 2 feet tall	Not a caterpillar food plant
	Purple-blue flowers rise 3–5 feet tall in early summer providing nectar for butterflies but also favored by bumble bees	Zones 4–10 perennial with 4- foot-tall flower spikes	Painted Lady, Silvery Blue
	Showy white, purple, or pink flowers have a long nectar season in summer	Zones 4–8 perennial reaching 48 inches tall	Not a caterpillar food plant
	Pink to rosy- purple blooms in summer; good nectar plant	Zones 5–9 perennial growing 2–4 feet tall	West Coast Lady, Common Checkered-Skipper
	Bright yellow fall flowers provide nectar for butterflies	Zones 3–9 perennial reaching 5 feet tall	Not a caterpillar food plant
	Not a nectar plant, flowers insignificant	Zones 3–10 perennial growing 2–4 feet tall	Red Admiral, Milbert's Tortoiseshell, West Coast Lady, Satyr Comma

continued overleaf

Table continued

SCIENTIFIC NAME	COMMON NAME	NATIVE RANGE
Shrubs		
Gaultheria shallon	Salal	Washington, Oregon, and California
Holodiscus discolor	Oceanspray	Westward from Montana, Idaho, Colorado, and New Mexico
Holodiscus dumosus	Rockspirea (also known as dwarf oceanspray)	Roughly east of Cascade and Sierra Nevada mountains through Rocky Mountains
Spirea betulifolia	White spirea (also known as shinyleaf spirea)	Oregon, Idaho, Montana, Minnesota, North Carolina
Spirea douglasii	Rose	Primarily Washington, Oregon, Northern California, and Idaho
Trees		
Acer macrophyllum	Bigleaf maple	Washington, Oregon, and California coastlines
Populus balsamifera	Black cottonwood	West from Montana, Idaho, Utah, and Nevada
Prunus emarginata	Bitter cherry	Primarily west from Arizona, Nevada, and Idaho
Salix lucida	Pacific willow	Westward from Montana, Idaho, Colorado, and New Mexico
Thuja plicata	Western red cedar	Montana, Idaho, Washington, Oregon, and California

FLOWER COLOR, FLOWER SEASON, AND NECTAR SOURCE	USDA HARDINESS ZONE	CATERPILLAR FOOD PLANT FREQUENTED BY GARDEN BUTTERFLIES
White to pink flowers in spring but are not a nectar source	Zones 6–10, evergreen shrub growing 1–5 feet	Spring Azure, Brown Elfin
White flowers May to August provide ample nectar	Zones 6–9 fast-growing shrub reaching 6–20 feet	Pale Swallowtail, Lorquin's Admiral, Spring Azure, Gray Hairstreak, Brown Elfin
White flowers in summer provide nectar	Zones 4–8 shrub growing 6–12 feet	Not a caterpillar food plant
White flowers in late spring to early summer provide ample nectar	Zones 4–9 shrub growing to 5 feet	Not a caterpillar food plant
Red-pink fragrant flowers bloom in summer, providing long season of nectar	Zones 5–8 shrub 2–7 feet tall that forms a thicket	Not a caterpillar food plant
Pale yellow flowers in early spring provide nectar for bees	Zone 6 tree reaching 60–100 feet	Western Tiger Swallowtail, possibly Mourning Cloak
Fragrant spring flowers, not a nectar source	Zones 4–8 tree reaching 60–180 feet	Western Tiger Swallowtail, Mourning Cloak, Lorquin's Admiral
White or pinkish flat-topped flower clusters in spring provide nectar	Shrub reaching 4–12 feet high or small tree up to 30 feet	Pale Swallowtail
White catkins in spring provide early nectar	Zones 3–9, shrub or small tree reaching 20–40 feet	Western Tiger Swallowtail, Mourning Cloak, Lorquin's Admiral
Insignificant flowers, not a nectar source	Zones 3–9 shade-tolerant tree reaching 60–200 feet	'Nelson's' Juniper Hairstreak

CHAPTER SIX

BUTTERFLY GARDENING

EASTERN

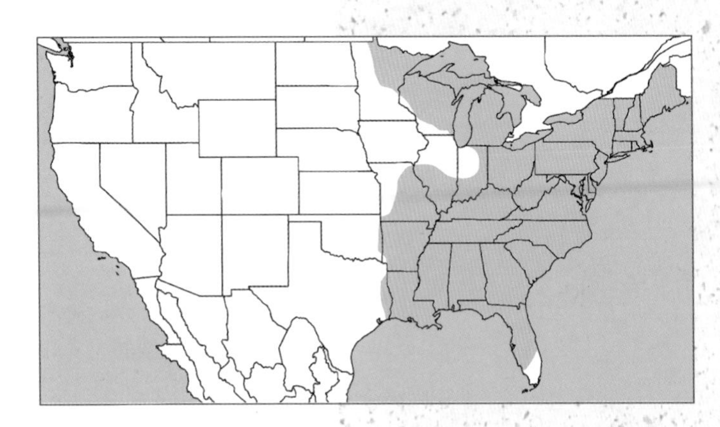

The Eastern Deciduous Forest region.

The Eastern Deciduous Forest ecosystem covers portions of 26 states from New England and southern Canada to Florida, extending west to Texas and Minnesota. Habitats vary within the forest range; each unique habitat supports its own diverse flora and fauna based, in part, on soils, elevations, temperatures, and rainfall. Despite these variations, butterfly gardeners throughout this large area recommend many of the same plants. When considering plants in the Eastern Deciduous Forest guide, check local and Internet resources, such as the Native Plant Society or Cooperative Extension Service websites specific to your state, to confirm that a given plant will thrive in your area. Different garden butterflies occur in different portions of this range, so before excitedly planting specific caterpillar food plants, consult a butterfly field guide or www.webutterfly.org to determine which butterflies are common to your location and likely to visit gardens.

BUTTERFLIES NEAR NEW YORK CITY

Wade and Sharon Wander watch and welcome all types of wildlife, including butterflies. Their butterfly garden is best described as a series of garden beds that meander throughout their 3-acre sloping property. By breaking the garden into patches, the Wanders have created a series of garden vignettes, where plant growth is optimized by matching the plants with the various soil and sun conditions found on the property; woods almost

WITH TREES

DECIDUOUS FOREST

surround the property and each garden bed receives differing amounts of sun over the course of the day.

Located in the Ridge and Valley Province of the Appalachian Mountains, Wade and Sharon's garden falls into USDA Hardiness Zone 6a, about 90 minutes west of New York City. Elevations in their county vary from 300 to 1,810 feet above sea level, the annual minimum temperature ranges from −5° to −10°F, and annual rainfall is about 45 inches. Although forested areas are not usually considered prime butterfly-garden territory (and their site is actually a 2-acre clearing within a largely forested matrix), Wade and Sharon demonstrate how to take advantage of trees and shrubs when creating butterfly habitat.

They started the garden in 1992 and so far it's attracted 84 species of butterflies—probably the highest total of any garden in New Jersey. Careful planting and watching for early-season butterflies is part of the strategy that has produced this garden's impressive species list. The Wanders live in a part of New Jersey known as the "Sussex County Snow Belt," which receives substantially more snow than the rest of New Jersey. Many of their plant choices are tough native plants that survive cold, wet winters and therefore can be useful in butterfly gardens across wide sections of the country.

Along one of their forest edges the Wanders have planted eastern redbud—a native tree that flowers before its leaves emerge, providing some of the earliest nectar for spring butterflies,. Native to the lower Great Plains and eastern United States, eastern redbud is fast growing, reaching 20–30 feet at maturity. Many different butterflies will nectar at eastern redbud, but the Wanders particularly notice the first brood of Juniper Hairstreaks visiting the flowers in spring. As their name suggests, these hairstreaks use juniper trees as their caterpillar food plant. In New Jersey fields and forest edges, eastern redcedar (which grows naturally on the Wanders' property) is the Juniper Hairstreak caterpillar food plant of choice, but the butterfly nectars on nearby flowers. In July a second brood of Juniper Hairstreaks emerges, which the Wanders often see nectaring on hoary mountainmint. In fact, hoary mountainmint is one of the most popular summer nectar plants for a wide array of pollinators at the Wander garden. A second plant reported by other gardeners as favored by Juniper Hairstreak is butterfly milkweed.

OPPOSITE: Sourwood's fall red color is spectacular and its midsummer nectar production is profuse. Native to the eastern United States, sourwood requires acidic soils, similar to those needed by azaleas and rhododendrons. It can tolerate some shade but is intolerant of drought.

Juniper Hairstreak on mountainmint species.

Even small eastern redbuds will bloom in the spring. This one is being planted in honor of Earth Day.

CERTAIN VARIETIES OF EASTERN REDBUD are particularly well suited for hot or dry climates. For Texas and Oklahoma, the native variety commonly called Texas redbud is more drought tolerant than the straight species and has darker and brighter flowers. 'Oklahoma,' a selection of Texas redbud found naturally growing in the Sooner state, is often found for sale. With a more compact growth habit than eastern redbud, it reaches 12–18 feet at maturity. Both Texas redbud and its variety 'Oklahoma' are hardy only to USDA Zone 6, while eastern redbud can be grown much further north, into USDA Zone 4. A dwarf, weeping cultivar of eastern is also available that is ideal for smaller gardens and brings nectaring butterflies within easy view.

Native to Texas and Arizona and thus suitable for far southern locations, Mexican redbud is often shorter in stature than either eastern or Texas redbud and its leaves are smaller; it is quite tolerant of heat and has fairly low water requirements. And gardeners in California, Arizona, Utah, and Nevada can plant a native species, California redbud, that is well adapted to a number of native plant communities. So some version of redbud is an excellent choice for butterfly gardens throughout much of the United States in USDA Zones 4 and higher.

Northern spicebush—which grows naturally in a wetland on the Wanders' property—is a large shrub that provides caterpillar food for Spicebush Swallowtail. Although not considered a significant nectar source, before its leaves emerge it does produce a lovely haze of tiny, nectar-filled flowers that are welcome to early-flying butterflies such as Spring Azure. Northern spicebush is an easy-to-grow, deer-resistant shrub for a shady, preferably moist, location. It can be trimmed to maintain a small stature and can even be cut back entirely to just above ground level, which will cause it to regrow as a multistemmed shrub. It is one of a handful of caterpillar food plants for the Spicebush Swallowtail and gardeners will appreciate its golden-yellow blooms as true harbingers of spring.

Spring Azures fly early in the season when few nectar plants are blooming and will nectar on northern spicebush.

Attracting early-flying butterflies is important to the Wanders, and harlequin blueflag is one of their favorite early-season nectar plants, established in a small artificial pond. Native to the northeastern quarter of the United States, this iris requires ample moisture but is easy to grow and attracts early pollinators. Bumble bees and carpenter bees are the primary pollinators of harlequin blueflag, and although its showy purple-blue flowers will attract spring-flying skippers and early migrants such as American Lady, little actual pollination is performed by butterflies.

Bumble bees, with their short tongues, must get up close and personal with flowers in order to drink nectar. When drinking from harlequin blueflag, bees also collect pollen on their bodies and thus cross-pollinate the irises.

Zabulon Skippers have long tongues and do not need to crawl into the flower in order to drink its nectar—they are able to perch on the large sepals and probe for nectar.

Harlequin blueflag flowers have a lower set of "petals" that in the iris world are commonly called *falls* and in the larger botanical world are called *sepals*. These large, showy sepals make the flower attractive to humans but also help to draw pollinators by displaying darker veinlike markings along their length that serve as nectar guides to direct the attention of pollinators toward the center of the flower. Bees follow the nectar guides through a tunnel-like opening between the sepal and the pistil (the female part of the plant's reproductive structure) to reach the nectar, gathering pollen on their bodies as they proceed. On future visits to nearby harlequin blueflag flowers the bees will deposit the pollen clinging to their bodies, resulting in cross pollination.

Growing in semishade, spotted geranium blooms in midspring and is a great plant for skippers in the Wander garden. Indian and Hobomok skippers and

Pincushion flower blooms all summer and attracts many butterflies, including this Indian Skipper.

Wild Indigo and Juvenal's duskywings are all early-flying skippers that will visit spotted geranium. It can be a challenge to identify skippers but Sharon Wander insists that, with the help of close-focusing binoculars and a good butterfly field guide, you can learn to identify the skippers in your garden. First check the field guide for flight times so you know which butterflies to expect in any given month; figuring out which species are likely to be in flight is the first step in identification of skippers, and other butterflies as well. Putting some effort into learning the fine points of butterfly identification is a really fun way to get the mental stimulation that we all need to keep our minds sharp!

Pincushion flower and catmint are two other great flowering nectar plants to include if you like to watch for skippers, although other butterflies will visit them as well. Although pincushion flower and catmint are not native plants, the Wanders suggest them as tough, long-blooming nectar plants for the summer. Occasional deadheading during the summer will keep these two plants looking fresh and blooming longer. To complete a plant grouping for season-long skipper-watching, fall-blooming blue mistflower also grows fairly low and, along with spotted geranium, pincushion flower, and catmint could be the fourth plant for a season-long, easy-care nectar planting.

The Wanders name eastern purple coneflower as one of their favorite nectar plants. Its bright flowers attract many different types of butterflies, like this Eastern Tiger Swallowtail, and it is easy to grow.

Spicebush Swallowtails range throughout most of the Eastern Deciduous Forest. This pair is nectaring on bottlebrush buckeye, a native shrub that blooms midsummer and can tolerate light shade conditions.

BUTTERFLY GARDENING WITH TREES

Wade and Sharon's property backs up to woods and although shade is not often associated with butterfly gardening, the woods sustain butterflies in a number of ways. A large number of trees and shrubs found within the mixed deciduous woodlands serve as caterpillar food and some provide nectar. The naturally growing plants in the forest bordering the Wander garden expand the extent of butterfly-friendly habitat beyond their landscaped area. Oaks and hickories provide food for hairstreak and duskywing caterpillars, and the adults nectar in their flower beds; tuliptree and black cherry bring them Eastern Tiger Swallowtails; Spicebush Swallowtails lay eggs on the sassafras trees along the forest edge; woodland grasses support Northern Pearly-eye, which doesn't nectar but which they look for in clearings with dappled shade and bare soil; thanks to common hackberries they are often greeted by Tawny and Hackberry emperors; and a volunteer black locust is a favorite host plant for Silver-spotted Skipper.

Even though trees and shrubs are an integral part of butterfly habitats, not everyone has the space or inclination to plant a tree or shrub. If your garden is small or not situated near a wild space like Julie O'Donald's or abutting a stand of native woodlands like the Wanders', protecting the trees and shrubs already in your general location is vital to butterflies and their survival. Wade Wander feels there are opportunities for homeowners to preserve habitat by simply taking inventory of their trees and shrubs. When home environs are "cleaned up" or landscaped to suit a homeowner's style, leaving mature trees and shrubs that serve butterflies and their caterpillars is a free and easy way to help them. After all, before embarking on any work that involves digging, everyone is urged to call 811 to ensure that no underground utilities will be damaged—if the same caution were applied before digging up trees and shrubs to ensure no butterfly habitat would be damaged, think of all the habitat that could be saved! It's wise to learn what is in your existing landscape before making wholesale changes.

Butterfly habitat in public and private landscapes is important to note and protect. This cemetery is graced by a sizable black cherry that provides butterfly and wildlife habitat while offering shade and scenery to cemetery visitors.

SAMPLINGS OF THE NATIVE TREES THAT FEED CATERPILLARS AND SURROUND THE WANDERS' GARDEN

~ Northern Red Oak: the flowers and leaves feed Banded Hairstreak, Juvenal's Duskywing, and Horace's Duskywing caterpillars
~ Blackhaw: the flower buds of this small tree in the Honeysuckle Family provide food for Spring Azure caterpillars
~ Black Cherry: the leaves feed Eastern Tiger Swallowtail and Red-spotted Purple caterpillars while the flowers and fruit support caterpillars of Coral and Striped hairstreaks.
~ Eastern Redcedar: Juniper Hairstreak caterpillars feed on the branch tips
~ Common Hackberry: Hackberry Emperor and Tawny Emperor caterpillars commonly feed on the tree's leaves; American Snout, Mourning Cloak, and Question Marks may also use common hackberry as caterpillar food
~ Northern Spicebush: the preferred caterpillar food for Spicebush Swallowtail
~ Sassafras: fine, short hairs on the leaves make sassafras a less preferred but still commonly used caterpillar food for Spicebush Swallowtail
~ Tuliptree: One of many trees used by Eastern Tiger Swallowtail caterpillars
~ River Birch: Mourning Cloak and Compton Tortoiseshell caterpillars eat birch leaves while living communally up in the tree canopy
~ Black Locust: Silver-spotted Skipper caterpillars enjoy this tree's leaves

Spicebush Swallowtail caterpillar.

LEFT: A number of butterflies thrive in and around the Eastern Deciduous Forest. Although not considered common garden butterflies, all use trees as caterpillar food and may be locally common—Spicebush Swallowtail, Red-spotted Purple (pictured here), Hackberry and Tawny emperors, Compton Tortoiseshell, and American Snout.

BUTTERFLIES IN MASSACHUSETTS

For almost 15 years, Tom Gagnon has set out a butterfly banquet in a field of vegetables. Surrounded on all sides by a grid of garden beds planted primarily with vegetables for people, Tom's two double garden plots at the Northampton Community Garden in Northampton, Massachusetts, produce food for butterflies. While Tom's garden does not include caterpillar host plants, his plantings are circled by densely planted wooded areas and vegetable crops, many of which do provide caterpillar food.

A long-time birder and butterfly watcher, Tom stopped by the Northampton Community Garden on a whim many years ago when he noticed that the sunny field contained some flowers scattered among the 440 vegetable plots. His hunch that it might be a good spot to watch butterflies was rewarded during his first visit when he spotted a Common Checkered-Skipper, which at the time was not listed as occurring in Massachusetts. Inspired by the sighting, he visited the Community Garden a few more times that fall and signed up for a garden plot for the following year.

Each of Tom's 20 × 40-foot plots is planted primarily with purpletop vervain, which is allowed to reseed from year to year. Around the beginning of June, the small vervain seedlings start to appear on the soil surface. Gardening in USDA Hardiness Zone 5a, with average annual minimum winter temperatures ranging from −15° to −20°F, means that the growing season is short and the soil is slow to warm up in the spring. During the second week of June, Tom—using a string to maintain straight rows and orderly spacing—starts to organize the volunteer seedlings into evenly spaced rows with the plants 8–9 inches apart. The transplanting of 800–1,000 small purpletop vervains takes some time! After each row is lined up, the plants are watered deeply. Tom feels that the work early in the season is well worth the effort. If the volunteer plants were allowed to grow where they sprouted each year, the resulting plot would have an unkempt, weedy look rather than the inviting, gardenlike feel that results when the plants are evenly spaced. Transplanting the seedlings also allows them to grow taller than they would if left in a more crowded arrangement.

Tom also includes zinnias—always tall, single varieties—in the two garden plots. He has noticed that the larger butterflies like Eastern Tiger Swallowtail and Great Spangled Fritillary prefer the taller zinnias over purpletop vervain, as they provide stable landing platforms from which to nectar. Over the years, Tom has chosen to feature different colors of zinnias. In the past he planted only red zinnias along one side of the plot, while in recent years he has used a mixture of tall yellow and orange varieties. Many sources suggest that flower color influences butterflies in their choices of which flowers to nectar at, but Tom has not noticed that one zinnia color is preferred over another. When they are bordering a sea of purpletop vervain, it is likely that any color of zinnia would be attractive to butterflies.

By the third week of July, the garden plot is in full bloom, with the vervain and zinnias attracting a wide variety of butterflies. Tom's gardens offer nectar to draw as many butterflies as possible, and a nearby garden bench also accommodates butterfly watchers. A box attached to the underside of the bench holds a plastic bag containing a stenographer's notebook and a pen. Garden visitors can record their butterfly sightings in the notebook, creating a record of the number and variety of butterflies that have visited the garden. Just as importantly, the notebook serves to inform arriving butterfly watchers of what species to watch for during their visit.

Beyond serving as reminders of what groceries to pick up at the store, lists can serve as a springboard for garden inspiration. Many people photograph butterflies as a way to document their sightings, but Tom finds that keeping lists suits him better. By recording the number of butterflies as well as the date, he is preserving information that can help him see trends.

Planting a butterfly garden that focuses only on adult butterflies is unusual, as the traditional concept of planting for butterflies includes feeding caterpillars as well. This all-nectar, all-annual garden within the Deciduous Forest Ecosystem is an unqualified success—both supporting butterflies and creating community through shared information and a bench thoughtfully provided for all.

RECOMMENDED BUTTERFLY PLANTS FOR EASTERN DECIDUOUS FOREST GARDENS

The table on pages 182–7 highlights plants found alluring to butterflies by NABA members in parts of the Eastern Deciduous Forest region. While suited to butterflies in this region, these plants may also thrive and attract butterflies elsewhere.

Gardeners in this region may also wish to consult the list of recommended butterfly plants for Grasslands in chapter 7 as many of those plants are suited to the Eastern Deciduous Forest states.

To determine whether a plant from the list will grow in your area, consult the Native Plant Society or Cooperative Extension Service websites specific to your state. To determine if a butterfly from the list has a range that includes your garden, consult a butterfly field guide or www.webutterfly.org.

Tom Gagnon's community garden plots in 2012.

SCIENTIFIC NAME	COMMON NAME	NATIVE RANGE
Annuals		
Tithonia rotundifolia	Clavel de muerto or Mexican sunflower	Not native to US
Verbena bonariensis	Purpletop vervain	Not native to US
Zinnia elegans	Zinnia	Not native to US
Perennials and Vines		
Aristolochia macrophylla	Pipevine	Eastern US
Asclepias tuberosa	Butterfly milkweed	Throughout US except northwestern states
Asclepias incarnata	Swamp milkweed	Most of the US excluding far western states
Anaphalis margaritacea	Western pearly everlasting	Most of the US excluding Oklahoma and southeastern states
Antennaria neglecta	Field pussytoes	Eastern US and parts of the Midwest
Conoclinium coelestinum	Blue mistflower	Eastern and lower Midwestern states
Geranium maculatum	Spotted geranium	Eastern US
Iris versicolor	Harlequin blueflag	Eastern US and parts of the Midwest
Liatris spicata	Dense blazing star	Eastern and midwestern US

FLOWER COLOR, FLOWER SEASON, AND NECTAR SOURCE	USDA HARDINESS ZONE	CATERPILLAR FOOD PLANT FREQUENTED BY GARDEN BUTTERFLIES
Orange flowers provide profuse amounts of nectar from late summer until frost	Annual reaching up to 6 feet tall	Not a caterpillar food plant
Purple flowers produce nectar from midsummer until frost	Annual reaching up to 4 feet tall	Not a caterpillar food plant
Many different flower colors provide nectar from early summer through frost	Annual reaching up to 4 feet tall	Not a caterpillar food plant
Yellow, green, or purple flowers in late spring do not provide nectar for butterflies	Zones 4–8 vine growing up to 30 feet tall	Pipevine Swallowtail
Bright orange flowers from early to midsummer are a favorite nectar source	Zones 3–9 perennial reaching 18 inches tall	Monarch
Mauve or pink flowers provide weeks of nectar in summer	Zones 3–6 perennial growing 5 feet tall	Monarch
White flowers in summer provide nectar to many butterflies	Zones 3–8, perennial plant growing 2–3 feet	American Lady
White flowers in spring are not considered a source of butterfly nectar	Zone 3–7 perennial reaching 4 inches tall	American Lady
Purple flowers from late summer through fall provide nectar	Zones 5–10 perennial reaching 3 feet tall	Not a caterpillar food plant
Purple flowers in spring months provide nectar	Zones 3–8 perennial reaching 12 inches tall	Not a caterpillar food plant
Deep blue flowers in May, June, July provide nectar	Zones 3–6 perennial reaching 3 feet tall	Not a caterpillar food plant
Pinkish-purple flowers provide weeks of nectar in midsummer	Zones 3–8 perennial growing 2–4 feet tall, prefers moist soils	Not a caterpillar food plant

continued overleaf

Table continued

SCIENTIFIC NAME	COMMON NAME	NATIVE RANGE
Annuals *continued*		
Monarda didyma	Scarlet beebalm	Eastern US
Monarda fistulosa	Wild bergamot	Most of the US
Nepeta spp.	Catmint	Not native to US
Petroselinum crispum	Parsley	Not native to US
Pycnanthemum incanum	Hoary mountainmint	Eastern US
Ruta graveolens	Common rue	Not native to US
Scabiosa columbaria	Pincushion flower	Not native to US
Solidago speciosa	Showy goldenrod	Eastern and central US
Symphyotrichum novae-angliae	New England aster	Most of the US
Grasses		
Panicum virgatum	Switchgrass	Most of the US excluding far western states
Schizachyrium scoparium	Little bluestem	Most of the US

RECOMMENDED BUTTERFLY PLANTS

FLOWER COLOR, FLOWER SEASON, AND NECTAR SOURCE	USDA HARDINESS ZONE	CATERPILLAR FOOD PLANT FREQUENTED BY GARDEN BUTTERFLIES
Bright red flowers produce nectar in summer	Zones 4–9 perennial growing to 4 feet	Not a caterpillar food plant
Lavender-pink flowers provide a lot of nectar in summer	Zones 3–9 perennial growing to 4 feet	Not a caterpillar food plant
Purple flowers from spring to fall provide nectar mostly for smaller butterflies	Zones 4–9 perennial reaching 30 inches tall	Not a caterpillar food plant
Yellow flowers in second year from planting	Zones 3–9 biennial reaching 18 inches tall	Black Swallowtail
White flowers with light purple tinge in summer provide nectar	Zones 4–8 perennial reaching 36 inches tall	Not a caterpillar food plant
Pale yellow flowers in summer are not visited by butterflies	Zones 4–8 perennial growing to 3 feet tall	Black Swallowtail, Giant Swallowtail
Blue-purple flowers in summer provide nectar over a long time frame	Zones 4–10 perennial reaching 12 inches tall	Not a caterpillar food plant
Large yellow flowerheads provide nectar in fall	Zones 3–8 perennial growing 5 feet tall	Not a caterpillar food plant
Purple flowers in the fall provide nectar	Zones 4–8 perennial growing 6 feet tall	Pearl and Northern crescents
Not a nectar plant, flowers insignificant	Zones 5–9 perennial grass growing 6 feet tall	Indian, Delaware, and Hobomok skippers
Not a nectar plant, flowers insignificant	Zones 3–9 grass reaching 4 feet tall	A number of grass-skippers use little bluestem as a caterpillar food but most are not regular garden visitors

continued overleaf

Table continued

SCIENTIFIC NAME	COMMON NAME	NATIVE RANGE
Shrubs and Trees		
Aesculus parviflora	Bottlebrush buckeye	New Jersey, Pennsylvania, New York, Alabama, Georgia, South Carolina
Betula nigra	River birch	Eastern US
Celtis occidentalis	Common hackberry	Eastward from Montana, Utah, and New Mexico
Cercis canadensis	Eastern redbud	Lower Great Plains and eastern US
Juniperus virginiana	Eastern redcedar	Eastern US
Lindera benzoin	Northern spicebush	Eastern US and parts of the Midwest
Liriodendron tulipifera	Tuliptree	Eastern US
Oxydendrum arboreum	Sourwood	Eastern US
Prunus serotina	Black cherry	Eastern half of US, Washington State, Arizona, and New Mexico
Quercus rubra	Northern red oak	Eastern US westward through Minnesota and Iowa, south to eastern Oklahoma
Robinia pseudoacacia	Black locust	Entire US
Sassafras albidum	Sassafras	Eastward from Texas, Kansas, Iowa, and Wisconsin
Viburnum prunifolium	Blackhaw	Eastern and central US

FLOWER COLOR, FLOWER SEASON, AND NECTAR SOURCE	USDA HARDINESS ZONE	CATERPILLAR FOOD PLANT FREQUENTED BY GARDEN BUTTERFLIES
White flowers are held above foliage in June and July providing nectar over a few weeks	Zones 4–8 large shrub or tree reaching 8–12 feet tall	Not a caterpillar food plant
Not a nectar plant, flowers insignificant	Zones 4–9 tree growing 70 feet tall	Mourning Cloak, Compton Tortoiseshell
Insignificant flowers, not a nectar source	Zones 2–9 tree reaching 60 feet tall	Hackberry Emperor, Tawny Emperor, American Snout, Mourning Cloak, Question Mark
Pink flowers in early spring offer nectar	Zones 4–8 tree reaching 30 feet tall	Not a caterpillar food plant
Needled evergreen: no nectar	Zones 2–9 tree reaching 65 feet	Juniper Hairstreak
Yellow flowers in very early spring provide nectar	Zones 4–9 small tree/large shrub to 12 feet	Spicebush Swallowtail
Showy flowers high up in treetop provide nectar	Zones 4–9 tree growing 90 feet tall	Eastern Tiger Swallowtail
Pendulous clusters of white flowers in summer provide nectar over a few weeks	Zones 5–9 tree growing 20–50 feet tall	Not a caterpillar food plant
Lot of white flowers in spring provide nectar	Zones 3–9 tree reaching 60 feet tall	Eastern Tiger Swallowtail, Red-spotted Purple, Coral Hairstreak, Striped Hairstreak
Not a nectar plant, flowers insignificant	Zones 4–8 tree reaching 75 feet tall	Banded Hairstreak, Juvenal's Duskywing, Horace's Duskywing
Showy, fragrant flowers provide nectar but are not visited by butterflies	Zones 3–8 tree growing to 50 feet tall	Silver-spotted Skipper
Yellow flowers in spring are not known to be visited by butterflies	Zones 4–9 tree growing 60 feet tall	Spicebush Swallowtail, Eastern Tiger Swallowtail
White flowers in May and June provide spring nectar	Zones 3–9 small tree reaching 15 feet tall	Spring Azure

CHAPTER SEVEN PRAIRIE-PLANT INSPIRED

THE GRASSLANDS

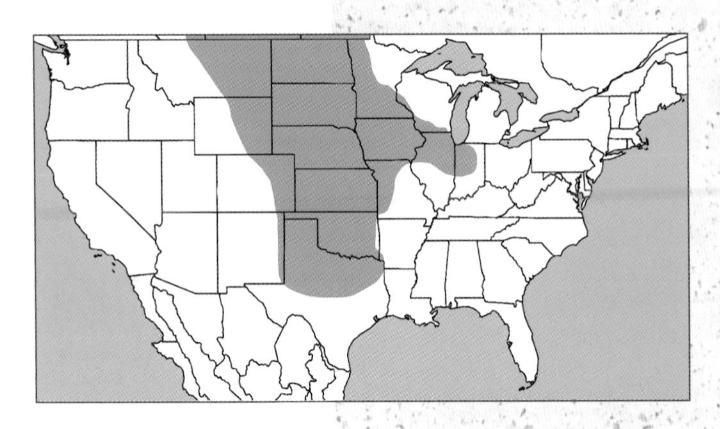

The Grasslands region.

This butterfly garden region is based loosely on the historic outline of two prairie ecosystems—the tallgrass and shortgrass prairies. A third type, the mixed-grass prairie (where the tallgrass and shortgrass prairies merge) is also included.

Ironically, butterfly gardening in the grasslands includes very little grass! The majority of recommended butterfly-attracting plants for gardens are flowering plants native to the tallgrass prairie. Very few gardeners have the resources to "re-create" extensive grassland habitats, but by using native grassland plant materials (that are also beautiful garden plants) they can attract butterflies, create a modest amount of habitat, and produce stunning gardens that benefit all pollinators.

BUTTERFLIES NEAR CHICAGO

The path that led Stephanie Walquist to butterfly gardening was slow and steady; its course traveled across two states and a number of years. Stephanie started out as a "typical" gardener, one who enjoyed choosing garden plants from catalogs based on their attractiveness. She was living in a newly built home in a New Hampshire housing development that featured large lawns. When their lawn became too much to take care of, Stephanie and her husband decided to let part of it revert back to its original, more natural state.

Once the mowing ceased, native wildflowers started to return to the wild section of lawn; common boneset was one of the first to appear and with it, butterflies. Over time, more wildflowers sprang up, attracting increasing numbers of butterflies and fueling Stephanie's curiosity about what was happening in the yard. Stephanie began as a gardener who relished the beauty of flowers, but as the wildflower meadow at her New Hampshire home grew and evolved, and she observed the dynamic life that revolved around the wilder edges of her property, her gardening ethos evolved to include the impact of her activities on the wider environment. Not only was the meadow beautiful to look at but it also demonstrated how different gardening practices, such as the elimination

BUTTERFLY GARDENS

of mowing, allowed the garden to evolve into a more diverse and interesting landscape. Butterflies became a primary focus of her gardening, and to support them her love of regionally native plants developed.

The publication of *Bringing Nature Home* broadened Stephanie's perspective on the plants she chose for her garden, and a move from the meadow of New Hampshire to an urban home in Oak Park, Illinois, led her to refine the plants she could include for butterflies. While *Bringing Nature Home* emphasizes the value of native plants for home landscapes, her new urban home in Illinois had no room for the meadow to which she was accustomed; in fact, it had very little outside space at all. Undaunted, Stephanie continued to garden for butterflies but on a much smaller scale. Using some of the same plants she was familiar with from New Hampshire, she scaled back the size of her garden and watched to see which butterflies would be attracted to her new home.

In addition to her home garden, Stephanie started a butterfly garden at her children's elementary school as well as small gardens at other public locations around Oak Park. For public gardens, she creates "pocket prairies"—small, densely grouped patches of plants that serve as fuel stops for passing pollinators. While the specific plants selected for each pocket prairie are based on local soil conditions and available sunlight, she relies mainly on a group of plants that are native to her area and that require little attention once they are acclimated to the new garden site. Since the pocket-prairie plantings are on public land and do not receive daily attention, they must be able to grow with minimal care and be well adapted to the Illinois climate.

Stephanie has discerned over time that the best plants to attract a wide variety of butterflies in her urban environment are native species that are components of the tallgrass prairie ecosystem, which was once predominant in her

Showy goldenrod, skyblue aster, and little bluestem create a bright fall color combination. These prairie plants do well in larger gardens where they can intermingle.

Native prairie flowers include bright orange butterfly milkweed, white spiky rattlesnake master, and pale purple coneflower.

part of Illinois. Using the plants that historically were native to a particular ecosystem has many virtues for butterfly gardening, allowing the gardener to provide an array of nectar and caterpillar food plants that will be attractive to butterflies over the entire growing season. By choosing regionally native plants that are known to feed butterflies and their caterpillars, the gardener is mimicking a food web, one that it is hoped will support local butterflies. In creating pocket prairies, Stephanie is working to bridge the gap between suburban and urban private gardens and wilder spaces with islands of habitat. Although her efforts spring from her own curiosity about the natural world, the plantings become examples to others of the small opportunities that are present all around us for fostering butterflies and other pollinators.

Pale purple coneflower.

The butterfly nectar season in the pocket prairie begins with pale purple coneflower, which blooms in June, followed by eastern purple coneflower in July. Depending on the soil conditions, Stephanie plants a few different milkweeds, including swamp milkweed, which she has found will grow well with a bit of shade (and tends to withstand drier soil when grown in the shade). Butterfly, whorled, and prairie milkweeds are also commonly used in the pocket prairies.

All the plants that Stephanie uses in her pocket prairies are natives that have not been bred or selected for any special characteristics. By using such plants, whose seeds will produce offspring similar to their parents, Stephanie is also creating a sustainable resource for her community. She collects large amounts of their seed in the fall for use in creating future pocket prairies.

By grouping the plants close together and mulching heavily the first year, Stephanie is able to launch her pocket prairies with ease. Aside from initial planting, each pocket prairie requires only an hour or so of care every few weeks during the first year while the plants are becoming established. Heavy mulch at this time helps conserve water. Stephanie likes to keep much of the dead, dry plant material in the garden over the winter, and so, where possible, she does not cut back the plants in the fall or winter.

Two plants from the Mint Family, scarlet beebalm and wild bergamot, feature in the pocket prairies as nectar plants. Both plants spread underground to form mats of stems that help tie the pocket prairie together. They not only provide nectar in the summer but also function as a ground cover in the spring and cooler

The mat of next year's growth is visible on scarlet beebalm during a late-winter thaw. Creeping through last year's fallen leaves, the new growth remains low through spring, holding the soil in place and suppressing weeds.

ABOVE: Scarlet beebalm grows skywards and produces bright red flowers in summer. It is extremely adaptable, as seen here growing with eastern purple coneflower in a parking strip near Chicago.

parts of the year, when their shallow, dense root systems produce small amounts of low-to-the-ground foliage. In many climates, the shoots of these Mint Family plants will be visible during the winter.

New England aster, a few types of blazing stars, and a variety of goldenrods are also mainstays of Stephanie's Illinois pocket prairies. Although the plants chosen for pocket prairies are ones that would naturally occur in an expansive sea of grass, owing to the space constraints of their urban location these pocket prairies do not often include grasses. In a setting with more space available, adding distinctive native grasses such as little bluestem, Indiangrass, or switchgrass as accent plants would enhance the look of the garden and more accurately embody the pocket prairie theme.

BUTTERFLIES IN OHIO

For many years, Jan Dixon had a large garden in the Toledo, Ohio, area—so large that she removed the backyard lawn entirely and replaced it with a wildlife-supporting landscape. At her current home, also in the Toledo area, her homeowner association frowns on such gestures and all new garden beds need to be preapproved by the association if lawn is to be removed. Yet, even with restrictions, Jan still attracts butterflies galore. Despite the surrounding sterile expanse of lawn, Jan has seen the adage "plant it and they will come" borne out time and again in her butterfly gardens. She plants as many caterpillar food plants as possible, maintains dense plantings of nectar plants in carefully edged garden beds, and credits a nearby park as instrumental in providing additional habitat for butterflies.

Many grass-skippers use switchgrass (and other native grasses) as caterpillar food, although only a few, such as Hobomok, Tawny-edged, and Northern Broken-Dash, are likely to frequent gardens. Placing native grasses in your garden adds interesting structure and a visual break from flowering plants while also supplying seed for birds and shelter for butterflies as well as other creatures.

Common sneezeweed blooms for many weeks in the fall. To keep it a manageable size that will not need staking, clip the plant back to about 6 inches tall in the late spring/early summer, which will cause the plant to make lateral shoots that are stockier and shorter. Smaller butterflies such as this Meadow Fritillary tend to visit common sneezeweed in Jan Dixon's Ohio garden.

The USDA Hardiness Zone for Ohio is now Zone 6 (with a minimum winter temperature of −10°F), reflecting a revision in the zone designations (until a few years ago, Ohio was placed in Zone 5, with a minimum winter temperature of −20°F). Many gardeners feel that it is safest to still consider the colder minimum temperature as a possibility and choose plants accordingly. Jan uses a wide variety of plants and for the most part sticks with native species that will survive the cold winters no matter how the zones shift. Ohio lies in the eastern edge of the tallgrass prairie and many of the plants that work so well for Jan are prairie natives.

Eastern purple coneflower, three different milkweeds (swamp, common, and butterfly), hoary verbena, swamp verbena, wild bergamot, New Jersey tea, and common sneezeweed are prairie-native nectar plants that Jan provides to butterflies. Many gardeners install these plants in large groups that mimic prairies or wilder spaces; Jan grows them in long flowerbeds that average 3–4 feet deep. She relies on vigilant deadheading to keep the plants from spreading seed, which is particularly important with the hoary and swamp verbenas, both prolific seed producers.

In addition to native plants, Jan particularly likes two nonnative plants that she uses both for their butterfly-attracting qualities and for the colorful beauty that the flowers add to her garden beds. Each spring, Jan purchases lantana bedding plants from local nurseries. Red or pink varieties are her favorite and seem to do a good job at attracting butterflies. She plants long swaths of lantana, which allows butterflies to easily visit many flowers with little effort. In Ohio, lantana is used as an annual bedding plant as it is killed by the first frost in the fall. Jan also plants orange eye butterflybush—in fact at her previous, large garden she had nine of these plants! The combination of lantana, which comes from the nursery already in bloom, and orange eye butterflybush, which starts to bloom in the middle of summer, provides continuous, season-long nectar. Jan assiduously deadheads both these plants during the entire growing season so that fresh flowers are in constant supply.

Large swaths of lantana bloom throughout the butterfly garden season. Nectar is always available!

Partridge pea's bright yellow flowers appear in the summer. The blue-green, dissected foliage provides caterpillar food for Cloudless Sulphurs in Jan Dixon's garden. In other parts of the country, partridge pea is eaten by the caterpillars of Sleepy Orange, Little Yellow, Gray Hairstreak, and Ceraunus Blue.

Jan Dixon's granddaughter waiting for a newly emerged Monarch to take its maiden flight. She sends each butterfly off with the benediction "Good luck!"

Pussytoes, partridge pea, stinging nettle, northern spicebush, common rue, parsley, tuliptree, and common hop are just some of the caterpillar food plants in Jan's Ohio gardens that have attracted butterflies to come and lay eggs. Spicebush Swallowtail seems to be the most common swallowtail in Jan's area so she planted multiple northern spicebush shrubs. Both caterpillar food plants and butterfly nectar plants are well represented in Jan's garden. She enjoys observing the entire butterfly life cycle, which she shares with her grandchildren, who now grow caterpillar food plants at their own homes!

Over time, Jan has developed a practice of rearing caterpillars inside enclosures. She began protecting them when she realized that many of the caterpillars she was watching in her garden disappeared before forming chrysalides. Now she regularly takes some caterpillars inside to rear to adulthood, while always leaving some behind to fend for themselves as part of her garden food web. Most often using small glass aquariums with screen tops, Jan places each species of caterpillar in its own enclosure (although there may be many caterpillars of the same species in one enclosure), and feeds them daily using the same plant from the garden on which she originally found them. The aquariums are housed next to a window inside Jan's garage, where the caterpillars seem quite content to eat and grow. The butterfly species that Jan raises in her aquariums include Pipevine, Black, and Eastern Tiger swallowtails; Question Mark; Monarch; and American Lady.

RECOMMENDED BUTTERFLY PLANTS FOR GRASSLAND GARDENS

The table on pages 196–203 highlights plants that NABA members in the Grasslands have found to be alluring to butterflies. While suited to butterflies in this region, these plants may also thrive and attract butterflies in other locations.

Gardeners in the Grasslands may wish to consult the list of recommended butterfly plants for the Eastern Deciduous Forest in chapter 6; many of these

SCIENTIFIC NAME	COMMON NAME	NATIVE RANGE
Annuals		
Chamaecrista fasciculata	Partridge pea	Eastern and central US
Lantana camara	Lantana	Not native to US
Petroselinum crispum	Parsley	Not native to US
Tithonia rotundifolia	Clavel de muerto or Mexican sunflower	Not native to US
Verbena bonariensis	Purpletop vervain	Not native to US
Zinnia elegans	Zinnia	Not native to US
Grasses		
Panicum virgatum	Switchgrass	Most of the US excluding far western states

plants are suited to the Grassland states. The list of recommended butterfly plants for the Central Monarch Flyway in chapter 8 should also be consulted for possible plants.

To determine whether a plant from the list will grow in your area, consult the Native Plant Society or Cooperative Extension Service websites specific to your state. To determine if a butterfly from the list has a range that includes your garden, consult a butterfly field guide or www.webutterfly.org.

	FLOWER COLOR, FLOWER SEASON, AND NECTAR SOURCE	USDA HARDINESS ZONE	CATERPILLAR FOOD PLANT FREQUENTED BY GARDEN BUTTERFLIES
	Yellow flowers in summer do not provide nectar	Annual plant growing up to 40 inches tall	Cloudless Sulphur, Little Yellow, Gray Hairstreak
	Flowers of many different colors provide nectar from summer until frost	Annual (perennial in Zones 10–11) reaching up to 4 feet	Not a caterpillar food plant
	Yellow flowers in second year from planting	Zones 3–9 annual or biennial reaching 18 inches tall	Black Swallowtail
	Orange flowers provide profuse amounts of nectar from late summer until frost	Annual reaching up to 6 feet tall	Not a caterpillar food plant
	Purple flowers produce nectar from midsummer until frost	Annual reaching up to 4 feet tall	Not a caterpillar food plant
	Many different flower colors provide nectar from early summer through frost	Annual reaching up to 4 feet tall	Not a caterpillar food plant
	Not a nectar plant, flowers insignificant	Zones 5–9 perennial grass growing 6 feet tall	Common Wood-Nymph and some skippers

continued overleaf

Table continued

SCIENTIFIC NAME	COMMON NAME	NATIVE RANGE
Grasses *continued*		
Schizachyrium scoparium	Little bluestem	Most of the US
Perennials and Vines		
Antennaria neglecta	Field pussytoes	Eastern US and parts of the Midwest
Aristolochia macrophylla	Pipevine	Eastern US
Asclepias incarnata	Swamp milkweed	Most of the US excluding far western states
Asclepias sullivantii	Prairie milkweed	Central US
Asclepias tuberosa	Butterfly milkweed	Throughout US except northwestern states
Asclepias verticillata	Whorled milkweed	Washington, Oregon, Idaho, Nevada, Utah, and California
Echinacea pallida	Pale purple coneflower	Central eastern and central midwestern states
Echinacea purpurea	Eastern purple coneflower	Eastward from Iowa in the north, Colorado in the west, and Texas in the south
Eryngium yuccifolium	Rattlesnake master	Eastern and central US

PLANTS FOR GRASSLAND GARDENS

	FLOWER COLOR, FLOWER SEASON, AND NECTAR SOURCE	USDA HARDINESS ZONE	CATERPILLAR FOOD PLANT FREQUENTED BY GARDEN BUTTERFLIES
	Not a nectar plant, flowers insignificant	Zones 3–9 grass reaching 4 feet tall	A number of skippers use little bluestem as a caterpillar food but most are not regular garden visitors
	White flowers in spring are not considered a source of butterfly nectar	Zone 3–7 perennial reaching 4 inches tall	American Lady
	Yellow, green, or purple flowers in late spring do not provide nectar for butterflies	Zones 4–8 vine growing up to 30 feet tall	Pipevine Swallowtail, in southern portions of this region
	Mauve or pink flowers provide weeks of nectar in summer	Zones 3–6 perennial growing 5 feet tall	Monarch
	Pink flowers produce nectar in summer	Zones 3–7 perennial growing 3 feet	Monarch
	Bright orange flowers from early to midsummer are a favorite nectar source	Zones 3–9 perennial reaching 18 inches tall	Monarch
	White flowers produce nectar	Zones 4–9 perennial growing 3 feet	Monarch
	Pale pink flowers with drooping petals provide nectar	Zones 3–8 perennial growing 3 feet tall	Not a caterpillar food plant
	Purple flowers with orange centers are one of the most popular summer nectar plants	Zones 3–8 perennial growing 1–3 feet	Not a caterpillar food plant
	Round white flowers produce a lot of summer nectar	Zones 3–8 perennial growing 5 feet tall	Not a caterpillar food plant

continued overleaf

Table continued

SCIENTIFIC NAME	COMMON NAME	NATIVE RANGE
Perennials and Vines *continued*		
Eupatorium perfoliatum	Common boneset	Eastern and central US
Helenium autumnale	Common sneezeweed	Entire US
Liatris ligulistylus	Rocky Mountain blazing star	Central US
Liatris pycnostachya	Prairie blazing star	Central and southeastern US
Monarda didyma	Scarlet beebalm	Eastern US
Monarda fistulosa	Wild bergamot	Most of the US
Pycnanthemum incanum	Hoary mountainmint	Eastern US
Ruta graveolens	Common rue	Not native to US
Solidago speciosa	Showy goldenrod	Eastern and central US
Symphyotrichum novae-angliae	New England aster	Most of the US
Symphyotrichum oolentangiense	Skyblue aster	Eastern and central US

PLANTS FOR GRASSLAND GARDENS

FLOWER COLOR, FLOWER SEASON, AND NECTAR SOURCE	USDA HARDINESS ZONE	CATERPILLAR FOOD PLANT FREQUENTED BY GARDEN BUTTERFLIES
Numerous white flowers in late summer attract butterflies	Zones 3–8 perennial growing 6 feet tall	Not a caterpillar food plant
Yellow flowers provide nectar in late summer and fall	Zones 3–8 perennial growing to 3 feet tall	Not a caterpillar food plant
Rose-purple flowers in July to September provide nectar	Zones 3–8 growing to 2 feet tall, prefers dry to medium- moist soils.	Not a caterpillar food plant
Lilac-purple flowers in July and August provide ample nectar	Zones 3–9 perennial growing 2–5 feet tall, prefers wet to medium-moist soils	Not a caterpillar food plant
Bright red flowers produce nectar in summer	Zones 4–9 perennial growing to 4 feet	Not a caterpillar food plant
Lavender- pink flowers provide a lot of nectar in summer	Zones 3–9 perennial growing 4 feet tall	Not a caterpillar food plant
White flowers with light purple tinge in summer provide nectar	Zones 4–8 perennial reaching 36 inches tall	Not a caterpillar food plant
Pale yellow flowers in summer are not visited by butterflies	Zones 4–8 perennial growing to 3 feet tall	Black Swallowtail, Giant Swallowtail
Large yellow flowerheads provide nectar in fall	Zones 3–8 perennial growing 5 feet tall	Not a caterpillar food plant
Purple flowers in the fall provide nectar	Zones 4–8 perennial growing 6 feet tall	Pearl and Northern crescents
Purple-blue flowers pump out nectar in the fall	Zones 3–8 perennial growing 3 feet tall	Pearl Crescent

continued overleaf

Table continued

SCIENTIFIC NAME	COMMON NAME	NATIVE RANGE
Perennials and Vines *continued*		
Urtica dioca	Stinging nettle	Not native to US
Verbena hastata	Swamp verbena	Entire US
Verbena stricta	Hoary verbena	Most of the US
Trees and Shrubs		
Celtis occidentalis	Common hackberry	Eastward from Montana, Utah and New Mexico
Cercis canadensis	Eastern redbud	Lower Great Plains and eastern US
Lindera benzoin	Northern spicebush	Eastern US and parts of the Midwest
Liriodendron tulipifera	Tuliptree	Eastern US
Prunus serotina	Black cherry	Eastern half of US, Washington State, Arizona, and New Mexico
Robinia pseudoacacia	Black locust	Entire US

PLANTS FOR GRASSLAND GARDENS

	FLOWER COLOR, FLOWER SEASON, AND NECTAR SOURCE	USDA HARDINESS ZONE	CATERPILLAR FOOD PLANT FREQUENTED BY GARDEN BUTTERFLIES
	Not a nectar plant, flowers insignificant	Zones 3–10 perennial growing to 2–4 feet tall	Red Admiral, Eastern Comma, Question Mark, Milbert's Tortoiseshell
	Purplish-blue flowers July to September provide butterfly nectar	Zones 3–8 perennial growing 2–6 feet tall can spread aggressively by rhizome and self-seeding	Not a caterpillar food plant
	Blue-purple flowers throughout summer provide nectar for butterflies	Zones 4–7 perennial growing 2–4 feet	Not a caterpillar food plant
	Insignificant flowers, not a nectar source	Zones 2–9 tree reaching 60 feet tall	Hackberry Emperor, Tawny Emperor, American Snout, Mourning Cloak, Question Mark
	Pink flowers in early spring offer nectar	Zones 4–8 tree reaching 30 feet tall	Not a caterpillar food plant
	Yellow flowers in very early spring provide nectar	Zones 4–9 small tree/large shrub to 12 feet	Spicebush Swallowtail
	Showy flowers high up in treetop provide nectar	Zones 4–9 tree growing 90 feet tall	Eastern Tiger Swallowtail
	Lots of white flowers in spring provide nectar	Zones 3–9 tree reaching 60 feet tall	Eastern Tiger Swallowtail, Red-spotted Purple, Coral Hairstreak, Striped Hairstreak
	Showy fragrant flowers provide nectar but not visited by butterflies	Zones 3–8 tree growing to 50 feet tall	Silver-spotted Skipper

CHAPTER
EIGHT

PLANTING WITH THE CENTRAL

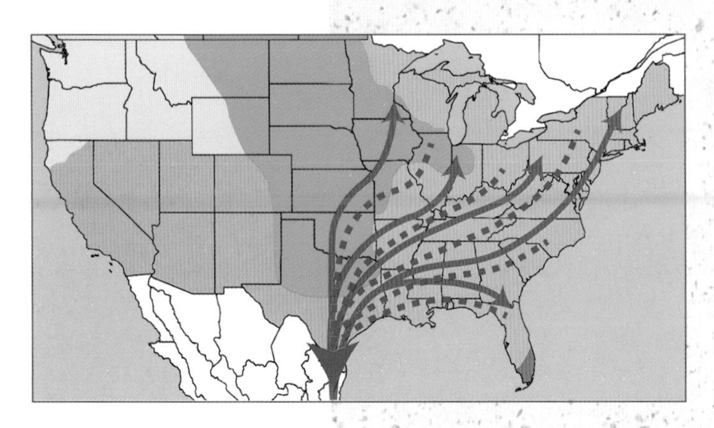

The Central Monarch Flyway. Red lines indicate the path of spring migration while blue lines show the fall migration.

The Central Monarch Flyway is not a distinct geographic region; it is defined as the flight path traveled by Monarchs in the eastern portion of the United States. Like the Monarch migration itself, the flyway boundaries are broad and ever shifting, depending on many variables, including the number of Monarchs in any particular year and the weather. The potential area encompassed by the flyway includes most of the United States east of the Rocky Mountains.

In the spring, Monarchs leaving their overwintering roosts in Mexico travel northward, with the Sierra Madre Oriental mountains to the west and the Gulf of Mexico to the east compressing their route through Mexico to a narrow flight path. Once they reach Texas and Oklahoma, the flight path starts to widen as Monarchs disperse across the central and eastern United States. Monarchs on their spring migration are in need of nectar to fuel their movement northward and of milkweed on which to lay eggs for the next generation.

In fall the migration is reversed, with Monarchs funneling southward from as far north as Canada and as far east as Maine. As with their spring migration, physical land features compress the flight path, this time with the Rocky Mountains acting as a barrier to the west and the Gulf of Mexico to the south. As the migration approaches Texas and Oklahoma, the density of Monarchs increases, creating a beautiful sight for residents as well as an opportunity for gardeners to take actions that will provide Monarchs with their most basic needs—nectar to build up reserves needed for their winter rest and milkweed for egg laying that continually replenishes the Monarch population.

The Monarch migration provides butterfly gardeners throughout the United States with particular pleasure, but those in areas where the "funnel" effect of the mass migration produces spring and fall concentrations of these magnificent butterflies have a special fondness and are highly attuned to the need to provide "fuel stops" for Monarchs. Fuel for Monarchs is simply nectar and—in spring—milkweeds in amounts that can provide for the large numbers of butterflies that pass through the area.

PURPOSE

MONARCH FLYWAY

Monarchs might be considered a "gateway butterfly"—once gardeners become aware of the importance of providing fuel for Monarchs, an interest in caring for all butterflies follows, as exemplified by the gardeners interviewed in the Central Monarch Flyway.

BUTTERFLIES NEAR HOUSTON

"Carefully curated" best describes the garden near Houston, Texas, that Don Dubois has been cultivating for more than a decade. Average high temperatures in winter are above 60°F yet freezing temperatures do occur on occasion. But it is the high summer heat (along with typically scarce rainfall) that impacts Don's gardening choices—plants in his garden must provide for butterflies while surviving extreme summer conditions. The Houston area straddles two USDA Plant Hardiness Zones: southern sections fall in zone 9a (with minimum annual temperatures of 20°–25°F) while northern Houston is designated zone 8b (with minimum annual temperatures of 15°–20°F).

This Eastern Tiger Swallowtail stopped for a drink of nectar—and perhaps also to look for a mate. Black cherry leaves feed Eastern Tiger Swallowtail caterpillars as well as those of Red-spotted Purple, while the spring blossoms provide nectar for early-flying adults.

OPPOSITE FROM TOP TO BOTTOM: Hackberry Emperor, American Snout, and Tawny Emperor.

Caterpillars that feed on common hackberry include those of Hackberry and Tawny emperors, which feed on the leaves as a group and spend the winter as caterpillars rolled up inside of dead leaves. American Snout and Question Mark caterpillars eat young common hackberry leaves, and the adults of both species overwinter in the southern parts of the United States. Mourning Cloak caterpillars live in a communal web while feeding on common hackberry leaves, and adults overwinter.

Sugarberry, a tree closely related to common hackberry, will also host the same suite of caterpillars. Its native range extends farther south and west than common hackberry, making it a good choice for southern and western states (although states in the far west are beyond the range of Question Mark and Tawny Emperor.

Don's garden features native plants as its backbone—natives are the plants that seem to thrive in his location while also being the most attractive to butterflies. Black cherry and common hackberry are two trees that Don considers "must haves" for butterfly gardens, since they serve as host plants for seven different butterflies found in the Houston area.

Shrubs play a large role in framing Don's garden—they not only create habitat for butterflies but also serve as a visual link between the taller trees and the herbaceous garden plants below, while also helping to moderate the garden's microclimate by decreasing wind speeds. For gardeners, the shrub layer opens opportunities to work with a wider number of decorative plants both for garden design and for butterfly needs. For wildlife such as birds and butterflies, shrubs provide both shelter and food. While herbaceous perennials are often thought of as the backbone of a butterfly garden, shrubs are essential if a wide variety of passing butterflies are going read the landscape as "home." In a long growing season such as Houston's, shrubs play an essential role in providing nectar for the entire growing season.

Blooming summer through fall, flame acanthus is root hardy to USDA Hardiness Zone 7.

Flame acanthus is a native shrub that draws both butterflies and hummingbirds. It is hardy as far north as Dallas, Texas, although in colder areas it will die back to the roots and reemerge each year, acting as a perennial plant rather than a shrub. It can also be used as a container plant in colder locations. Flame acanthus is so attractive to nectaring butterflies that Don suggests this plant as a perfect shrub for beginning butterfly gardeners. It is also one of the caterpillar food plants for Texan Crescent, which can be found in gardens from southern California eastward across the southern states to Florida.

Don's second shrub recommendation for beginning butterfly gardeners is sweet almond verbena. Intensely fragrant for nearby humans and nectar-rich for passing butterflies, this nonnative plant can be grown as a shrub in Houston, as a perennial plant in USDA Plant Hardiness Zone 8, and as a container plant farther north. The foliage can be coarse and can cause allergic skin reactions in sensitive individuals, so place the plant where it can be appreciated without touching. When planted in southern locations, sweet almond verbena benefits from trimming spent blooms halfway through the growing season in order to encourage a flush of new flowers.

Whitebrush (below) is at home in meadowlike setting. A Gulf Fritillary (below right) nectars on West Indian shrubverbena, also known as Texas lantana, which blooms throughout the summer.

Choosing nonnative sweet almond verbena over whitebrush, a similar but native plant, highlights the variety of choices when gardening for butterflies. Over time, Don has found that in his garden, sweet almond verbena is more attractive to butterflies than its native cousin. Sweet almond verbena is also more commonly found in local nurseries, while whitebrush can be difficult to track down.

With lantanas, Don chooses native over nonnative. The native lantana species, West Indian shrubverbena (also known as Texas lantana), is more attractive to butterflies and shows more resilient growth in Houston's scorching summers. Native from California across to Florida, this lantana species is immensely popular all along the southern border of the United States and is often sold under the common name of Texas lantana or calico bush. The nonnative *Lantana camara*, which simply goes by the common name lantana, is similar but has become invasive in parts of Hawaii and Florida and is considered a problem in Texas.

Spider milkweed is a western native plant that exemplifies how careful plant selection can be used in public places to enhance butterfly habitat. The plant's native habitat is rocky or sandy soil where regular moisture may be lacking. Spider milkweed should be considered for planting in road medians, public rights-of-way, and other less-than-pampered locations. Monarchs, as well as other butterflies, need as much habitat as possible! To meet their needs, look beyond individual gardens and seek other opportunities for increasing habitat.

Houston is in the funnel of the central Monarch flyway, so in addition to providing nectar, Don makes sure to have enough milkweed available for egg-laying when Monarchs are passing through on their way north. Butterfly milkweed will grow well in Houston, but Don has found that nonlocal plants (those shipped from other locations) do not thrive in Houston's hot conditions. He is not certain why potted transplants do not thrive for him, but starting butterfly milkweed from locally collected seed allows Don to grow this native species successfully.

Green antelopehorn milkweed is vitally important for Monarchs in the Houston area. Texas has a diversity of climatic conditions, with heat and rainfall varying widely, and as a result, different species of milkweeds occur in different locations. To the south of Houston, zizotes milkweed becomes more prevalent, and to the west, spider milkweed is one of the choice milkweeds to plant for Monarchs. Swamp milkweed and common milkweed have not been successful in Don's garden.

Blue mistflower is easy to find in plant nurseries and catalogs/websites. Also called hardy ageratum, it has a tendency to spread by underground stems, so if you place it in a garden bed among other plants, plan to divide it every two or three years to control its spread. It prefers well-drained soil and requires additional watering in very dry conditions, but is generally adaptable.

In the northern United States, blue mistflower produces an abundant fall bloom of lilac-blue flowers. Planted farther south, flowers appear in the summer, and in Houston, it starts to bloom in spring, continuing into early summer. If cut back after the summer flowers fade, this composite will bloom again in the fall. Blue mistflower fulfills the basic requirement of a butterfly garden nectar plant: nectar that is attractive to butterflies and produced over a long period on a plant that will thrive in a wide variety of settings. Considering its easy cultural requirements, most people would stop with just this one plant.

Blue mistflower attracts and fuels Monarchs.

Yet Don is growing two similar species to further extend the season of bloom. His second choice, palmleaf thoroughwort, more commonly known as Gregg's mistflower, has cultural requirements similar to blue mistflower but its primary bloom time in Houston is late spring to summer. As with blue mistflower, a summer trimming will induce some fall blooms.

To ensure ample fall nectar, Don includes a third mistflower-like plant called Jack in the bush, also known as fragrant mistflower. Although it is a coarser-looking garden plant than Don's other two mistflowers, its late bloom period ensures a vital source of nectar for fall-migrating Monarchs. From mid-October until mid-November, the fragrant flowers of Jack in the bush not only hold the attention of Monarchs but also accommodate the influx of other butterflies that come to Houston in the fall.

Don's Houston butterfly garden is filled with perennial plants that might seem exotic to gardeners in other parts of the United States. Many plants grown as shrubs in Houston are sold as annual plants in more northern regions and will rarely reach shrublike proportions when grown as potted plants. Sweet almond verbena is used in public butterfly displays because it is aromatic to visitors as well as attractive to butterflies, and lantana is commonly sold for Northerners' patio planters each spring.

In other warm parts of the world, many of these nectar plants grow so robustly that they are considered pernicious. In India, both Jack in the bush and lantana are invasive weeds that romp through agricultural fields and natural areas, displacing everything in their paths. Since virtually any plant can become problematic given the right conditions, perhaps all plants purchased from retailers should come with a warning label! Agronomists in India have examined composting Jack in the bush and lantana in a mixture with other plant materials to create a finished product that is high in the nutrients needed for potato production. Any positive use that can be derived from an existing invasive species problem should be applauded and can perhaps be applied in other climates. As the scope of our knowledge about butterfly plant preferences grows and is applied, gardeners need to become cognizant of the materials they are using and the possible immediate impacts of each plant.

RECOMMENDED BUTTERFLY PLANTS FOR HOUSTON AREA GARDENS

The table on pages 212–17 highlights plants found by NABA members near Houston to be alluring to butterflies. While suited to butterflies in this region, these plants may also thrive and attract butterflies in other locations.

Gardeners near Houston may wish to consult the list of recommended butterfly plants for the Grasslands in chapter 7 as many of these plants may be suitable.

To determine whether a plant from the list will grow in your area, consult the Native Plant Society or Cooperative Extension Service websites specific to your state. To determine if a butterfly from the list has a range that includes your garden, consult a butterfly field guide or www.webutterfly.org.

Queen, a butterfly closely related to the Monarch, nectars on Gregg's mistflower. Like Monarchs, Queens use milkweed as their caterpillar food plant. Queens are common in South Florida and southern Texas, as well as along the Mexican border in New Mexico, Arizona, and southern California. Additionally, they may be seen north of their range as regular immigrants. Like Monarchs, Queens migrate southward in the fall; some years the number of migrating Queens is in the millions, yet unlike Monarchs, no one knows where the Queens go!

SCIENTIFIC NAME	COMMON NAME	NATIVE RANGE
Annuals		
Chamaecrista fasciculata	Partridge pea	Eastern and central US
Pentas lanceolata	Egyptian starcluster, or better known as pentas	Not native to US
Zinnia elegans	Zinnia	Not native to US
Perennials and Vines		
Aristolochia fimbriata	White-veined hardy Dutchman's pipe	Not native to US
Aristolochia tomentosa	Woolly Dutchman's pipe	Eastern and south-central US
Asclepias asperula	Spider milkweed	Western US
Asclepias curassavica	Tropical milkweed	Not native to US
Asclepias oenotheroides	Zizotes milkweed	Texas, Arizona, New Mexico, Oklahoma, Colorado, Louisiana
Asclepias tuberosa	Butterfly milkweed	Throughout US except northwestern states

PLANTS FOR HOUSTON AREA

	FLOWER COLOR, FLOWER SEASON, AND NECTAR SOURCE	USDA HARDINESS ZONE	CATERPILLAR FOOD PLANT FREQUENTED BY GARDEN BUTTERFLIES
	Yellow flowers in summer do not provide nectar	Annual plant growing up to 40 inches tall	Cloudless Sulphur, Little Yellow, Gray Hairstreak, Ceraunus Blue
	Red, pink, lavender, or white flowers produce large amounts of nectar throughout the growing season	Zones 8–11 perennial but may be treated as annual in areas that experience frost	Not a caterpillar food plant
	Many different flower colors provide nectar from early summer through frost	Annual reaching up to 4 feet tall, depending on variety	Not a caterpillar food plant
	Yellow-green, pipe shaped flowers with burgundy rim do not provide nectar	Zones 7a–9b perennial ground cover	Pipevine Swallowtail
	Greenish-yellow flowers do not provide nectar	Zones 5–8 vine growing up to 30 feet tall	Pipevine Swallowtail
	White-green flowers produce nectar from spring through fall	Zones 6–10 perennial growing 2 feet tall	Monarch, Queen
	Red or yellow flowers provide nectar over a long growing season	Zones 8b–11 perennial; north of Zone 8b grown as annual that often self-seeds, height up to 48 inches	Monarch, Queen
	Green flowers tinged with purple provide nectar from spring through summer	Zones unknown growing to 2 feet tall	Monarch, Queen
	Bright orange flowers from early to midsummer are a favorite nectar source	Zones 3–9 perennial reaching 18 inches tall	Monarch, Queen

continued overleaf

Table continued

SCIENTIFIC NAME	COMMON NAME	NATIVE RANGE
Perennials and Vines *continued*		
Asclepias viridis	Green antelopehorn milkweed	Midwest and southern US
Chromolaena odorata	Jack in the bush, also known as fragrant mistflower or crucita	Texas, Florida
Conoclinium coelestinum	Blue mistflower, also called hardy ageratum	Eastern and lower Midwestern states
Conoclinium greggii	Palmleaf thoroughwort, also known as Gregg's mistflower	Texas, Arizona, New Mexico
Echinacea purpurea	Eastern purple coneflower	Eastward from Iowa in the north, Colorado in the west, and Texas in the south
Gaillardia pulchella	Firewheel	Much of the US
Lantana urticoides	West Indian shrubverbena, also known as Texas lantana	Southern tier US including California
Monarda fistulosa	Wild bergamot	Most of the US
Passiflora incarnata	Purple passionflower	Eastern US
Phyla nodiflora	Turkey tangle fogfruit	Lower half of US
Grasses		
Panicum virgatum	Switchgrass	Most of the US excluding far western states

FLOWER COLOR, FLOWER SEASON, AND NECTAR SOURCE	USDA HARDINESS ZONE	CATERPILLAR FOOD PLANT FREQUENTED BY GARDEN BUTTERFLIES
Greenish flowers produce nectar from late spring through summer	Zones 4–9 perennial growing to 3 feet	Monarch, Queen
Purple flowers in fall produce large amounts of nectar	Zones 8–11 perennial growing 6 feet tall	Not a caterpillar food plant
Purple flowers from late summer through fall provide nectar	Zones 5–10 perennial reaching 3 feet tall	Not a caterpillar food plant
Blue flowers spring through fall produce large amounts of nectar	Zones 8–10 perennial growing 18 inches tall	Not a caterpillar food plant
Purple flowers with orange centers are one of the most popular summer nectar plants	Zones 3–8 perennial growing 1–3 feet	Not a caterpillar food plant
Yellow-orange-red flowers produce a lot of nectar from spring through summer	Annual that may reseed	Not a caterpillar food plant
Yellow-orange flowers produce nectar from spring through fall	Zones 8–11 perennial growing to 3 feet tall	Not a caterpillar food plant for garden butterflies
Lavender- pink flowers provide lot of nectar in summer	Zones 3–9 perennial growing 4 feet tall	Not a caterpillar food plant
Purple flowers provide some nectar	Zones 5–9 vine reaching 8 feet tall	Gulf Fritillary, Zebra Heliconian, Variegated Fritillary
White flowers appear all year in warmer locations and provide nectar for a large number of butterflies	Zones 6–11 perennial ground cover growing 3–6 inches tall	Common Buckeye, Phaon Crescent
Not a nectar plant, flowers insignificant	Zones 5–9 perennial grass growing 6 feet tall	Grass- skippers

continued overleaf

Table continued

SCIENTIFIC NAME	COMMON NAME	NATIVE RANGE
Grasses *continued*		
Schizachyrium scoparium	Little bluestem	Most of the US
Shrubs and Trees		
Aloysia gratissima	Whitebrush	Texas, Arizona, New Mexico
Aloysia virgata	Sweet almond verbena	Not native to US
Anisacanthus quadrifidus var. *wrightii*	Flame acanthus	Texas
Celtis laevigata	Sugarberry	Southern and western US
Celtis occidentalis	Common hackberry	Eastward from Montana, Utah, and New Mexico
Eysenhardtia texana	Texas kidneywood	Texas
Hamelia patens var. *patens*	Scarletbush, also known as firebush	Florida
Persea borbonia	Redbay	Texas and coastal states as far east as North Carolina
Prunus serotina	Black cherry	Eastern half of US, Washington State, Arizona, and New Mexico

	FLOWER COLOR, FLOWER SEASON, AND NECTAR SOURCE	USDA HARDINESS ZONE	CATERPILLAR FOOD PLANT FREQUENTED BY GARDEN BUTTERFLIES
	Not a nectar plant, flowers insignificant	Zones 3–9 grass reaching 4 feet tall	A number of skippers use little bluestem as a caterpillar food but most are not regular garden visitors
	White flowers produce abundant nectar in spring, summer, and fall, particularly after rain	Zones 8–11 shrub growing to 10 feet tall	Not a caterpillar food plant
	White flowers produce fragrant nectar spring through fall	Zones 8–11 shrub growing to 10 feet tall	Not a caterpillar food plant
	Red-orange flowers provide nectar summer through fall	Zones 7–11 shrub growing to 5 feet tall	Texan Crescent
	Insignificant flowers, not a nectar source	Zones 6–9 tree growing to 80 feet tall	Hackberry Emperor, Tawny Emperor
	Insignificant flowers, not a nectar source	Zones 2–9 tree reaching 60 feet tall; sugarberry is an alternative choice for dry, hot locations	Hackberry Emperor, Tawny Emperor, American Snout, Mourning Cloak, Question Mark
	Fragrant white flowers in spring, summer, and fall	Zones 8–11 medium to large shrub growing to 10 feet tall	Not a caterpillar food plant
	Red flowers are a nectar favorite for butterflies, blooming spring through fall in Zone 9 and nearly year-round in Zones 10 and 11	Zones 9–11 shrub in warmer areas, perennial that dies back in colder areas, and also used as annual in cold areas	Not a caterpillar food plant
	Inconspicuous yellow-green flowers are not nectar sources	Zone 8–11 tree growing to 40 feet tall	Palamedes Swallowtail
	Lot of white flowers in spring provide nectar	Zones 3–9 tree reaching 60 feet tall	Eastern Tiger Swallowtail, Red-spotted Purple

BUTTERFLIES NEAR KANSAS CITY

Aromatic aster 'Raydon's Favorite' is a very popular selection—it received a five-star rating in a comparative study of cultivated asters by the Chicago Botanic Garden. This selection has a mounding habit and shows good resistance to powdery mildew.

With more than 20 species of asters growing in his garden, Alan Branhagen might seem like a gardener who is interested only in a spectacular fall display, but the number of different asters growing around his 3-acre property also reflects a deep understanding of a plant's niche within a garden habitat. From the rhizomatous roots of common blue wood aster that help hold soil in place to New England aster's prolific blooms full of late-season nectar, each different species fills a particular ecological role in the garden environment. Even though the Kansas City area is not in the narrow "funnel" portion of the Monarch flyway, it is in a part of the country where the number of Monarchs during spring and fall migrations can be dense, and fall asters provide nectar to fuel the Monarchs southward.

Aromatic aster is one of Alan's favorite fall asters and easy to find for sale. The name is slightly misleading—the flowers of aromatic aster do not have a scent, but the leaves and stems do produce an herbal fragrance if crushed. Over time, the plants spread by underground stems to form a colony and will grow in dry or poor soil. When adding an aromatic aster to a garden, pay attention to soil and sun—in rich organic soil, neighboring plants with faster growth rates can easily crowd out this aster.

Blooms of aromatic aster change color as they age. In full bloom, 'Raydon's Favorite' is covered with clear, bright purple flowers that turn a burnt reddish-purple once they pass their prime. Both flower colors are pleasant to look at and the plant blooms for weeks. To insects, though, the changing flower color is more than decorative. As the nectar flow ends in each flower, the petals change color, from bright to burnt, as if to say to potential pollinators, "the diner is closed, don't bother to stop here." Seeing the reddish-purple color, nectar-seeking insects will not waste precious energy visiting the nectarless flowers.

New England aster is beloved by butterfly gardeners and recommended when planting specifically for fall-migrating Monarchs. Often growing 6 feet tall and 3 feet wide, it is capable of producing an enormous number of nectar-producing flowers on each plant, and as a bonus, the caterpillars of Pearl and Northern crescents eat its foliage. Adaptable to growing in most of the United States, it performs best in full sun. In Alan's Missouri garden, New England aster grows in drier, more exposed locations, although in the eastern United States, New England aster does well in moist to average soils.

If an aster beauty contest were held, common blue wood aster would be only a third runner-up for title of "most dramatic fall floral display," but it fills an important niche in the shady edges of Alan's garden. At the end of the growing season, when many weeds and wildflowers are

New England aster is big, bright, and needs room to roam; it can spread 2–3 feet wide.

no longer in bloom, common blue wood aster explodes with a multitude of small, daisylike flowers. While not as showy as other asters, common blue wood aster will bloom happily in dry shade—a notoriously difficult spot to grow any plant, much less a productive nectar source. It is a strong grower and can be placed near other plants that also have a robust growth habit.

Commonly repeated advice for beginning butterfly gardeners is to choose a location that receives at least 6 hours of full sun a day. Sunlight is an essential component of butterflies' lives, providing the warmth these cold-blooded creatures need to become active enough to fulfill their mission of mating and feeding. Like most butterfly gardens, however, Alan's has a variety of habitats, some of which include shade. By seeking out plants adapted to thrive in less than full sun, Alan includes a vast number of beautiful landscape plants that also support butterflies (which will nectar in shade in hot weather).

The small flowers of common blue wood aster are complemented by the hairawn muhly (also know as pink muhly grass) growing nearby.

BUTTERFLIES NEAR KANSAS CITY

Many milkweeds will grow and thrive in Kansas, but purple milkweed is one of Alan's favorites. He recommends growing it in light shade and finds that it does not spread as widely as common milkweed. Blooming early, around the summer solstice, a good stand of purple milkweed will feed Monarch caterpillars while also providing nectar for numerous butterflies such as swallowtails, skippers, and fritillaries.

Regularly offered for sale at garden centers, common, butterfly, and swamp milkweeds will all thrive in the Kansas City area, as well as throughout most of the Plains States. Common milkweed is the most widespread milkweed species in the midwestern and northeastern United States and the one most routinely used by Monarchs in the east. Showy milkweed and prairie milkweed are two less commonly available milkweeds that are wonderful plants to consider for Monarchs in the Plains region. Both species are similar to common milkweed in appearance but exhibit some differences that gardeners may wish to note: prairie milkweed has larger flowers and does not spread as quickly as common milkweed, and showy milkweed has the largest flowers of the three milkweeds (in fact, it has the largest flowers of any United States milkweed).

With its relatively short stature, vibrant flower color, and copious nectar production, butterfly milkweed is a favorite among gardeners, yet some observations and early studies have suggested that female Monarchs do not prefer this milkweed for egg-laying. If planting for Monarchs is a primary goal, you can still include butterfly milkweed, as it has many virtues, but you would be wise to include other milkweeds in other parts of the garden. Follow the example set by Alan's placement of asters: include many milkweed species and site the plants around the garden based on their cultural requirements.

Common milkweed is loved by butterflies and the flowers are incredibly fragrant, but the plant can spread aggressively.

Indian woodoats seed heads.

A shade-tolerant grass that makes a good ground cover is Indian woodoats. It is not a candidate for a traditional garden border or flowerbed because it aggressively self-seeds, but it can be used as a ground cover in a shaded area. Try using this native grass in a dry location, which tends to curb some of its enthusiasm for spreading.

Alan finds that Indian woodoats is the perfect ground cover to plant underneath his common hackberry trees—it is both attractive and a host plant for Northern Pearly-eye, a butterfly commonly associated with woodland edges, and for a variety of grass-skippers such as Common Roadside-Skipper. Some sources mention other satyrs as using Indian woodoats as a caterpillar food plant, but the reports are not widespread, leaving an opening for "shady" butterfly gardeners to photodocument the true extent to which this beautiful grass feeds caterpillars.

Indian woodoats is a cool-season species that will grow and flower earlier than many other ornamental grasses. The leaves emerge in spring and can be 2 feet tall before summer gets under way. Its decorative seed heads appear in summer, and the dried plant remains a tawny brown throughout winter. Planted under trees such as common hackberry, a ground cover of Indian woodoats left over the winter can provide a safe haven for overwintering caterpillars of Hackberry and Tawny emperors that may fall from the tree.

Common hackberry is a favorite tree that Alan recommends since both Hackberry and Tawny emperors are common in his area. American Snout and Question Mark also use common hackberry in the Midwest. Alan's second-favorite tree is one that most butterfly gardeners agree on—black cherry. In the Kansas City area, this tree provides caterpillar food for Eastern Tiger Swallowtail, Red-spotted Purple, and Coral Hairstreak as well as spring nectar for many other butterflies.

Two additional smaller trees, American plum and fragrant sumac, are also important spring nectar sources in the Midwest. American plum provides caterpillar food for Red-spotted Purple and Coral Hairstreak as well as nectar for early-flying Red Admirals, Question Marks, Eastern Commas, and Juniper Hairstreaks.

Although not considered a "common" garden butterfly, Red-spotted Purple can be found in suburbia, and its caterpillars will eat the leaves of both American plum and black cherry. Coral Hairstreak is even less common but

possible in gardens within its range (butterfly milkweed is one of its favorite nectar plants), and its caterpillars will also use American plum and black cherry leaves—demonstrating that when planting for "common" garden butterflies, other species also benefit, and the likelihood increases that less-common butterflies may appear in your garden. Plant it and they will come!

Fragrant sumac is one of the best nectar plants in the spring, but the flowers are very small so gardeners often overlook it. Its clusters of flowers often open

ABOVE AND LEFT: Fragrant sumac sports spring flowers, beautiful fall foliage, and food for Red-banded Hairstreaks.

at almost exactly the same time Spring Azures emerge, and Alan reports seeing Henry's Elfin nectaring on them. This spring-flying elfin is locally common throughout its flight range in the eastern and southern United States. Its caterpillars feed on a variety of plants, including eastern redbud, blueberries, hollies, and American plum, with different populations specializing on one or a few related host plants. In addition to displaying beautiful fall leaf color, fragrant sumac is also used by the caterpillars of Red-banded Hairstreak, which feed mainly on dead leaves underneath the plant (so don't be a neat freak in your garden!).

At heart, Alan is a plantsman, but his advice to the beginning butterfly gardener in the Midwest is not about plants! He suggests that a butterfly feeder is a great first start to observing butterflies. Alan's simple setup is a hanging birdbath with one alteration—he replaces the chains that come with most of these birdbaths with UV-stabilized nylon cord, which prevents raccoons and opossums from climbing into the feeder. He keeps his butterfly feeder simple by filling it with fruit scraps—peaches, apples, bananas, or even mango—finding that just about any fruit attracts butterflies.

SCIENTIFIC NAME	COMMON NAME	NATIVE RANGE
Annuals		
Asclepias curassavica	Tropical milkweed	Not native to US
Chamaecrista fasciculata	Partridge pea	Eastern and central US
Verbena bonariensis	Purpletop vervain	Not native to US
Zinnia elegans	Zinnia	Not native to US

RECOMMENDED BUTTERFLY PLANTS FOR KANSAS CITY AREA GARDENS

The table on pages 224–9 highlights plants found by NABA members in the Kansas City region to be alluring to butterflies. While suited to butterflies in this region, these plants may also thrive and attract butterflies in other locations.

Gardeners in the Kansas City region may wish to consult the list of recommended butterfly plants for the Eastern Deciduous Forest in chapter 6; many of these plants are suited to the Kansas City region. The list of recommended butterfly plants for the Grasslands in chapter 7 should also be consulted for possible plants.

To determine whether a plant from the list will grow in your area, consult the Native Plant Society or Cooperative Extension Service websites specific to your state. To determine if a butterfly from the list has a range that includes your garden, consult a butterfly field guide or www.webutterfly.org.

FLOWER COLOR, FLOWER SEASON, AND NECTAR SOURCE	USDA HARDINESS ZONE	CATERPILLAR FOOD PLANT FREQUENTED BY GARDEN BUTTERFLIES
Red or yellow flowers provide nectar over a long growing season	Zones 8b–11 perennial, north of Zone 8b grown as annual that often self-seeds, height up to 48 inches	Monarch
Yellow flowers in summer do not provide nectar	Annual plant growing up to 40 inches tall	Cloudless Sulphur, Little Yellow, Gray Hairstreak
Purple flowers produce nectar from midsummer until frost	Annual reaching up to 4 feet tall	Not a caterpillar food plant
Many different flower colors provide nectar from early summer through frost	Annual flower reaching up to 4 feet tall	Not a caterpillar food plant

continued overleaf

Table continued

SCIENTIFIC NAME	COMMON NAME	NATIVE RANGE
Perennials and Vines		
Aristolochia tomentosa	Woolly Dutchman's pipe	Eastern and south-central US
Asclepias purpurascens	Purple milkweed	Eastern and central US excluding Florida, Alabama, and South Carolina
Asclepias speciosa	Showy milkweed	Midwest and western states
Asclepias sullivantii	Prairie milkweed	Central US
Asclepias syriaca	Common milkweed	Most of eastern US and Oregon
Asclepias tuberosa	Butterfly milkweed	Throughout US except northwestern states
Conoclinium coelestinum	Blue mistflower	Eastern and lower midwestern states
Echinacea pallida	Pale purple coneflower	Nebraska to Texas and east, with a number of gaps
Ruta graveolens	Common rue	Not native to US
Symphyotrichum cordifolium	Common blue wood aster	Eastern and central US
Symphyotrichum novae-angliae	New England aster	Most of the US
Symphyotrichum oblongifolium	Aromatic aster	Northeast and central US

PLANTS FOR KANSAS CITY AREA GARDENS

	FLOWER COLOR, FLOWER SEASON, AND NECTAR SOURCE	USDA HARDINESS ZONE	CATERPILLAR FOOD PLANT FREQUENTED BY GARDEN BUTTERFLIES
	Greenish-yellow flowers do not provide nectar	Zones 5–8 vine growing up to 30 feet tall	Pipevine Swallowtail
	Purple-pink flowers provide nectar in summer	Zones 3–8 perennial reaching 3 feet	Monarch
	Pinkish-purple flowers provide weeks of nectar in early summer	Zones 3–9 perennial reaching 4 feet tall	Monarch
	Pink flowers produce nectar in summer	Zones 3–7 perennial growing 3 feet	Monarch
	Mauve flowers in summer provide nectar	Zones 3–7 perennial growing 3 feet tall	Monarch
	Bright orange flowers from early to midsummer are a favorite nectar source	Zones 3–9 perennial reaching 18 inches tall	Monarch
	Purple flowers from late summer through fall provide nectar	Zones 5–10 perennial reaching 3 feet tall	Not a caterpillar food plant
	Pale pink drooping flowers provide nectar	Zones 3–8 perennial growing 3 feet tall	Not a caterpillar food plant
	Pale yellow flowers in summer are not visited by butterflies	Zones 4–8 perennial growing to 3 feet tall	Black Swallowtail, Giant Swallowtail
	Flowers in shades of blue provide nectar in the fall	Zones 3–8 perennial reaching 5 feet	Not a caterpillar food plant
	Purple flowers in the fall provide nectar	Zones 4–8 perennial growing 6 feet tall	Pearl and Northern crescents
	Blue-purple flowers in late summer through fall provide nectar	Zones 3–8 perennial growing to 3 feet tall	Not a caterpillar food plant

continued overleaf

Table continued

SCIENTIFIC NAME	COMMON NAME	NATIVE RANGE
Grasses		
Chasmanthium latifolium	Indian woodoats	Eastern US
Panicum virgatum	Switchgrass	Most of the US excluding far western states
Schizachyrium scoparium	Little bluestem	Most of the US
Shrubs and Trees		
Asimina triloba	Pawpaw	Eastern US
Celtis occidentalis	Common hackberry	Eastward from Montana, Utah, and New Mexico
Cercis canadensis	Eastern redbud	Lower Great Plains and eastern US
Prunus americana	American plum	Eastern and central US
Prunus serotina	Black cherry	Eastern half of US, Washington State, Arizona, and New Mexico
Rhus aromatica	Fragrant Sumac	Eastern and central US
Sassafras albidum	Sassafras	Eastward from Texas, Kansas, Iowa, and Wisconsin

PLANTS FOR KANSAS CITY AREA GARDENS

FLOWER COLOR, FLOWER SEASON, AND NECTAR SOURCE	USDA HARDINESS ZONE	CATERPILLAR FOOD PLANT FREQUENTED BY GARDEN BUTTERFLIES
Not a nectar plant, flowers insignificant	Zones 3–8 grass growing to 5 feet tall	Northern Pearly-eye, grass-skippers
Not a nectar plant, flowers insignificant	Zones 5–9 perennial grass growing 6 feet tall	Grass-skippers
Not a nectar plant, flowers insignificant	Zones 3–9 grass reaching 4 feet tall	A number of skippers use little bluestem as a caterpillar food but most are not regular garden visitors
Purple flowers in spring do not provide nectar	Zones 5–9 tree growing to 30 feet tall	Zebra Swallowtail
Insignificant flowers, not a nectar source	Zones 2–9 tree reaching 60 feet tall	Hackberry Emperor, Tawny Emperor, American Snout, Mourning Cloak, Question Mark
Pink flowers in early spring offer nectar	Zones 4–8 tree reaching 30 feet tall	Henry's Elfin (not a common garden butterfly but is possible in certain areas)
White flowers in early spring provide volumes of nectar	Zones 3–8 tree growing to 25 feet tall	Red-spotted Purple, Coral Hairstreak
Lots of white flowers in spring provide nectar	Zones 3–9 tree reaching 60 feet tall	Eastern Tiger Swallowtail, Red-spotted Purple, Coral Hairstreak
Yellow flowers attract butterflies with early season nectar	Zones 3–9 shrub growing 2–6 feet tall	Red-banded Hairstreak
Yellow flowers in spring are not known to be visited by butterflies	Zones 4–9 tree growing 60 feet tall	Spicebush Swallowtail, Eastern Tiger Swallowtail

CHAPTER NINE

YEAR-ROUND BUTTERFLY GARDENING

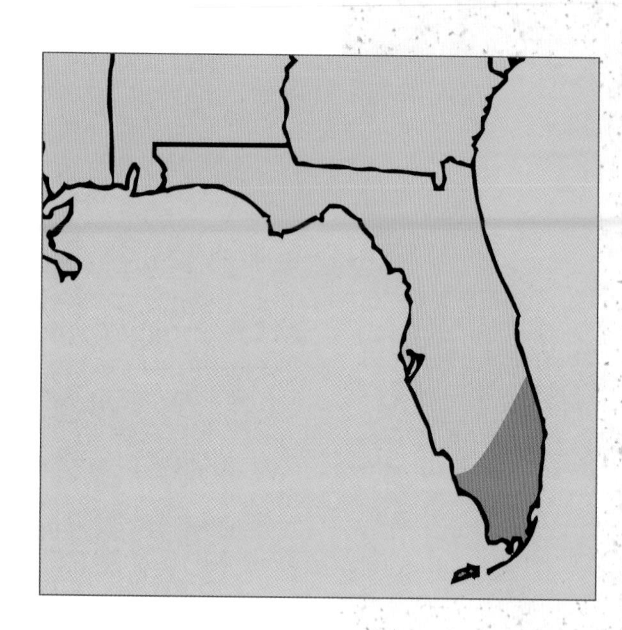

The northern portion of Florida is covered by the Subtropical Evergreen Region of the Eastern Deciduous Forest while the southern tip of the state is characterized by flooded grasslands and enjoys a subtropical climate.

NABA has recorded approximately 186 butterfly species in Florida. While Texas boasts the largest state list of butterfly species with 459, Florida is unique in the butterfly gardening world. In addition to the high number of species, many of which fly year-round, Florida has the third-largest human population in the United States and a climate conducive to nearly year-round gardening in many areas, encouraging a large fellowship of butterfly gardeners to flourish. It is no surprise that Florida's five NABA chapters are the largest number of any state.

Florida is a mosaic of habitats, each with different plant communities that support butterflies. Many of these varied lands are under constant threat by the push of development to support the state's burgeoning population. Given the resulting important and urgent large-scale butterfly conservation needs, home and public gardens can help by promoting native plantings—these will provide respite both for butterflies and for many other creatures displaced by development. Luckily for Florida gardeners, a large number of beautiful native plants are available that support butterflies.

Most of Florida's land falls in the southernmost portion of the Eastern Deciduous Forest, where the vegetation is further classified as Subtropical Evergreen. South of about Jupiter on Florida's east coast and Fort Myers on the west coast, the native vegetation cover becomes dominated by swamps and flooded savannas and the climate is considered tropical. To suggest butterfly-friendly plants for a gardening oasis like Florida with its enormous range of habitats is beyond the scope of this book, but with the help of NABA chapters across the state, local information abounds. The plants highlighted in this Florida garden guide represent the variety of plants that are widely grown in the state and that support the most common garden butterflies.

BUTTERFLIES IN A PUBLIC GARDEN

Visiting established butterfly gardens, whether on a private tour or at a public garden, is one of the best ways for gardeners of all experience levels to increase

OPPORTUNITY

IN FLORIDA

White Peacock is a common, year-round butterfly in south Florida gardens but is uncommon in northern parts of the state.

BELOW: Wide, flat paths allow everyone to enjoy the LaBrie Butterfly Garden.

their knowledge of local butterflies and the plants they use. In 1995 the NABA Sarasota County Butterfly Club embraced the educational opportunity offered by public gardens by establishing the Catherine & Richard LaBrie Butterfly Garden on the grounds of the Sarasota Garden Club. Named after a former club president and her husband who are both still active in the chapter, the garden measures 20 × 150 feet and makes it easy for visitors to view butterflies and their caterpillars year-round.

Brazilian Dutchman's pipevine engulfs the garden's arbor, where Polydamas Swallowtail caterpillars feed.

The garden plantings, which are maintained by club volunteers, include corkystem and purple passionflowers, tropical and butterfly milkweeds, herb of grace, sennas, blue porterweed, zinnias, and Brazilian Dutchman's pipevine. Chapter volunteers meet each Friday morning to tend the garden, but when they are not present, interested garden visitors can get in touch and learn more about butterflies thanks to club brochures provided in a mailbox stationed along the main path.

Members' enthusiasm for sharing their love of butterfly gardening, combined with a climate that promotes luxuriant plant growth, makes this chapter's garden a "must see" location. To encourage butterfly watchers to linger in the garden, the club has installed 7 benches, making the garden a "must sit" location as well.

The gardeners consider their inputs carefully—forgoing pesticides, watering with reclaimed water, mulching plant beds to conserve water, and sourcing native plants from growers who have not treated the plants with pesticides. The result is a garden that brings a small taste of the natural world to a city park.

BUTTERFLIES IN A SMALL GARDEN

When Nancy Soucy moved to Florida, she knew she wanted to continue to grow flowers as she had for many years at her Connecticut home, but it took some experimentation before she achieved her goal. Her first attempts were unsuccessful—most of her plant choices did not survive, and Florida's gardening conditions challenged her Zone 6 knowledge. She took some time to read about gardening in Florida, added plants she had never grown before, and—after a few years of trial and error—began to notice that the plants that grew most reliably in her sandy soil were Florida natives. At the same time, she began to notice and appreciate the wide variety of wildlife attracted to her plantings. Through this combination of gardening experimentation and observation, a butterfly gardener was born!

Nancy Soucy's property is not large—her lot is 50 × 80 feet, which includes the area occupied by her home—but she has attracted 31 butterfly species by carefully selecting the plants she grows. Living in central coastal Florida in Plant Hardiness Zone 10a, where the minimum winter temperatures range between 30° and 35°F, Nancy has found that experimentation is the key to success. Her culling system is rigorous—if a plant does not grow vigorously or attract the expected butterflies, then another plant takes its place. But if a plant attracts butterflies that create a new generation in the garden, Nancy enthusiastically adds more of that plant. Keeping a list of butterflies seen in her garden is one way Nancy keeps track of how well her plantings are attracting visitors. Butterflies are active throughout the year in central coastal Florida, so rather than count any butterfly that she sees "in" the garden, Nancy records only butterflies that she sees "on" the garden—in other words, to make Nancy's garden list, the butterfly must stop and alight on a plant.

Her most common garden butterflies are a handful of species regularly found in central and south Florida gardens: Monarch, Gulf Fritillary, Polydamas Swallowtail, Orange-barred Sulphur, Long-tailed Skipper, Ceraunus and Cassius blues, and Zebra Heliconian. Two of her "must have" butterfly garden plants are climbing vines that serve as caterpillar food for three of these: Dutchman's pipe for Polydamas Swallowtail and passionflower for Zebra Heliconian and Gulf Fritillary. Using vertical trellises allows her to grow a lot of caterpillar food in a small space.

Nancy grows a nonnative Dutchman's pipe for Polydamas Swallowtails, which are very common in her area. The vine she has chosen is attractive for its large, showy, maroon flowers, but she notes that this species of Dutchman's pipe is toxic to Pipevine Swallowtails—they may lay eggs on the plant but the resulting caterpillars will not survive. In her small garden, she enjoys the drama that the large-flowered nonnative Dutchman's pipe brings, and she does not live in an area where Pipevine Swallowtails are common. Her choice of a nonnative caterpillar food plant reflects an understanding of the size constraints of her garden (she has room for only one Dutchman's pipe plant), the relative abundance of Polydamas Swallowtails over Pipevine Swallowtails (through her observations Nancy knows that Pipevine Swallowtails are rare visitors to her garden), and a garden aesthetic that pleases her (she appreciates the visual excitement created by the large marbled maroon-and-white nonnative Dutchman's pipe flowers.)

In general, Pipevine Swallowtails are more common in northern Florida gardens while Polydamas Swallowtails are more common in the south. Of course, in some areas both species are likely garden visitors, which leaves butterfly gardeners facing a dilemma—do they want to include a pipevine species that Pipevine Swallowtails will not survive on? Two common native Dutchman's pipes that support the caterpillars of both swallowtails are not well suited to widespread use in Florida but may work in some situations. Woolly Dutchman's pipevine will feed both swallowtail species but grows best in the colder regions of Florida. Once established, woolly Dutchman's pipevine is a vigorous plant,

YEAR-ROUND OPPORTUNITY

IN MOST OF THE UNITED STATES, planting for Pipevine Swallowtail is straightforward; if your garden is within the flight range of this species, determine which native pipevine species is common in your location, find a strong trellis or structure for support if planting one of the vigorous Dutchman's pipes, plant the vine, and wait. Sometimes Pipevine Swallowtails will come to a garden quite quickly after it is planted, although many gardeners wait years before they spot one; the occurrence of Pipevine Swallowtail throughout its range is localized, yet most butterfly gardeners feel this is a species worth planting for. Aside from the beauty of the butterfly, the large caterpillars are voracious eaters that are fun to watch. In fact, an immature Dutchman's pipe plant may very well be too small to sustain the caterpillars, so that neither the plant nor the caterpillars will survive! When faced with dwindling caterpillar food, many butterfly gardeners reach out to their circle of contacts (such as NABA chapters or Facebook groups) to request additional Dutchman's pipe leaves or to "rehome" eggs and young caterpillars to other gardens.

but many gardeners (across the United States as well as in Florida) report that getting the plant established and growing vigorously can be difficult. Virginia snakeroot is another native Dutchman's pipe species and found in wilder woodland areas of Florida, but in a garden setting it is slow to grow, does not produce a lot of caterpillar food per plant, and it is not commercially available. Both plants, however, are worth experimenting with in areas where both Pipevine and Polydamas swallowtails are common.

Non-native Dutchman's pipe are widely sold in Florida but not all of them will support both Pipevine and Polydamas swallowtails. Elegant Dutchman's pipe, also known as calico flower, is widely sold and is relished by Polydamas Swallowtail but is toxic to Pipevine Swallowtail caterpillars. Also, it is listed as a Category II invasive exotic by the Florida Exotic Pest Plant Council, meaning that it has the potential to adversely affect Florida plant communities. Many nonnative Dutchman's pipe are sold across the United States, as the large-flowered ornamental vines make striking garden features, but butterfly gardeners should be aware that Pipevine Swallowtail caterpillars cannot survive on them.

Other commonly sold nonnative Dutchman's pipe that will support Polydamas Swallowtail but not Pipevine Swallowtail are pelicanflower and Brazilian Dutchman's pipe. For gardeners who wish to attract and feed both Pipevine and Polydamas swallowtails, two nonnative Dutchman's pipe species to try are bejuco de Santiago, also known as vine of St. James, and white-veined hardy Dutchman's pipe.

Nancy's first choice among passionflowers is the native corkystem passionflower, native in Florida and Texas. Purple passionflower is another good choice and has a larger native range that spans much of the eastern and central United States. Both grow well in her location, flower profusely, and serve as caterpillar food for Gulf Fritillaries and Zebra Heliconians. As a rule of thumb, Zebra Heliconians lay eggs on passionflowers grown in the shade, while Gulf Fritillaries lay their eggs on plants in the sun, so plant at least two.

Polydamas Swallowtail laying eggs in Nancy Soucy's garden.

Pipevine Swallowtail laying eggs.

Practically every list of Florida butterfly garden plants includes scarletbush, also sometimes called firebush, a nectar plant that tops Nancy's list as well. It is a large shrub that flowers throughout the year and attracts butterflies in droves, making it a must-have even in a small garden. It can be grown in USDA Zones 11, 10, and the warmer portions of 9. Reddish-orange flowers and slightly hairy leaves characterize the native species. Mexican firebush, which has yellow, orange-based flowers and smooth leaves, will attract butterflies and is sold in Florida nurseries, but it is a nonnative species that can hybridize with wild scarletbush, causing concern for native stands. A third species, Bahama firebush, has yellow, bell-shaped flowers but is not attractive to butterflies. Seek out the native scarletbush!

Cape leadwort, also known as blue plumbago, is another shrub that fits in Nancy's small garden. Bright blue flowers provide nectar throughout the year and Cassius Blue caterpillars feed on the foliage. Other species of plumbago, such as the red-blooming whorled plantain, are also valuable in Florida butterfly gardens and feed Cassius Blue as well. Filling small spaces in Nancy's

	CHAPMAN'S SENNA	PARTRIDGE PEA
Plant Type	Evergreen shrub	Annual
Flower color and flower season	Yellow, year-round flowers with heaviest flowering in fall and winter months.	Yellow, summer through fall
Nectar plant	Yes, nectar for butterflies.	Floral nectar is not present but nectar is produced outside of flowers in extrafloral nectaries (small glands at the base of each leaf). Ants seek nectar from these plants but butterflies rarely do.
Caterpillar food plant for Florida butterflies	Orange-barred Sulphur, Cloudless Sulphur, Sleepy Orange	Cloudless Sulphur, Sleepy Orange, Little Yellow, Ceraunus Blue, and Gray Hairstreak.
Garden use	Specimen shrub, part of a border, or can be planted in masses	Used for erosion control and improving soil fertility. Fits well in large borders and naturalized settings.
USDA Hardiness Zones	10,11	Annual that can reseed

At night, Zebra Heliconians roost together. They return to the same roost night after night, which provides safety from predators.

garden are herbaceous nectar plants including spotted beebalm, beach sunflower, and sweet alyssum.

Two genera of plants in the Pea Family, *Cassia* (senna spp.) and *Chamaecrista* (sensitive pea spp.), are important caterpillar food plants for sulphurs and gossamer-wing butterflies in Florida, as well as across the United States. Nancy prefers Chapman's senna in her garden, which grows well in Hardiness Zones 10 and 11 and feeds Orange-barred Sulphurs, which are frequent garden visitors, as well as the Cloudless Sulphurs and Sleepy Oranges that occasionally stop by. Gardeners across the United States have a number of available choices with sennas and sensitive peas—so plant selection should be based on what butterflies are common in the area as well as on the space available in the garden. Both Chapman's senna and partridge pea will grow in central coastal Florida and feed the caterpillars of common garden butterflies, but each plant will fill a different niche in the garden.

RECOMMENDED BUTTERFLY PLANTS FOR FLORIDA GARDENS

The table on pages 238–43 highlights plants found by NABA members in Florida to be alluring to butterflies. While suited to butterflies in this region, these plants may also thrive and attract butterflies in other locations.

Florida gardeners may wish to contact a NABA chapter for suggestions on which plants are loved by butterflies on a local level.

To determine whether a plant from the list will grow in your area, consult the Native Plant Society or Cooperative Extension Service websites specific to your state. To determine if a butterfly from the list has a range that includes your garden, consult a butterfly field guide or www.webutterfly.org.

SCIENTIFIC NAME	COMMON NAME	NATIVE RANGE
Annuals		
Chamaecrista fasciculata	Partridge pea	Eastern and central US
Gaillardia pulchella	Firewheel	Much of the US
Lobularia maritima	Sweet alyssum	Not native to US
Petroselinum crispum	Parsley	Not native to US
Tithonia rotundifolia	Clavel de muerto or Mexican sunflower	Not native to US
Zinnia elegans	Zinnia	Not native to US
Perennials		
Asclepias curassavica	Tropical milkweed	Not native to US
Asclepias tuberosa	Butterfly milkweed	Throughout US except northwestern states
Bacopa monnieri	Herb of grace, also known as water hyssop	Southern tier of US including California and East Coast as far north as Delaware

FLOWER COLOR, FLOWER SEASON, AND NECTAR SOURCE	USDA HARDINESS ZONE	CATERPILLAR FOOD PLANT FREQUENTED BY GARDEN BUTTERFLIES
Yellow flowers in summer do not provide nectar	Annual growing up to 40 inches tall	Cloudless Sulphur, Orange Sulphur, Little Yellow, Gray Hairstreak, Ceraunus Blue
Yellow-orange-red flowers produce a lot of nectar from spring through summer	Annual that may reseed	Not a caterpillar food plant
Many different flower colors provide nectar from early summer through frost	Annual flower with sprawling growth habit reaching 12–14 inches tall	Not a caterpillar food plant
Yellow flowers in second year from planting	Zones 3–9 biennial reaching 18 inches tall; dill and fennel are also used to feed Black Swallowtail caterpillars	Black Swallowtail
Orange flowers provide profuse amounts of nectar from late summer until frost	Annual reaching up to 6 feet tall but can become larger in Florida's long growing season	Not a caterpillar food plant
Many different flower colors provide nectar from early summer through frost	Annual flower reaching up to 4 feet tall	Not a caterpillar food plant
Red or yellow flowers provide nectar over a long growing season	Zones 8b–11 perennial; north of Zone 8b grown as annual that often self-seeds, height up to 48 inches	Monarch, Queen, Soldier
Bright orange flowers from early to midsummer are a favorite nectar source	Zones 3–9 perennial reaching 18 inches tall, grows best in northern Florida	Monarch, Queen, Soldier
Small white flowers provide nectar from spring through fall, flowering all year in Florida	Zones 8b–11 perennial ground cover reaching up to 6 inches tall	White Peacock

continued overleaf

Table continued

SCIENTIFIC NAME	COMMON NAME	NATIVE RANGE
Perennials *continued*		
Clitoria ternatea	Asian pigeonwings, also known as butterfly pea	Not native to US
Helianthus debilis	Cucumberleaf sunflower, also called beach sunflower	Southeast and Gulf Coast states
Monarda punctata	Spotted beebalm	Eastern and central US and California
Pentas lanceolata	Egyptian starcluster, or better known as pentas	Not native to US
Phyla nodiflora	Turkey tangle fogfruit	Lower half of US
Senna mexicana var. *chapmanii*	Chapman's senna	South Florida
Shrubs and Trees		
Duranta erecta	Golden dewdrops	Florida, Louisiana, Texas, Arizona, California
Hamelia patens var. *patens*	Scarletbush, also known as firebush	Florida
Plumbago auriculata	Cape leadwort, also known as blue plumbago	Not native to US

FLOWER COLOR, FLOWER SEASON, AND NECTAR SOURCE	USDA HARDINESS ZONE	CATERPILLAR FOOD PLANT FREQUENTED BY GARDEN BUTTERFLIES
Deep blue flowers	Zones 11–12 perennial vine, may be grown as an annual in colder zones	Long-tailed Skipper
Yellow flowers produce nectar from spring into late fall or early winter	Perennial in frost-free zones 8b–11 and self-seeding annual in areas that freeze; grows 18–24 inches, spreading as a ground cover	Not a caterpillar food plant
Yellow or purple flowers with purple spots provide nectar in late spring through summer	Zones 3–8 perennial reaching 2 feet tall	Not a caterpillar food plant
Red, pink, lavender, or white flowers produce large amounts of nectar throughout the growing season	Zones 8–11 perennial but may be treated as annual in areas that experience frost	Not a caterpillar food plant
White flowers appear all year in warmer locations and provide nectar for a wide number of butterflies	Zones 6–11 perennial ground cover growing 3–6 inches tall	Common Buckeye, White Peacock, Phaon Crescent
Yellow flowers produce nectar year round	Zones 10–11 shrub reaching 4 feet tall, a south Florida favorite	Orange-barred Sulphur, Cloudless Sulphur, Sleepy Orange
Bluish-purple flowers provide nectar over the entire year	Zones 9b and higher shrub or small tree up to 18 feet	Not a caterpillar food plant
Red flowers are a nectar favorite for butterflies, blooming spring through fall in Zone 9 and nearly year-round in Zones 10 and 11	Zones 9a–11 shrub growing to 12 feet tall, not hardy in northern Florida	Not a caterpillar food plant
Rich blue flowers provide nectar throughout most of the year	Zones 9–11 small shrub growing to 4 feet. May grow in central Florida but will be affected by freezing weather	Cassius Blue

continued overleaf

Table continued

SCIENTIFIC NAME	COMMON NAME	NATIVE RANGE
Shrubs and Trees *continued*		
Plumbago indica	Whorled plantain	Not native to US
Stachytarpheta jamaicensis	Light-blue snakeweed, also known as blue porterweed	Native to south Florida
Asimina triloba	Pawpaw	Eastern US
Celtis occidentalis	Common hackberry	Eastward from Montana, Utah, and New Mexico
Magnolia virginiana	Sweetbay	Eastern US
Vines		
Aristolochia fimbriata	White-veined hardy Dutchman's pipe	Not native to US
Aristolochia gigantea	Brazilian Dutchman's pipe	Not native to US
Aristolochia tomentosa	Woolly Dutchman's pipe	Eastern and south-central US
Aristolochia triloba	Vine of St. James (bejuco de Santiago)	Not native to US
Passiflora incarnata	Purple passionflower	Eastern US
Passiflora suberosa	Corkystem passionflower	Florida and Lower Rio Grande Valley, Texas

	FLOWER COLOR, FLOWER SEASON, AND NECTAR SOURCE	USDA HARDINESS ZONE	CATERPILLAR FOOD PLANT FREQUENTED BY GARDEN BUTTERFLIES
	Scarlet flowers provide nectar in fall through spring	Zones 8a–11 spreading shrub grows to 7 feet	Cassius Blue
	Blue flowers provide nectar all year although fewer flowers in winter	Zones 9a–11 subshrub ground cover growing to 1 foot tall	Tropical Buckeye
	Purple flowers in spring do not provide nectar	Zones 5–9 tree growing to 30 feet tall, *A. triloba* for northern Florida or *A. parviflora* for south Florida	Zebra Swallowtail
	Insignificant flowers, not a nectar source	Zones 2–9 tree reaching 60 feet tall, best suited to northern Florida	Hackberry Emperor, Tawny Emperor, American Snout, Question Mark
	Showy white flowers do not provide nectar	Zones 5–10 tree growing to 35 feet tall	Eastern Tiger Swallowtail, Spicebush Swallowtail
	Yellow-green, pipe-shaped flowers with burgundy rim do not provide nectar	Zones 7a–9b	Pipevine Swallowtail, Polydamas Swallowtail
	Large maroon flowers do not provide nectar	Zones 10–12 vine growing to 20 feet with support	Polydamas Swallowtail
	Greenish-yellow flowers do not provide nectar	Zones 5–8 vine growing up to 30 feet tall	Pipevine Swallowtail, Polydamas Swallowtail
	Pale green, pipe- shaped flowers with burgundy rim are not a nectar source.	Zones 10a–11 vine growing to 30 feet, not hardy in northern Florida	Pipevine Swallowtail, Polydamas Swallowtail
	Purple flowers provide some nectar	Zones 5–9 vine reaching 8 feet tall	Gulf Fritillary, Zebra Heliconian, Variegated Fritillary
	Greenish-yellow flowers provide some nectar	Root hardy to Zone 8	Gulf Fritillary, Zebra Heliconian, Variegated Fritillary

CHAPTER
TEN

WATER-SAVING

THE WESTERN STATES

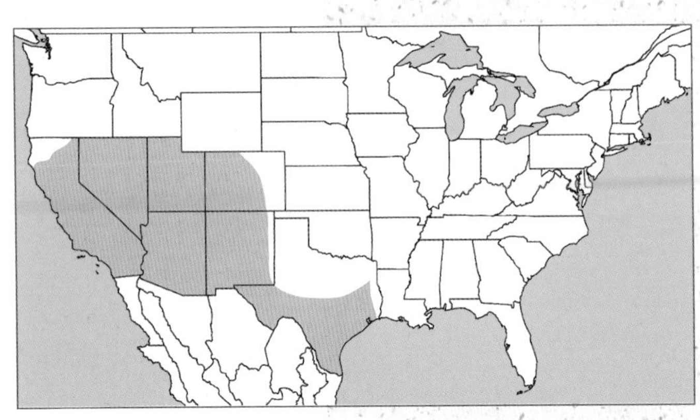
The western states.

BUTTERFLIES NEAR LOS ANGELES

Saving natural resources can be accomplished through many small steps. What better way to encourage the first steps and increase awareness for water conservation than to offer financial incentives? In the arid western states, many municipalities offer cash rebates to residents who remove water-guzzling grass lawns and install water-efficient landscaping in its place. One NABA member saw this offer as more than a cash rebate—he saw an opportunity to increase butterfly habitat.

Water-conservation programs do not cover the entire cost of re-landscaping a residential property, but Chris Leslie of Ventura, California, used the program as it was intended, as an incentive to do more to conserve water in the region. His new, lawn-free landscape is a mixture of California native plants that are adapted to low water conditions, plants native to nearby Mexico, and some nonnative plants. Weeds are also included in Chris's planting scheme, with common dandelion (for nectar), common mallow (for West Coast Lady caterpillars), and fennel (for Anise Swallowtail caterpillars).

Gardeners across much of the United States intentionally plant fennel for Anise or Black Swallowtail caterpillars (depending on location), yet across much of southern and coastal California, fennel is a problematic perennial weed that

Chris Leslie's lawnless landscape is alive with color and life.

BUTTERFLY GARDENS

outcompetes native plants for nutrients, light, and water. Once established in wild areas, fennel can be difficult to eradicate, but Chris finds that in a suburban yard, fennel does not pose a problem. It does produce large amounts of easily dispersed seeds over a long growing season, so that curbing its potential invasiveness requires constant vigilance. In a home garden, deadheading flowers after they bloom but before seed is set is the best way to prevent the plant from spreading. In Chris's garden, fennel supports Anise Swallowtail caterpillars. If deadheading fennel is not possible, a large swath of parsley or dill is easy to grow and will also feed Anise Swallowtails.

Common mallow is another widespread weed, in arid western states as well as in most other parts of the United States. Where soil has been disturbed and exposed, common mallow is an opportunistic weed and it can invade lawns (if you have a lawn!). Many common garden butterflies will lay eggs on common mallow including West Coast Lady, Common Checkered-Skipper, Gray Hairstreak, and Painted Lady, all of which are on the list of butterflies that have visited Chris's yard. If the weedy nature of common mallow does not appeal, consider other plants in the Mallow Family that can thrive in a low-water garden, such as desert mallow and checkerblooms, both favored by West Coast Lady and Common Checkered-Skipper caterpillars.

To create a meadowlike feel throughout the lawnless landscape behind his house, Chris has planted a mixture of nectar-producing annuals and perennials that have sprawling habits and grow 1–2 feet tall. Exserted Indian paintbrush (a caterpillar food plant for Variable Checkerspot) with deep rose-purple flowers, baby blue eyes with sky-blue flowers, and fivespot with blue-tipped white flowers are just a few of the California wildflowers that bloom on his property after the spring rains.

Shrubs of all sizes play an important role in the front of Chris's house, giving the landscape structure, providing color

Nick Dean's design for a California home shows that a strip of land between driveway and sidewalk can flourish with native plants for bees and butterflies. Bright orange California poppies provide only pollen, no nectar for butterflies, but are a vibrant addition to any wildflower mixture. Lilac verbena, bush monkeyflowers, and elegant clarkia add nectar and brilliant color, while the red flowers on a bottlebrush tree call all pollinators to attention.

throughout the year, and feeding butterflies and caterpillars. Removing the lawn left plenty of room for shrubby plants, so Chris often groups more than one of a species into blocks of nectar and caterpillar food that are easy for butterflies to find. The following are just some of the butterfly-supporting shrubs that Chris has success with—all have low water requirements, flower profusely, and some feed caterpillars in addition to providing nectar.

- **Buckwheats** provide nectar as well as caterpillar food. The primary genus of butterfly caterpillars that feed on buckwheats, *Euphilotes*, are often referred to as buckwheat blues. Within many of these species, individual populations are localized, exhibiting specific flight times and particular buckwheat choices, making it difficult to predict whether a garden planting of buckwheat will support the caterpillars of your local blues. Buckwheats, however, are worth including in a butterfly garden for the structure they provide to plant groupings, the color and nectar their flowers provide, and their low water requirements. Acmon Blue, although not in the genus of buckwheat blues, is a common garden butterfly that will feed on buckwheats.
  - **Redflower buckwheat** is a short shrub, growing around 2 feet tall with reddish-pink flowers from June to October.
  - **Sulphur-flower buckwheat** is a low-growing shrub, or in some locations can be treated as an herbaceous perennial; it produces yellow flowers from spring to early summer.
  - **Seacliff buckwheat** is another short shrub that fills in where the lawn is gone. White flowers rise above its sprawling foliage.
  - **Eastern Mojave buckwheat** grows to 3 feet tall, with white flowers that bloom from spring through fall.
- **Christmasbush**, also called Christmas senna, provides yellow flowers in fall and early winter as well as caterpillar food for Cloudless Sulphur (which Chris has seen in his garden) as well as the less common Sleepy Orange (which he is still waiting for).
- **False indigo bush** (feeds Southern Dogface and Gray Hairstreak caterpillars) and California false indigo (feeds California Dogface caterpillars) provide fragrant purple flowers in spring and summer.
- **Ceanothus** are wonderful shrubs for dry western gardens. Depending on the species planted, they provide nectar in the spring and early summer from blue flowers. Two eastern species, New Jersey tea and Jersey tea, produce white flowers in spring. Both are good butterfly garden plants, although not terribly common in the nursery trade, but they are not

recommended for western gardens. The variety of choices for arid West gardens is vast—in addition to many straight species, a number of hybrids and cultivars are available—so it's no problem to forgo the two eastern species. Hedgerow Hairstreak and Pale Swallowtail lay eggs on ceanothus—consult a butterfly field guide to determine if your location is within their ranges. California Tortoiseshell is rare to uncommon within its range but in some years experiences a huge population irruption and migration. Since ceanothus is the caterpillar food for California Tortoiseshell, in boom years it might attract one of these beauties to your garden.

- **Blue plumbago** has rich blue flowers that bloom intermittently throughout the year. Marine Blue caterpillars eat the flowers and seedpods.
- **Orange bush monkeyflower** has orange flowers spring through fall; Variable Checkerspot and Common Buckeye use this plant as caterpillar food.
- **Lantana** is also planted throughout Chris's front yard and is a beloved nectar plant.

OPPOSITE: Seaside buckwheat is a gardenworthy plant that is commercially available.

RECOMMENDED BUTTERFLY PLANTS FOR CALIFORNIA GARDENS

The table on pages 248–53 highlights plants found by NABA members in California to be attractive to butterflies. While specifically suited to butterflies in this region, these plants may also thrive and attract butterflies in other locations.

California gardeners who live in the northern portion of the state may wish to also consult the list of recommended butterfly plants for gardens in the Pacific Northwest in chapter 5, and all California gardeners may benefit from perusing the water-saving plants suggested later in this chapter where Arizona gardens are highlighted.

To determine whether a plant from the list will grow in your area, consult the Native Plant Society or Cooperative Extension Service websites specific to your state. To determine if a butterfly from the list has a range that includes your garden, consult a butterfly field guide or www.webutterfly.org.

Ceanothus 'Ray Hartman' is commonly found for sale in California. This hybrid ceanothus grows as a large shrub or small tree and is tolerant of a wide variety of growing conditions.

SCIENTIFIC NAME	COMMON NAME	NATIVE RANGE
Annuals		
Castilleja exserta	Exserted Indian paintbrush, also known as purple owl's clover	California, Arizona, New Mexico
Clarkia amoena	Farewell to spring	California, Oregon, Washington, New York
Clarkia unguiculata	Elegant clarkia	California
Lupinus succulentus	Hollowleaf annual lupine, also known as arroyo lupine	California, Arizona
Nemophila maculata	Fivespot	California, Oregon, Utah
Nemophila menziesi	Baby blue eyes	California, Oregon, Nevada, Wyoming
Petroselinum crispum	Parsley	Not native to US
Phacelia tanacetifolia	Lacy phacelia	California Oregon, Nevada, Colorado, Kansas, New Mexico, Maine, Michigan, Pennsylvania
Perennials and Vines		
Aristolochia californica	California Dutchman's pipe	California
Asclepias curassavica	Tropical milkweed	Not native to US

PLANTS FOR CALIFORNIA GARDENS

FLOWER COLOR, FLOWER SEASON, AND NECTAR SOURCE	USDA HARDINESS ZONE	CATERPILLAR FOOD PLANT FREQUENTED BY GARDEN BUTTERFLIES
Rose-purple flowers provide nectar in spring	Annual growing 1 foot tall	Not a caterpillar food plant
Pinkish-red-purple flowers provide nectar in summer	Annual flower growing 2 feet	Not a caterpillar food plant
Rose-lavender flowers provide nectar in spring	Annual flower growing 2 feet	Not a caterpillar food plant
Blue flowers bloom in spring to summer and are not a butterfly nectar source	Annual growing 24–48 inches tall	Silvery Blue, Orange Sulphur, Acmon Blue
Blue-tipped white flowers produce nectar in spring to early summer	Annual growing 1 foot tall	Not a caterpillar food plant
Blue flowers produce nectar throughout spring	Annual growing 1 foot tall	Not a caterpillar food plant
Yellow flowers in second year from planting	Annual or Zones 3–9 biennial reaching 18 inches tall	Black Swallowtail, Anise Swallowtail
Blue flowers with white dots provide nectar	Annual flower 12–24 inches tall	Not a caterpillar food plant
Yellowish-purple flowers are not a nectar source	Zones 8–10 vine growing to 4 feet	Pipevine Swallowtail
Red or yellow flowers provide nectar over a long growing season	Zones 8b–11 perennial, north of Zone 8b grown as annual that often self-seeds, height up to 48 inches	Monarch

continued overleaf

Table continued

SCIENTIFIC NAME	COMMON NAME	NATIVE RANGE
Perennials and Vines *continued*		
Asclepias linaria	Pineneedle milkweed	California, Arizona, New Mexico
Asclepias speciosa	Showy milkweed	Midwest and western states
Corethrogyne filaginifolia	California sandaster	California, Oregon
Echinacea purpurea	Eastern purple coneflower	Eastward from Iowa in the north, Colorado in the west, and Texas in the south
Lantana camara	Lantana	Not native to US
Nepeta spp.	Catmint	Not native to US
Sidalcea malviflora	Dwarf checkerbloom	California, Oregon, Washington
Sphaeralcea ambigua	Desert globemallow	California, Nevada, Arizona, Utah
Symphyotrichum chilense	Pacific aster	California, Oregon, Washington
Shrubs and Trees		
Amorpha californica	California false indigo	California, Arizona
Amorpha fruticosa	False indigo bush	Most of the US but is listed as invasive in many locations

PLANTS FOR CALIFORNIA GARDENS

	FLOWER COLOR, FLOWER SEASON, AND NECTAR SOURCE	USDA HARDINESS ZONE	CATERPILLAR FOOD PLANT FREQUENTED BY GARDEN BUTTERFLIES
	White flowers spring through fall provide nectar	Zones 8–10 perennial growing up to 5 feet tall	Monarch
	Pinkish-purple flowers provide weeks of nectar in early summer	Zones 3–9 perennial reaching 4 feet tall	Monarch
	Lavender flowers in summer provide nectar	Zone unknown perennial growing to 3 feet	Northern Checkerspot
	Purple flowers with orange centers are one of the most popular summer nectar plants	Zones 3–8 perennial growing 1–3 feet	Not a caterpillar food plant
	Flowers of many different colors provide nectar from summer until frost	Annual (perennial in Zones 10–11) reaching up to 4 feet	Not a caterpillar food plant
	Purple flowers from spring to fall provide nectar mostly for smaller butterflies	Zones 4–9 perennial reaching 30 inches tall	Not a caterpillar food plant
	Pink to rosy purple blooms in summer; good nectar plant	Zones 5–9 perennial growing 2–4 feet tall	West Coast Lady, Common Checkered- Skipper
	Orange flowers throughout the year provide nectar	Zones 4–10 perennial growing 2–5 feet tall	Painted Lady, West Coast Lady, Common Checkered- Skipper
	Blue, nectar- filled flowers bloom summer through fall	Zones 6–10 perennial growing 3 feet tall	Field Crescent, Northern Checkerspot
	Fragrant purple flowers provide nectar in spring and summer	Zones 6–10 shrub growing to 10 feet	California Dogface
	Fragrant purple flowers in spring through early summer provide nectar	Zones 4–9 shrub growing to 12 feet	Southern Dogface, Silver-spotted Skipper, Gray Hairstreak

continued overleaf

Table continued

SCIENTIFIC NAME	COMMON NAME	NATIVE RANGE
Shrubs and Trees *continued*		
Buddleja marrubiifolia	Woolly butterflybush	Texas
Ceanothus spp.	Ceanothus species	Western US
Diplacus aurantiacus	Orange bush monkeyflower	California, Oregon
Ericameria nauseosa	Rubber rabbitbrush	Western US
Eriogonum fasciculatum	Eastern buckwheat, also called California buckwheat	California, Nevada, Arizona, Utah
Eriogonum latifolium var. *rubrens*	Redflower buckwheat, also known as San Miguel Island buckwheat	California
Eriogonum parvifolium	Seacliff buckwheat	California
Eriogonum umbellatum	Sulphur-flower buckwheat	States west of the Rocky Mountains
Senna bicapsularis	Christmasbush, also known as Christmas senna	Not native to US
Senna covesii	Coues' cassia	California, Nevada, Arizona, New Mexico

PLANTS FOR CALIFORNIA GARDENS

	FLOWER COLOR, FLOWER SEASON, AND NECTAR SOURCE	USDA HARDINESS ZONE	CATERPILLAR FOOD PLANT FREQUENTED BY GARDEN BUTTERFLIES
	Orange flowers provide nectar summer through fall	Zones 8–11 shrub growing to 6 feet	Not a caterpillar food plant
	Blue or white flowers in spring through midsummer provide nectar	Zones and sizes vary based on species	Not a caterpillar food plant for common garden butterflies
	Orange flowers provide nectar spring through fall but are not a butterfly favorite	Zones 8 and above, shrub blooms early summer through late fall	Common Buckeye, Chalcedon Checkerspot
	Yellow flowers in fall are a favorite butterfly nectar plant	Zones 4–10 shrub growing to 5 feet tall, possibly taller	Not a caterpillar food plant
	White flowers provide nectar spring to early fall	Zones 7–10 shrub growing 3 feet tall	Acmon Blue, Gray Hairstreak, many other butterflies not common to gardens
	Pinkish-red flowers provide nectar from June through October	Zones 8–10 shrub reaching 2 feet tall	Acmon Blue, Gray Hairstreak, many other butterflies not common to gardens
	White flowers in summer provide nectar	Zones unknown shrub reaching 2 feet tall	Acmon Blue, Gray Hairstreak, many other butterflies not common to gardens
	Yellow flowers in summer provide nectar	Zones 3–8 small shrub growing 6–12 inches tall makes a good ground cover	Acmon Blue, Gray Hairstreak, many other butterflies not common to gardens
	Yellow flowers do not produce nectar	Zones 9–11 shrub or small tree reaching to 12 feet tall	Sleepy Orange, Cloudless Sulphur
	Yellow flowers bloom April through October; does not provide nectar	Zones 6–10 small shrub reaching 24 inches	Sleepy Orange, Cloudless Sulphur

Bright red flowers of lantana and clear yellow flowers of velvet leaf senna in the foreground leave no doubt that arid gardens can be beautiful. Purple flower spikes of Mexican bush sage, with ornamental oregano at its base spilling over into the gravel path, add more color (and nectar!). Clinging along a wire fence in the background, bluecrown passionflower provides caterpillar food for Gulf Fritillaries.

BUTTERFLIES IN ARIZONA

The arid West is a mosaic of habitats, encompassing cool, high deserts such as the lands around Albuquerque, New Mexico; Flagstaff, Arizona; and Grand Junction, Colorado; as well as the cold, semiarid foothills of Colorado Springs, Colorado; and Santa Fe, New Mexico. Even within each piece of the mosaic one finds wide variations in garden parameters such as rainfall and temperature, which means that butterfly gardeners may have to experiment to find plants that thrive in unique locations.

The Chihuahuan Desert is a warm desert that stretches off the Mexican Plateau into southeast Arizona and New Mexico, with abrupt changes in altitude where desert meets the mountains at 5,000 feet. A desert may sound like an unlikely spot for an extensive butterfly garden, but Robert Behrstock and Karen LeMay have found it ideal.

Cottage-style gardening, with big blowsy flowers, was the original plan for the Behrstock/LeMay garden. The flowers flourished but the gardeners wilted under the demanding watering regime required to keep the garden alive. So they transitioned to a garden style that encompasses native plants in a setting that reflects the land's distinctive features, and shifted to focusing on attracting all creatures—birds and pollinators in particular. Many plants in the original garden attracted butterflies but did not satisfy the gardeners—eastern purple coneflower required too much water, orange eye butterflybush needed constant deadheading, and Russian sage was invasive. The shift toward low-maintenance, low-input plants (for both water and soil amendments) has been a success—butterflies, hummingbirds, moths, bats, and birds are attracted to an array of garden plants that thrive on the natural rainfall of 30 inches a year.

Zinnias (the large, tall, old-fashioned varieties) used to be part of the garden, but Robert and Karen are always looking for plants with low water requirements and have found that Peruvian zinnia fills in nicely for their larger, thirstier relatives. Peruvian zinnia produces red-orange pastel flowers on plants that can grow 3–4 feet tall in rich garden soil but that in the Chihuahuan Desert reach about a foot tall. Blanketflowers are another group of nectar plants that thrive in the dry desert (as well as in many other locations across the United States) and are prominent in the garden. The various blanketflower species that Robert and Karen have planted over the years have been allowed to self-seed, creating a mix of blanketflowers that is unique to their garden. Sulphur cosmos is a third long-blooming annual that self-seeds around the garden, helping to add color and nectar.

Blanketflowers and sulphur cosmos mingle and spread throughout the garden.

Throughout the arid West, sparse and sporadic rainfall has a predominant impact on butterfly gardens—precipitation is seasonal and temperatures are high, creating a constant challenge to keep plants hydrated when water is at a premium. Because June is the hottest and driest month of the year in southern Arizona, the butterfly season does not get into full swing until temperatures moderate and the monsoon rains begin in July. As the rains allow the landscape to revive, Mexican sunflower starts to put on fast growth. Blooming from July to frost, Mexican sunflower often has a butterfly on every flower. In southern Arizona, it grows 6 feet tall and will self-seed. A similar species, tree marigold, also called tree tithonia, also puts on quick growth with the advent of rain—it grows up to 15 feet tall at lower elevations, but at an altitude of 5,000 feet, tree marigold is a more demure 8 or 10 feet tall. When they originally purchased tree marigold, Robert and Karen assumed it would live only until the first frost but it has performed as a perennial in their garden. With the help of rain, it flowers profusely—50 Queens have been spotted nectaring on one plant at the same time. And tree marigold provides other benefits, serving as host plant for Bordered Patch, a common butterfly in the region that lays eggs on its expansive foliage.

Providing for common garden butterflies is just the first step. Many butterfly gardeners find that a garden packed with nectar and caterpillar food plants lures less-common butterflies into view as well. Dorantes Longtail has a very restricted range in the United States and is uncommon within that range, but it visited Mexican sunflower in Robert and Karen's garden.

Lantana is another plant that behaves in unexpected ways when given space in the arid West. Considered invasive in many parts of the United States and not a prime nectar plant in northern climates, where plants do not get large enough to put on expansive floral displays, lantana in the arid West acts as a well-behaved perennial that dies back to the ground when winter arrives. In spring, even before the summer rains, lantana resprouts and its flowers attract early-season butterflies. It continues to flower during the summer but never as prolifically as in spring. Karen and Bob have never seen an errant seedling and so feel confident including this nectar powerhouse in their garden.

For her garden, Karen defines native plants as those originally found in the Chihuahuan Desert, which includes parts of Mexico, west Texas, and New Mexico in addition to Arizona. Many plants she considers native are not historically found in Arizona but they are native to the desert. This strategy crosses state and national borders by considering the underlying ecosystem: the local limestone-based soil, elevation, minimum winter temperatures (the desert receives killing frosts), and rainfall. *Bringing Nature Home* discusses the definition of what a native plant is and is not, and this book deeply influenced Karen's gardening ethos. There is no one universally accepted definition of "native plant"—some sources restrict native status to state lines, while others consider naturalized plants as native (a definition that would include many European weeds). Karen's view is based on many factors, with the ultimate goal to provide plants that will serve pollinators native to her home. Native status is not a black-and-white issue, and Karen feels so strongly about the promotion and protection of native pollinators that she has started a nonprofit, Pollinator Corridors Southwest, that educates about pollinators and their needs.

When choosing native milkweeds, Robert and Karen have a wealth of choices—their location, including the nearby mountains, supports 17 native milkweed species. The diversity of plant forms displayed by desert-growing milkweeds is astounding, from the needlelike leaves on pineneedle milkweed to the practically leafless stems of rush milkweed. Many milkweeds of the arid West have extensive taproots, which makes them hard to establish in a garden, and they are notoriously tricky to transplant,

Woolly butterflybush, a native cousin to the controversial orange eye butterflybush, is a valuable nectar plant for arid gardens. The shrub has low water requirements and its fuzzy gray foliage and sparkling orange flowers create a focal point wherever it is planted.

Like all passionflower species, bluecrown passionflower has a beautifully complex flower.

but these desert-adapted species hold such value as nectar and caterpillar food plants that Robert and Karen purchase seedlings whenever they come across them. Their value is reflected in the number of species grown by Robert and Karen: fringed twinevine and wavyleaf twinevine are two plants in the milkweed family that support butterflies, along with Arizona, spider, tropical, Lemmon's, pineneedle, Mojave, showy, horsetail, and butterfly milkweeds.

Beyond milkweeds, caterpillar food plants abound in and around the Behrstock/LeMay garden:

- Three different species of senna—Coues' cassia, Wislizenus' senna, and woolly senna, all of which feed Cloudless Sulphur and Sleepy Orange caterpillars.
- Hackberry trees are found in the lands adjacent to the garden, bringing American Snout, Empress Leilia, and Tawny and Hackberry emperors to the garden.
- Watson's Dutchman's pipe is a sprawling vine that feeds Pipevine Swallowtails.
- Three passionflower species are grown to feed Gulf Fritillaries. The native cupped and Arizona passionflowers do not seem to be used as regularly as the nonnative bluecrown, but more importantly, the native species produce shorter vines than bluecrown passionflower, which in warm climates can grow 30 feet of caterpillar-feeding foliage.

Plants found in the arid West have many adaptations—deep taproots store water and nutrients, allowing milkweeds and bluecrown passionflower to regrow after very hot or very cold weather stops their aboveground growth. Other plants have adapted leaf structures; for example, the needlelike leaves of (nonnative) rosemary contain fewer pores (called *stomata*), resulting in less evaporative loss of water. Many desert-adapted plants have gray-green or silvery leaves owing to fuzzy or scaly coatings that provide shade from the sun and reduce wind speed, both of which cut down on moisture loss. Many plants with this gray-silver coloration are found in arid-West butterfly gardens—for example, catmint, lilac chastetree (also known as vitex), woolly butterflybush, and rubber rabbitbrush.

Each fall, the Southeast Arizona Butterfly Club (the local NABA chapter), holds a field trip when rubber rabbitbrush is in bloom. It grows wild throughout the area and its nectar flow seems magnetic to butterflies—nearly 50 different species are often sighted during the fall field trip. However, despite its spectacular butterfly-attracting quality, many gardeners feel that rubber rabbitbrush is too coarse-looking to plant in a flowerbed.

Arlene Ripley, who gardens 60 miles north of Robert and Karen's garden, has an unusual approach to growing rubber rabbitbrush in her garden—she prunes it to 12 inches tall in the spring, similar to pruning woolly butterflybush. This produces a tidy shrub that fits into her smaller garden. Rubber rabbitbrush is a prolific self-seeder so she also prunes the plant after it flowers. Constant pruning over years takes a toll and the plants eventually die out, but Arlene replenishes them from the many seedlings growing wild just outside her garden wall.

Gray foliage sets off catmint's purple-blue flowers. Easy to grow and tolerant of dry conditions, catmint is a butterfly-garden staple. After the first flush of flowers, cut the plant back by half to encourage new flowers to form. Catmint offers many species and cultivars to choose from.

Gulf Fritillary nectaring on rubber rabbitbrush in the fall.

Located in mesquite grassland that is a transition zone between two deserts, Arlene grows many of the same plants as Robert and Karen. Living at an altitude of 4,700 feet with little rain has made it hard to find plants that will survive her difficult conditions. In order to discover what to grow, she observes butterflies in the nearby mountains, and then researches their caterpillar food plants. Often it is an easy match—mesquite trees that grow throughout her area provide caterpillar food for Reakirt's, Marine, and Ceraunus blues. Matching some other butterflies with suitable caterpillar food plants has been more challenging.

Black Swallowtails visit gardens throughout the arid West, and although their nonnative caterpillar food plants are varied and easy to grow, Arlene desired a native plant that would not require supplemental water beyond rainfall. After much searching, she learned of rue of the mountains, a perennial in the Citrus Family that is adapted to her soil and climate. The plant has many similarities to common rue—both plants produce foliage with a medicinal or citrusy smell, the foliage of both plants may cause skin photosensitivity in susceptible individuals, and both plants feed Black Swallowtail caterpillars. Solving the puzzle of feeding caterpillars while working within the constraints of her environment is a pleasure for Arlene.

Water is a scarce commodity in arid lands but an important one for butterfly gardening, as well as for other types of habitat gardening. Arlene's home has a water-catchment system that collects rainwater from the house roof and stores it in two buried 500-gallon tanks until needed. Other small buildings, such as

the garage, are equipped with aboveground rain barrels that collect roof runoff. The only water available for butterflies and wildlife is from a birdbath and a small area where seasonal rain runoff collects when all her water-saving containers are full. It is striking that in an environment as seemingly unfriendly to butterfly gardening as the parched southwestern United States, an uncommon relative of common rue could be identified to feed caterpillars, and that a small birdbath could serve as a vital water source. Tailoring a garden to butterflies in any location not only creates habitat needed by butterflies but also creates essential connections between people and nature that impel us to think about aspects of the remarkable planet on which we live that otherwise might go unnoticed. The scale of the project can be grand or petite; its location can be in arid desert or the damp Pacific Northwest; it merely needs to be started.

As with most butterfly gardeners, Arlene uses a mixture of native and non-native plants to support butterflies. One of her favorite plants is rosemary, a typical plant of hot Mediterranean landscapes that survives for long stretches without rainfall—it blooms prolifically in the spring and then reblooms later in the season. Rosemary can grow upright as a shrub or trail to form a matlike ground cover, and it is often seen clipped into topiary structures. Arlene's rosemary is a shrub variety that has grown so large over the years that it is visible online on Google Earth—an apt metaphor for the dramatically large consequences of relatively small actions on behalf of the environment. It is hoped that in the not-too-distant future, more butterfly gardens will be significant enough to be seen from outer space.

Marine Blue (nectaring on woolly butterflybush, opposite) and Ceraunus Blue (nectaring on turkey tangle fogfruit, left) are both common garden visitors whose caterpillars thrive on nearby mesquite trees.

Acmon Blue.

SCIENTIFIC NAME	COMMON NAME	NATIVE RANGE
Annuals		
Gaillardia pulchella	Firewheel	Much of the US
Tithonia rotundifolia	Clavel de muerto or Mexican sunflower	Not native to US
Zinnia elegans	Zinnia	Not native to US
Zinnia peruviana	Peruvian zinnia	Native to Arizona, northern Florida, Georgia, and North and South Carolina
Perennials and Vines		
Anaphalis margaritacea	Western pearly everlasting	Most of the US excluding Oklahoma and southeastern states

RECOMMENDED BUTTERFLY PLANTS FOR ARID WEST GARDENS

The table on pages 262–7 highlights plants found by NABA members in the arid West to be attractive to butterflies. While specifically suited to butterflies in this region, these plants may also thrive and attract butterflies in other locations.

Gardeners throughout the arid West may also wish to consult the lists of recommended butterfly plants for other areas of the United States. The different mixtures of altitudes and rainfall make it hard to predict how plants will perform in many locations, and experimentation with a variety of plants will be necessary.

To determine whether a plant from the list will grow in your area, consult the Native Plant Society or Cooperative Extension Service websites specific to your state. To determine if a butterfly from the list has a range that includes your garden, consult a butterfly field guide or www.webutterfly.org.

	FLOWER COLOR, FLOWER SEASON, AND NECTAR SOURCE	USDA HARDINESS ZONE	CATERPILLAR FOOD PLANT FREQUENTED BY GARDEN BUTTERFLIES
	Yellow-orange-red flowers produce a lot of nectar from spring through summer	Annual that may reseed	Not a caterpillar food plant
	Orange flowers provide profuse amounts of nectar from late summer until frost	Annual reaching up to 6 feet tall	Not a caterpillar food plant
	Flowers in many different colors provide nectar from early summer through frost	Annual reaching up to 4 feet tall	Not a caterpillar food plant
	Red-orange flowers provide nectar summer through fall	Annual flower reaching up to 4 feet tall	Not a caterpillar food plant
	White flowers in summer provide nectar to many butterflies	Zones 3–8, perennial plant growing 2–3 feet	American Lady

continued overleaf

Table continued

SCIENTIFIC NAME	COMMON NAME	NATIVE RANGE
Perennials and Vines *continued*		
Aristolochia watsonii	Watson's Dutchman's pipe	Arizona, New Mexico
Asclepias linaria	Pineneedle milkweed	California, Arizona, New Mexico
Asclepias subulata	Rush milkweed	California, Arizona, Nevada
Asclepias verticillata	Whorled milkweed	Washington, Oregon, Idaho, Nevada, Utah, and California
Conoclinium greggii	Palmleaf thoroughwort, also known as Gregg's mistflower	Texas, Arizona, New Mexico
Lantana camara	Lantana	Not native to US
Nepeta spp.	Catmint	Not native to US
Passiflora caerulea	Bluecrown passionflower	Not native to US
Passiflora foetida	Fetid passionflower	Texas and Florida
Phyla nodiflora	Turkey tangle fogfruit	Lower half of United States
Scabiosa columbaria	Pincushion flower	Not native to US
Sidalcea malviflora	Dwarf checkerbloom	California, Oregon, Washington

PLANTS FOR ARID WEST GARDENS

FLOWER COLOR, FLOWER SEASON, AND NECTAR SOURCE	USDA HARDINESS ZONE	CATERPILLAR FOOD PLANT FREQUENTED BY GARDEN BUTTERFLIES
Purple-green flowers are not a nectar source	Zones 9–11 vine growing to 2 feet	Pipevine Swallowtail
White flowers spring through fall provide nectar	Zones 8–10 perennial growing up to 5 feet tall	Monarch, Queen
Cream-yellow flowers produced April through December provide nectar	Zones 8b–11 perennial reaching 2–4 feet tall	Monarch, Queen
White flowers produce nectar	Zones 4–9 perennial growing 3 feet	Monarch, Queen, Soldier
Blue flowers spring through fall produce large amounts of nectar	Zones 8–10 perennial growing 18 inches tall	Not a caterpillar food plant
Flowers of many different colors provide nectar from summer until frost	Annual (perennial in Zones 10–11) reaching up to 4 feet	Not a caterpillar food plant
Purple flowers from spring to fall provide nectar mostly for smaller butterflies	Zones 4–9 perennial reaching 30 inches tall	Not a caterpillar food plant
Purple-white flowers produce nectar	Perennial vine reaching 30 feet	Gulf Fritillary, Zebra Heliconian, Variegated Fritillary
Dramatic yellow-purple flowers provide nectar	Zones 9–11 vine, length varies	Gulf Fritillary
White flowers appear all year in warmer locations and provide nectar for many butterflies	Zones 6–11 perennial growing 3–6 inches tall	Common Buckeye, White Peacock, Phaon Crescent
Blue-purple flowers in summer provide nectar over a long time frame	Zones 4–10 perennial reaching 12 inches tall	Not a caterpillar food plant
Pink to rosy purple blooms in summer; good nectar plant	Zones 5–9 perennial growing 2–4 feet tall	West Coast Lady, Common Checkered- Skipper

continued overleaf

Table continued

SCIENTIFIC NAME	COMMON NAME	NATIVE RANGE
Perennials and Vines *continued*		
Sphaeralcea ambigua	Desert globemallow	California, Nevada, Arizona, Utah
Thamnosma texana	Rue of the mountains	Texas, New Mexico, Arizona, Colorado
Tithonia diversifolia	Tree marigold, also called tree tithonia	Not native to US
Shrubs and Trees		
Buddleja marrubiifolia	Woolly butterflybush	Texas
Cercis canadensis var. *mexicana*	Mexican redbud	Texas and Arizona
Ericameria nauseosa	Rubber rabbitbrush	Western US
Eriogonum umbellatum	Sulphur-flower buckwheat	States west of the Rocky Mountains
Eysenhardtia orthocarpa	Tahitian kidneywood, also called kidneywood	Arizona, New Mexico
Eysenhardtia texana	Texas kidneywood	Texas
Prunus serotina	Black cherry	Eastern half of US, Washington State, Arizona, and New Mexico
Senna covesii	Coues' cassia	California, Nevada, Arizona, New Mexico

PLANTS FOR ARID WEST GARDENS

FLOWER COLOR, FLOWER SEASON, AND NECTAR SOURCE	USDA HARDINESS ZONE	CATERPILLAR FOOD PLANT FREQUENTED BY GARDEN BUTTERFLIES
Orange flowers throughout the year provide nectar	Zones 4–10 perennial growing 2–5 feet tall	Painted Lady, West Coast Lady, Common Checkered- Skipper
Small purple, white, or yellow flowers in spring to early summer	Zone unknown perennial growing to 1 foot tall	Black Swallowtail
Yellow flowers bloom summer through fall and provide nectar	Zones 9–11 perennial growing to 20 feet tall in some locations	Bordered Patch
Orange flowers provide nectar summer through fall	Zones 8–11 shrub growing to 6 feet	Not a caterpillar food plant
Pink flowers in early spring offer nectar	Zones 5–9 small tree reaching 15 feet	Not a caterpillar food plant
Yellow flowers in fall are a favorite butterfly nectar plant	Zones 4–10 shrub growing to 5 feet, possibly taller	Not a caterpillar food plant
Yellow flowers in summer provide nectar	Zones 3–8 small shrub growing 6–12 inches tall makes a good ground cover	Acmon Blue, Gray Hairstreak, and many other butterflies not common to gardens
White flowers attract butterflies after monsoon rain	Zones unknown tree growing 15 feet or more	Arizona Skipper
Fragrant white flowers in spring, summer, and fall	Zones 8–11 medium to large shrub growing to 10 feet tall	Southern Dogface
Lots of white flowers in spring provide nectar	Zones 3–9 tree reaching 60 feet tall	Red-spotted Purple, Two-tailed Swallowtail
Yellow flowers bloom April through October; does not provide nectar	Zones 6–10 small shrub reaching 24 inches	Sleepy Orange, Cloudless Sulphur

PLANT INVENTORY

The following list includes all plants mentioned in this book. Although this list represents some of the most popular butterfly gardening plants in the United States, these plants represent just a sampling of the interesting choices available to curious butterfly gardeners.

Alfalfa/*Medicago sativa*
American plum/*Prunus americana*
Arizona milkweed/*Asclepias angustifolia*
Arizona passionflower/*Passiflora arizonica*
Aromatic aster/*Symphyotrichum oblongifolium*
Asian pigeonwings/*Clitoria ternatea*
Aster species/*Symphyotrichum* spp.
Baby blue eyes/*Nemophila menziesi*
Bahama firebush/*Hamelia cuprea*
Beach sunflower/*Helianthus debilis*
Beebalm species/*Monarda* spp.
Bejuco de Santiago/*Aristolochia triloba*
Bigleaf lupine/*Lupinus polyphyllus*
Bigleaf maple/*Acer macrophyllum*
Birdfoot violet/*Viola pedata*
Bitter cherry/*Prunus emarginata*
Black cherry/*Prunus serotina*
Black cottonwood/*Populus balsamifera*
Black locust/*Robinia pseudoacacia*
Blackeyed Susan/*Rudbeckia hirta*
Blackhaw/*Viburnum prunifolium*
Blacksamson echinacea/*Echinacea angustifolia*
Blanketflower/*Gaillardia aristata*
Blazing star species/*Liatris* spp.
Blue giant hyssop/*Agastache foeniculum*
Blue mistflower/*Conoclinium coelestinum*
Blue plumbago/*Plumbago auriculata*
Bluecrown passionflower/*Passiflora caerulea*
Bluehead gilia/*Gilia capitata*
Bottlebrush buckeye/*Aesculus parviflora*
Brazilian Dutchman's pipe/*Aristolochia gigantea*
Brazilian vervain/*Verbena brasiliensis*
Bush monkeyflower species/*Diplacus* spp.
Bush's purple coneflower/*Echinacea paradoxa*
Butterfly milkweed/*Asclepias tuberosa*
Calico flower/*Aristolochia littoralis* (syn. *elegans*)
California Dutchman's pipe/*Aristolochia californica*
California false indigo/*Amorpha californica*
California poppy/*Eschscholzia californica*
California redbud/*Cercis orbiculata*
California sandaster/*Corethrogyne filaginifolia*
California sycamore/*Platanus racemosa*
Canada goldenrod/*Solidago canadensis*
Cape leadwort/*Plumbago auriculata*
Cardinalflower/*Lobelia cardinalis*
Catmint species/*Nepeta* spp.
Ceanothus species/*Ceanothus* spp.
Chapman's senna/*Senna mexicana* var. *chapmanii*
Checkerbloom species/*Sidalcea* spp.
Cheeseweed mallow/*Malva parviflora*
Christmasbush/*Senna bicapsularis*
Clavel de muerto/*Tithonia rotundifolia*
Coastal hedgenettle/*Stachys chamissonis*
Common blue violet/*Viola sororia*
Common blue wood aster/*Symphyotrichum cordifolium*
Common boneset/*Eupatorium perfoliatum*
Common buttonbush/*Cephalanthus occidentalis*
Common dandelion/*Taraxacum officinale*
Common hackberry/*Celtis occidentalis*
Common hop/*Humulus lupulus*
Common hoptree/*Ptelea trifoliata*

Common mallow/*Malva neglecta*
Common milkweed/*Asclepias syriaca*
Common plantain/*Plantago major*
Common pricklyash/*Zanthoxylum americanum*
Common rue/*Ruta graveolens*
Common sneezeweed/*Helenium autumnale*
Common woolly sunflower/*Eriophyllum lanatum*
Coontie/*Zamia pumila*
Corkystem passionflower/*Passiflora suberosa*
Coues' cassia/*Senna covesii*
Crownvetch/*Securigera varia*
Cucumberleaf sunflower/*Helianthus debilis*
Cupped passionflower/*Passiflora bryonioides*
Dense blazing star/*Liatris spicata*
Desert globemallow/*Sphaeralcea ambigua*
Dill/*Anethum graveolens*
Dotted blazing star/*Liatris punctata*
Dutchman's pipe/*Aristolochia* spp.
Dwarf checkerbloom/*Sidalcea malviflora*
Dwarf oceanspray/*Holodiscus dumosus*
Eastern Mojave buckwheat/*Eriogonum fasciculatum*
Eastern purple coneflower/*Echinacea purpurea*
Eastern redbud/*Cercis canadensis*
Eastern redcedar/*Juniperus virginiana*
Egyptian starcluster/*Pentas lanceolata*
Elegant clarkia/*Clarkia unguiculata*
Elegant Dutchman's pipe/*Aristolochia littoralis* (syn. *elegans*)
Exserted Indian paintbrush/*Castilleja exserta*
Fall phlox/*Phlox paniculata*
False indigo bush/*Amorpha fruticosa*
Farewell to spring/*Clarkia amoen*
Fennel/*Foeniculum vulgare*
Fetid passionflower/*Passiflora foetida*
Field pussytoes/*Antennaria neglecta*
Firebush/*Hamelia patens* var. *patens*
Firewheel/*Gaillardia pulchella*
Fivespot/*Nemophila maculata*
Flame acanthus/*Anisacanthus quadrifidus* var. *wrightii*
Fragrant sumac/*Rhus aromatica*
Fremont cottonwood/*Populus fremontii*
Fringed twinevine/*Funastrum cynanchoides*
Fringeleaf wild petunia/*Ruellia humilis*
Fuller's teasel/*Dipsacus fullonum*
Garden lovage/*Levisticum officinale*
Garden snapdragon/*Antirrhinum majus*
Giant hyssop species/*Agastache* spp.
Globethistle species/*Echinops* spp.
Golden Alexander/*Zizia aurea*
Golden dewdrops/*Duranta erecta*
Golden zizia/*Zizia aurea*
Goldenrod species/*Solidago* spp.
Green antelopehorn milkweed/*Asclepias viridis*
Gregg's mistflower/*Conoclinium greggii*
Hackberry species/*Celtis* spp.
Hairawn muhly/*Muhlenbergia capillaris*
Harlequin blueflag/*Iris versicolor*
Heartleaf rosemallow/*Hibiscus martianus*
Henderson's checkerbloom/*Sidalcea hendersonii*
Herb of grace/*Bacopa monnieri*
Hoary mountainmint/*Pycnanthemum incanum*
Hoary verbena/*Verbena stricta*
Hollowleaf annual lupine/*Lupinus succulentus*
Hollyhock species/*Alcea* spp.
Hookedspur violet/*Viola adunca*
Horsetail milkweed/*Asclepias subverticillata*
Indian woodoats/*Chasmanthium latifolium*
Indiangrass/*Sorghastrum nutans*
Jack in the bush/*Chromolaena odorata*

Japanese barberry/*Berberis thunbergii*
Japanese stiltgrass/*Microstegium vimineum*
Jeana garden phlox/*Phlox paniculata* 'Jeana'
Jersey tea/*Ceanothus herbaceus*
Lacy phacelia/*Phacelia tanacetifolia*
Lantana/*Lantana camara*
Lemmon's milkweed/*Asclepias lemmonii*
Light-blue snakeweed/*Stachytarpheta jamaicensis*
Lilac chastetree/*Vitex agnus-castus*
Lilac verbena/*Verbena lilacina*
Little bluestem/*Schizachyrium scoparium*
Mesquite species/*Prosopis* spp.
Mexican bush sage/*Salvia leucantha*
Mexican firebush/*Hamelia patens* var. *glabra*
Mexican redbud/*Cercis canadensis* var. *Mexicana*
Mexican sunflower/*Tithonia rotundifolia*
Mexican whorled milkweed/*Asclepias fascicularis*
Milkweed species/*Asclepias* spp.
Mojave milkweed/*Asclepias nyctaginifolia*
Monardella species/*Monardella* spp.
Mountainmint species/*Pycnanthemum* spp.
New England aster/*Symphyotrichum novae-angliae*
New Jersey tea/*Ceanothus americanus*
Northern red oak/*Quercus rubra*
Northern spicebush/*Lindera benzoin*
Oceanspray/*Holodiscus discolor*
Orange bush monkeyflower/*Diplacus aurantiacus*
Orange coneflower/*Rudbeckia fulgida*
Orange eye butterflybush/*Buddleja davidii*
Orange honeysuckle/*Lonicera ciliosa*
Ornamental oregano cultivars/*Origanum vulgare* cultivars
Oxeye daisy/*Leucanthemum vulgare*
Pacific aster/*Symphyotrichum chilense*
Pacific bleeding heart/*Dicentra formosa*
Pacific willow/*Salix lucida*
Pale purple coneflower/*Echinacea pallida*
Palmleaf thoroughwort/*Conoclinium greggii*
Parasol whitetop/*Doellingeria umbellata*
Parlin's pussytoes/*Antennaria parlinii*
Parsley/*Petroselinum crispum*
Partridge pea/*Chamaecrista fasciculata*
Passionflower species/*Passiflora* spp.
Pawpaw/*Asimina triloba*
Pelicanflower/*Aristolochia grandiflora*
Pennsylvania pellitory/*Parietaria pensylvanica*
Pentas/*Pentas lanceolata*
Peruvian zinnia/*Zinnia peruviana*
Pincushion flower/*Scabiosa columbaria*
Pineneedle milkweed/*Asclepias linaria*
Pipevine/*Aristolochia macrophylla*
Porterweed/*Stachytarpheta jamaicensis*
Prairie blazing star/*Liatris pycnostachya*
Prairie mallow 'Party Girl'/*Sidalcea* hybrid
Prairie milkweed/*Asclepias sullivantii*
Prairie violet/*Viola pedatifida*
Purple coneflower species/*Echinacea* spp.
Purple milkweed/*Asclepias purpurascens*
Purple passionflower/*Passiflora incarnata*
Purpletop vervain/*Verbena bonariensis*
Pussytoes species/*Antennaria* spp.
Rattlesnake master/*Eryngium yuccifolium*
Red clover/*Trifolium pratense*
Redbay/*Persea borbonia*
Redflower buckwheat/*Eriogonum latifolium* var. *rubrens*
Redosier dogwood/*Cornus sericea*
River birch/*Betula nigra*
Riverbank lupine/*Lupinus rivularis*
Rockspirea/*Holodiscus dumosus*
Rocky Mountain blazing star/*Liatris ligulistylus*
Rose spirea/*Spirea douglasii*
Rosemary/*Rosmarinus officinalis*
Rosy pussytoes/*Antennaria rosea*
Roundleaf ragwort/*Packera obovata*
Rubber rabbitbrush/*Ericameria nauseosa*
Rue of the mountains/*Thamnosma texana*
Rush milkweed/*Asclepias subulata*

PLANT INVENTORY

Russian sage/*Perovskia atriplicifolia*
Salal/*Gaultheria shallon*
Sassafras/*Sassafras albidum*
Scarlet beebalm/*Monarda didyma*
Scarletbush/*Hamelia patens* var. *patens*
Seacliff buckwheat/*Eriogonum parvifolium*
Seaside buckwheat/*Eriogonum latifoilium*
Shale barren pussytoes/*Antennaria virginica*
Shortspur seablush/*Plectritis congesta*
Showy goldenrod/*Solidago speciosa*
Showy milkweed/*Asclepias speciosa*
Sierra currant/*Ribes nevadense*
Sixangle foldwing/*Dicliptera sexangularis*
Skyblue aster/*Symphyotrichum oolentangiense*
Smallspike false nettle/*Boehmeria cylindrica*
Smooth blue aster/*Symphyotrichum laeve*
Solidago 'Little Lemon'/*Solidago* cultivar
Solidago rugosa 'Fireworks'/*Solidago rugosa* 'Fireworks'
Solidago sphacelata 'Golden Fleece'/*Solidago sphacelata* 'Golden Fleece'
Sourwood/*Oxydendrum arboreum*
Spider milkweed/*Asclepias asperula*
Spiderwort species/*Tradescantia* spp.
Spotted beebalm/*Monarda punctata*
Spotted geranium/*Geranium maculatum*
Stinging nettle/*Urtica dioca*
Sugarberry/*Celtis laevigata*
Sulphur cosmos/*Cosmos sulphureus*
Sulphur-flower buckwheat/*Eriogonum umbellatum*
Sunflower species/*Helianthus* spp.
Swamp milkweed/*Asclepias incarnata*
Swamp verbena/*Verbena hastata*
Sweet almond verbena/*Aloysia virgata*
Sweet alyssum/*Lobularia maritima*
Sweetbay/*Magnolia virginiana*
Switchgrass/*Panicum virgatum*
Texas kidneywood/*Eysenhardtia texana*
Texas lantana/*Lantana urticoides*
Texas redbud/*Cercis canadensis texensis*
Tree marigold/*Tithonia diversifolia*
Tree tithonia/*Tithonia diversifolia*
Tropical milkweed/*Asclepias curassavica*
Tuliptree/*Liriodendron tulipifera*
Turk's-cap lily/*Lilium superbum*
Turkey tangle fogfruit/*Phyla nodiflora*
Velvet leaf senna/*Senna lindheimeriana*
Vine of St. James/*Aristolochia triloba*
Virginia snakeroot/*Aristolochia serpentaria*
Watson's Dutchman's pipe/*Aristolochia watsonii*
Wavyleaf twinevine/*Funastrum crispum*
Wax mallow/*Malvaviscus arboreus*
West Indian shrubverbena/*Lantana urticoides*
Western azalea/*Rhododendron occidentale*
Western pearly everlasting/*Anaphalis margaritacea*
Western red cedar/*Thuja plicata*
White checkerbloom/*Sidalcea candida*
White clover/*Trifolium repens*
White spirea/*Spirea betulifolia*
White-veined hardy Dutchman's pipe/*Aristolochia fimbriata*
Whitebrush/*Aloysia gratissima*
Whorled milkweed/*Asclepias verticillata*
Whorled mountainmint/*Pycnanthemum verticillatum*
Whorled plantain/*Plumbago indica*
Wild bergamot/*Monarda fistulosa*
Willow species/*Salix* spp.
Wislizenus' senna/*Senna wislizeni*
Woman's tobacco/*Antennaria plantaginifolia*
Woolly butterflybush/*Buddleja marrubiifolia*
Woolly Dutchman's pipe/*Aristolochia tomentosa*
Woolly senna/*Senna hirsuta*
Wright's desert honeysuckle/*Anisacanthus quadrifidus* var. *wrightii*
Yellow passionflower/*Passiflora lutea*
Zinnia/*Zinnia elegans*
Zizotes milkweed/*Asclepias oenotheroides*

BUTTERFLY SCIENTIFIC

The following list includes all the butterflies mentioned in this book.

FAMILY PAPILIONIDAE, SWALLOWTAILS

Parnassius clodius/Clodius Parnassian
Battus philenor/Pipevine Swallowtail
Battus polydamas/Polydamas Swallowtail
Eurytides marcellus/Zebra Swallowtail
Papilio polyxenes/Black Swallowtail
Papilio joanae/Ozark Swallowtail
Papilio zelicaon/Anise Swallowtail
Papilio indra/Indra Swallowtail
Papilio cresphontes/Giant Swallowtail
Papilio glaucus/Eastern Tiger Swallowtail
Papilio rutulus/Western Tiger Swallowtail
Papilio multicaudata/Two-tailed Swallowtail
Papilio eurymedon/Pale Swallowtail
Papilio troilus/Spicebush Swallowtail
Papilio palamedes/Palamedes Swallowtail

FAMILY PIERIDAE, WHITES AND SULPHURS

Pieris rapae/Cabbage White
Anthocharis sara/Sara Orangetip
Colias philodice/Clouded Sulphur
Colias eurytheme/Orange Sulphur
Colias eurydice/California Dogface
Colias cesonia/Southern Dogface
Phoebis sennae/Cloudless Sulphur
Phoebis philea/Orange-barred Sulphur
Eurema lisa/Little Yellow
Eurema nicippe/Sleepy Orange

FAMILY LYCAENIDAE, GOSSAMER-WINGS

Feniseca tarquinius/Harvester
Lycaena phlaeas/American Copper
Eumaeus atala/Atala
Satyrium titus/Coral Hairstreak
Satyrium calanus/Banded Hairstreak
Satyrium saepium/Hedgerow Hairstreak
Callophrys augustinus/Brown Elfin
Callophrys henrici/Henry's Elfin
Callophrys gryneus/Juniper Hairstreak
(*C. g. nelsoni*)/'Nelson's' Juniper Hairstreak
Strymon melinus/Gray Hairstreak
Calycopis cecrops/Red-banded Hairstreak
Satyrium liparops/Striped Hairstreak
Leptotes cassius/Cassius Blue
Leptotes marina/Marine Blue
Hemiargus ceraunus/Ceraunus Blue
Hemiargus isola/Reakirt's Blue
Everes comyntas/Eastern Tailed-Blue
Everes amyntula/Western Tailed-Blue
Celastrina lado/Spring Azure

AND COMMON NAMES

Celastrina lado neglecta/'Summer' Spring Azure
Glaucopsyche lygdamus/Silvery Blue
Plebejus acmon/Acmon Blue

FAMILY RIODINIDAE, METALMARKS

Calephelis borealis/Northern Metalmark

FAMILY NYMPHALIDAE, BRUSHFOOTED BUTTERFLIES

Libytheana carinenta/American Snout
Agraulis vanillae/Gulf Fritillary
Heliconius charithonia/Zebra Heliconian
Heliconius erato/Erato Heliconian
Euptoieta claudia/Variegated Fritillary
Euptoieta hegesia/Mexican Fritillary
Speyeria cybele/Great Spangled Fritillary
Speyeria idalia/Regal Fritillary
Boloria bellona/Meadow Fritillary
Chlosyne lacinia/Bordered Patch
Chlosyne harrisii/Harris' Checkerspot
Phyciodes texana/Texan Crescent
Phyciodes phaon/Phaon Crescent
Phyciodes tharos/Pearl Crescent
Phyciodes selenis/Northern Crescent
Phyciodes campestris/Field Crescent
Euphydryas chalcedona/Variable Checkerspot
Polygonia interrogationis/Question Mark
Polygonia comma/Eastern Comma
Polygonia satyrus/Satyr Comma
Polygonia faunus/Green Comma
Polygonia gracilis/Hoary Comma
Polygonia oreas/Oreas Comma
Polygonia progne/Gray Comma
Nymphalis vaualbum/Compton Tortoiseshell
Nymphalis californica/California Tortoiseshell
Nymphalis antiopa/Mourning Cloak
Nymphalis milberti/Milbert's Tortoiseshell
Vanessa virginiensis/American Lady
Vanessa cardui/Painted Lady
Vanessa annabella/West Coast Lady
Vanessa atalanta/Red Admiral
Junonia coenia/Common Buckeye
Junonia genoveva/Tropical Buckeye
Anartia jatrophae/White Peacock
Limenitis arthemis arthemis/White Admiral
Limenitis arthemis astyanax/Red-spotted Purple
Limenitis archippus/Viceroy
Limenitis weidemeyerii/Weidemeyer's Admiral
Limenitis lorquini/Lorquin's Admiral
Anaea andria/Goatweed Leafwing
Asterocampa celtis/Hackberry Emperor
Asterocampa leilia/Empress Leilia
Asterocampa clyton/Tawny Emperor
Enodia anthedon/Northern Pearly-eye
Cercyonis pegala/Common Wood-Nymph
Danaus plexippus/Monarch
Danaus gilippus/Queen
Danaus eresimus/Soldier

FAMILY HESPERIIDAE, SKIPPERS

Epargyreus clarus/Silver-spotted Skipper
Urbanus proteus/Long-tailed Skipper
Urbanus dorantes/Dorantes Longtail
Thorybes pylades/Northern Cloudywing
Erynnis icelus/Dreamy Duskywing
Erynnis juvenalis/Juvenal's Duskywing
Erynnis horatius/Horace's Duskywing
Erynnis baptisiae/Wild Indigo Duskywing
Pyrgus communis/Common Checkered-Skipper
Pyrgus albescens/White Checkered-Skipper
Pyrgus sp./Common/White Checkered-Skipper
Pholisora catullus/Common Sootywing
Ancyloxypha numitor/Least Skipper
Thymelicus lineola/European Skipper
Hesperia sassacus/Indian Skipper
Polites themistocles/Tawny-edged Skipper
Wallengrenia egeremet/Northern Broken-Dash
Ochlodes sylvanoides/Woodland Skipper
Poanes hobomok/Hobomok Skipper
Poanes zabulon/Zabulon Skipper
Amblyscirtes vialis/Common Roadside-Skipper

ABOUT THE NORTH AMERICAN BUTTERFLY ASSOCIATION

The North American Butterfly Association (NABA), formed in 1992, is, by far, the largest group in North America (Canada, United States, and Mexico) interested in butterflies.

NONPROFIT ORGANIZATION

We are a membership-based 501(c)(3) not-for-profit organization working to increase public enjoyment and conservation of butterflies.

CONSERVATION

We are working to save butterfly species throughout North America. For example,

- NABA partnered with the University of Florida and the USFWS to help the endangered Schaus' Swallowtail in Florida.
- NABA successfully petitioned the State of Florida and the USFWS to declare Miami Blues an endangered species.
- NABA convinced the U.S. Army not to implement a plan that would have destroyed the last known viable colony of Regal Fritillaries east of the Mississippi River.
- NABA is on the steering committee of the Monarch Joint Venture, a governmental NGO partnership formed to conserve the spectacular migrations of Monarchs in North America.
- NABA is the only NGO member of the Florida Imperiled Butterfly Working Group.
- NABA has launched the Butterfly Habitat Network and is actively working to acquire habitat and save the rarest butterflies of North America.

ABOUT THE NORTH AMERICAN BUTTERFLY ASSOCIATION

NATIONAL BUTTERFLY CENTER

NABA owns and operates the National Butterfly Center (NBC), a 100-acre conservation, education, and research center in Mission, Texas. NABA has transformed what was an agricultural field, when acquired by NABA in 2002, into the largest botanical garden in the United States focused on using native plants in a garden setting. More than 230 species of wild butterflies have now been seen at the NBC. Each year, more than 5,000 school children come to the NBC to learn about the importance of butterflies and the plants and habitats on which they depend.

NABA BUTTERFLY MONITORING

NABA runs the NABA Butterfly Monitoring Program, including the 4th of July Butterfly Counts, and has amassed the largest database of butterfly occurrences and abundances in the world. These data are increasingly used by scientists to study butterfly population trends and to answer questions about butterfly biology.

BUTTERFLY GARDENING

NABA's Program for Butterfly Gardening and Habitats promotes the creation of habitats that increase the world's population of butterflies. You can help educate your neighbors about the importance of butterflies while directly helping butterfly conservation by certifying your garden with NABA. A Butterfly Garden Certification is available for individuals and institutions.

TAXONOMY

The NABA Names Committee, consisting of many of the top butterfly taxonomists in the world, evaluates new published data regarding butterfly taxonomy and, if warranted, makes changes to the *NABA Checklist and English Names of North American Butterflies*, which is published by NABA.

CHAPTERS

NABA has chapters throughout the United States. Various NABA chapters work at the state and local level to conserve butterflies and to educate the public about the importance of butterflies.

CULTURE

NABA is changing the way people view butterflies, moving people from an association with nets to an association with binoculars, cameras, gardening, and family fun. NABA's publications teach people how to find butterflies, how to identify them, how to create successful butterfly gardens, and how to photograph them. Your involvement with butterflies will help bring beauty and satisfaction to your life.

PLEASE JOIN US IN THESE EFFORTS WWW.NABA.ORG

RESOURCES

The following bibliography includes recent books about plant and butterfly identification. The butterfly field guides emphasize a modern approach to butterfly watching by including descriptions of particular butterflies and their habitats as well as the seasonal variations to watch for in butterfly life cycles. Another book not specifically about butterflies but that has influenced butterfly gardeners is Douglas W. Tallamy's *Bringing Nature Home: How You Can Sustain Wildlife with Native Plants* (Portland, OR: Timber Press, 2009).

BUTTERFLY FIELD GUIDES

Belth, Jeffrey E. *Butterflies of Indiana: A Field Guide.* Bloomington: Indiana University Press, 2013.

Betros, Betsy. *A Photographic Field Guide to the Butterflies in the Kansas City Region.* Kansas City, MO: Kansas City Star Books, 2008.

Chu, Janet R., and Stephen R. Jones. *Butterflies of the Colorado Front Range: A Photographic Guide to 80 Species.* Boulder, CO: Boulder County Nature Association, 2011.

Glassberg, Jeffrey. *Butterflies through Binoculars: A Field Guide to Butterflies in the Boston, New York, Washington Region.* New York: Oxford University Press, 1993.

Glassberg, Jeffrey. *Butterflies through Binoculars: The East.* New York: Oxford University Press, 1999.

Glassberg, Jeffrey. *Butterflies through Binoculars: The West: A Field Guide to the Butterflies of Western North America.* Oxford, UK: Oxford University Press, 2001.

Glassberg, Jeffrey. *A Swift Guide to Butterflies of North America.* Princeton, NJ: Princeton University Press, 2017.

Glassberg, Jeffrey, and Marc C. Minno. *Butterflies through Binoculars: Florida.* New York: Oxford University Press, 2000.

Heath, Fred, and Herbert Clarke. *An Introduction to Southern California Butterflies.* Missoula, MT: Mountain Press, 2004.

James, David G., and D. Nunnallee. *Life Histories of Cascadia Butterflies.* Corvallis: Oregon State University Press, 2011.

Shapiro, Arthur M. *Field Guide to Butterflies of the San Francisco Bay and Sacramento Valley Regions.* Berkeley: University of California Press, 2007.

Tveten, John L., and Gloria A. Tveten. *Butterflies of Houston & Southeast Texas.* Austin: University of Texas Press, 1996.

Venable, Rita. *Butterflies of Tennessee.* Franklin, TN: Maywood Publishing, 2014.

CATERPILLAR FIELD GUIDES

Allen, Thomas J., James P. Brock, and Jeffrey Glassberg. *Caterpillars in the Field and Garden: A Field Guide to the Butterfly Caterpillars of North America.* Oxford, UK: Oxford University Press, 2005.

Minno, Marc C., Jerry F. Butler, and Donald Hall. *Florida Butterfly Caterpillars and Their Host Plants.* Gainesville: University Press of Florida, 2005.

Wagner, David L. *Caterpillars of Eastern North America: A Guide to Identification and Natural History.* Princeton, NJ: Princeton University Press, 2005.

BUTTERFLY BIOLOGY, NATURAL HISTORY, AND BUTTERFLY GARDENING

Ajilvsgi, Geyata. *Butterfly Gardening for Texas*. College Station: Texas A&M University Press, 2013.

Burris, Judy, and Richards, Wayne. *The Life Cycles of Butterflies: From Egg to Maturity, A Visual Guide to 23 Common Garden Butterflies*. North Adams, MA: Storey Pub., 2006.

Cary, Steven J. *Butterfly Landscapes of New Mexico*. Albuquerque, NM: New Mexico Magazine, 2009.

Cech, Rick, and Guy Tudor. *Butterflies of the East Coast: An Observers Guide*. Princeton, NJ: Princeton University Press, 2007.

Dole, Claire Hagen. *The Butterfly Gardener's Guide*. Brooklyn, NY: Brooklyn Botanic Garden, 2003.

Glassberg, Jeffrey. *Butterflies of North America*. New York: Sterling, 2011.

Minno, Marc C., and Maria Minno. *Florida Butterfly Gardening: A Complete Guide to Attracting, Identifying, and Enjoying Butterflies of the Lower South*. Gainesville: University Press of Florida, 1999.

Ogard, Paulette Haywood, and Sara Bright. *Butterflies of Alabama: Glimpses into Their Lives*. Tuscaloosa: University of Alabama Press, 2010.

Stokes, Donald W., Lillian Q. Stokes, and Ernest H. Williams. *Stokes Butterfly Book: The Complete Guide to Butterfly Gardening, Identification, and Behavior*. New York: Little, Brown, 1991.

PLANT GUIDES AND GARDEN DESIGN

Hammer, Roger. *Attracting Hummingbirds and Butterflies in Tropical Florida: A Companion for Gardeners*. Gainesville: University Press of Florida, 2015.

Summers, Carolyn. *Designing Gardens with Flora of the American East*. New Brunswick, NJ: Rutgers University Press, 2010.

Holm, Heather. *Pollinators of Native Plants: Attract, Observe and Identify Pollinators and Beneficial Insects with Native Plants*. Minnetonka, MN: Pollination Press, 2014.

Sanders, Jack. *Secrets of Wildflowers: A Delightful Feast of Little-known Facts, Folklore, and History*. Guilford, CT: The Lyons Press, 2003.

Steiner, Lynn M. *Grow Native: Bringing Natural Beauty to Your Garden*. Minneapolis, MN: Cool Spring Press, 2016.

Wasowski, Sally. *Gardening with Prairie Plants: How to Create Beautiful Native Landscapes*. Minneapolis: University of Minnesota Press, 2002.

BUTTERFLY NOMENCLATURE

Gochfeld, Michael, and Joanna Burger. *Butterflies of New Jersey: A Guide to Their Status, Distribution, Conservation, and Appreciation*. New Brunswick, NJ: Rutgers University Press, 1997. Pages 15–27.

Miller, Jacqueline Y. *The Common Names of North American Butterflies*. Washington, DC: Smithsonian Institution Press, 1992.

North American Butterfly Association (NABA) Checklist & English Names of North American Butterflies. Morristown, NJ: NABA, 2001.

PHOTO CREDITS

©Alan Branhagen/Powell Gardens, pages 177, 223
©Annie's Annuals & Perennials, pages 56, 57, 164 (top), 246, 247
©Arlene Ripley, pages 259 (bottom), 260, 261, 262
©Beverly Z. Bowen, pages 71, 231 (top), 237
©Bonnie Ott, pages 44, 69, 82, 93
©Brad Guhr, pages 17, 54
©Bruce Newhouse, pages 100, 162, 163, 165
©Chris Leslie, pages 244 (bottom)
©Clay Sutton, page 75
©David Marsden/theanxiousgardener.com, page 139
©David Smitley, page 21
©Don DuBois, pages 148, 205, 207, 208, 210, 211
©Freda Moore/chiffonsigh.com, pages 158 (top), 170 (top), 188, 204, 230, 244 (top)
©Jan Dixon, pages 36, 49, 193, 194, 195
©Jane Hurwitz, pages 15, 20, 22, 26, 34, 70, 72, 73, 84, 85, 87, 97 (top), 115, 120, 121, 128, 131, 133, 137, 150, 152, 154, 180, 191
©Jeffrey Glassberg/*A Swift Guide to Butterflies of North America*, pages 35, 63–67
©Jim Springer, page 99
©John Flannery, pages 41 (bottom), 50, 51(right), 88, 89, 95, 116, 119, 178 (left)
©Julie O'Donald, pages 159, 160 (bottom)
©Kala King, page 77
©Karen Anthonisen Finch, page 232
©Karen LeMay, pages 254, 255, 256
©Karen Rosenbeck, page 231 (bottom)
©Ken Slade, pages 51 (left), 98
©Lenora Larson, pages 14, 59
©Luciano Guerra-National Butterfly Center, pages 28, 60, 101, 145, 146
©Mary Alice Tartler, page 144
©Mary Anne Borge/www.the-natural-web.org, pages 94, 103, 105, 172 (top), 173 (top), 176, 178 (right), 235 (bottom)
©Megan O'Donald, pages 158 (bottom), 160 (top), 161
©Michael Wetherford, pages 46, 52, 68, 74, 91
©Courtesy of Mt. Cuba Center, pages 32, 122, 123, 132
©Nancy Soucy, pages 235 (top)
©Nancy Witthuhn, page 81
©nickdeanlandscapedesign.com, pages 10, 245
©Noelle Johnson/www.azplantlady.com, page 257
©North American Butterfly Association, pages 12, 13 (right), 18
©Courtesy of North Creek Nurseries, Inc., pages 45, 53, 97 (bottom), 218, 219, 220, 221, 222, 259 (top)
©Pat Sutton, page 78
©Peter T. Volkmar, page 113
©pieceoflace photography, pages 2, 19, 37, 38, 41 (top), 58, 143
©Courtesy of Prairie Moon Nursery, pages 90, 140, 142, 189, 190, 192 (bottom)
©Courtesy of Reading Eagle/Mike Slater, pages 173 (bottom), 174 (top)
©Sharon Wander, pages 170 (bottom), 174 (bottom), 175
©Sonia Hill, page 129
©Susan Ford Collins/jungle mama, pages 24, 25
©Susan Martin, page 134
©Tom Halliwell, pages 27, 40, 42, 47, 48
©Wade Wander, page 86

FLICKR

Released into the Public Domain

Alan Schmierer, pages 13 (left), 55, 206 (middle)
Robb Hannawacker, pages 206 (top)

Used under a Creative Commons Attribution 2.0 Generic License

Andy Reago & Chrissy McClarren, pages 91, 206 (bottom)
K M, page 192 (top)
MgAgDept, page 172 (bottom)
Swallowtail Garden Seeds, page 258
Tom Hilton, page 164 (bottom)
USFWSmidwest, page 96

WIKIMEDIA COMMONS

Used under a Creative Commons Attribution-Share Alike 3.0 Unported

H. Zell, page 106
Stan Shebs, page 209

INDEX

PLANT INDEX

Page numbers in **bold** denote photos.

PLANT INDEX

PLANT INDEX

BUTTERFLY INDEX

Page numbers in **bold** denote photos or maps.

BUTTERFLY INDEX